Reason in Law

SIXTH EDITION

Lief H. Carter, LlB, PhD
The Colorado College

Thomas F. Burke, PhD
Wellesley College

Longman

New York   San Francisco   Boston
London   Toronto   Sydney   Tokyo   Singapore   Madrid
Mexico City   Munich   Paris   Cape Town   Hong Kong   Montreal

Publisher: Priscilla McGeehon
Senior Acquisitions Editor: Eric Stano
Associate Editor: Anita Castro
Marketing Manager: Megan Galvin-Fak
Senior Production Manager: Valerie Zaborski
Project Coordination, Text Design, and Electronic Page Makeup: The Clarinda Company
Cover Designer/Manager: Nancy Danahy
Cover Illustration/Photo: ©Noma/Stock Illustration Source, Inc.
Manufacturing Buyer: Roy Pickering
Printer and Binder: The Maple-Vail Book Manufacturing Group
Cover Printer: Phoenix Color Corps.

For permission to use copyrighted material, grateful acknowledgment is made to the copyright holders on p. 184, which is hereby made part of this copyright page.

Library of Congress Cataloging-in-Publication Data

Carter, Lief H.
    Reason in law / Lief H. Carter, Thomas F. Burke.—6th ed.
        p. cm.
    Includes bibliographical references and index.
    ISBN 0-321-08560-4 (pbk.)
    1. Law—United States—Methodology.   2. Law—United States—Interpretation and construction.   3. Stare decisis—United States.   4. Law and politics. I. Burke, Thomas Frederick. II. Title.

KF380 .C325 2002
340′.11—dc21

                                                                                                2001020414

Please visit our website at http://www.ablongman.com

ISBN 0-321-08560-4

2 3 4 5 6 7 8 9 10—MA—04 03 02 01

For Nancy, always

*To my father, Fred Burke, a man of uncommon
kindness, generosity, and spirit*

Contents

v

Preface

One day as an undergraduate, procrastinating on a term paper, I came across a book called *Contemporary Constitutional Lawmaking: The Supreme Court and the Art of Politics.* The book was fascinating. It wove together strands of constitutional law, legal philosophy, literary and aesthetic theory, and popular culture so elegantly that it inspired me to learn more about each. Along with a few other books and some wonderful teachers, it seduced me into the world of law and politics, and thence to graduate school and academia.

Reading that book, by Lief Carter, was just the first of many occasions on which Lief taught me about law. Years later, preparing to teach my first class at Wellesley College, I encountered another of Lief's books, *Reason in Law,* and found in it the same qualities that I had admired in his other writings. I made *Reason in Law* the centerpiece of my introductory law class and have enjoyed guiding students through the book nearly every semester for the past five years. Lief honored me greatly when he asked me to work with him to revise this classic book. The work has been a pleasure.

What did we do in this revision? Mostly we updated the cases, showing how *Reason in Law*'s principles can illuminate the legal conflicts familiar to today's students, from *Microsoft* and *Napster* to *Jones v. Clinton* and *Elian Gonzalez v. Reno,* from lawsuits over tobacco and guns to those involving gay rights and gender equality. We pay particular attention to *Bush v. Gore,* devoting an entire appendix to this landmark case and the election struggle that led to it.

We have also streamlined the book by cutting down the number of interesting, though inessential, detours it takes along the way. This makes the argument of the book more straightforward but still far from easy. There is no getting around it; to become expert in law, one must read very carefully some dense, not always graceful, texts. But more than that, to understand the argument of this book, one must wrestle with some fundamental puzzles about law, complexities that have befuddled legal scholars for many years.

Those puzzles come to the fore when controversy over legal reasoning becomes the stuff of national headlines, as in the case of *Bush v. Gore.* Reaction to that case was framed in part by the notion that law is a realm apart, a pure world that should remain unsullied by "politics." In this view, *Bush v. Gore* was a fall from grace, a moment when the Supreme Court exposed itself as low and partisan and thus unworthy of its high post. This view was, however, countered in the media by the equally stereotyped notion that law is "just politics," that justices are simply politicians with robes on, and that the words of judicial opinions are merely convenient rationalizations for the exercise of power. On this account, *Bush v. Gore* was just a more prominent example of what really happens in thousands of courtrooms across the nation every day.

Neither view satisfies. If legal reasoning is so unimportant, one wonders, why do so many bright people spend their lives poring over the nuances of legal texts? On the other hand, if law is supposed to have nothing to do with politics, why do people of good faith but differing political views often reach different answers to legal questions, as generations of political scientists have shown? *Reason in Law* answers these lingering questions by focusing on the role of legal reasoning. Our approach is postmodern in the modest sense that we don't believe that the law can ever produce "the one right answer" to a legal contest. Rather, we believe that people construct law just as they construct reality, through the languages they use to talk about their experiences and their relationships. Lief put it well in his preface to the fifth edition:

> People in all sorts of situations talk about law in all sorts of ways. Legal reasoning, one of many such ways, describes the way that lawyers and judges talk publicly and formally about the law. It is not the "correct" way, or even necessarily the best way, to talk about the law. However, legal reasoning is the way that those with official legal authority talk about law. Hence legal reasoning describes a particularly powerful set of legal realities. In the liberal democracy we inhabit, those of us who don't hold legal power nevertheless retain the civic right and duty to decide whether we accept the realities that official law talk creates. This book seeks to give readers the tools for doing that job.

The key to unlocking this book's meaning is this: Our legal language *does* give us the tools to tell the difference between impartial legal decisions and partisan political decisions. We can tell when sports referees seem improperly to favor one team. By mastering legal reasoning, we can also tell when judges fail to play their proper role as impartial umpires in the political game.

Reason in Law is at one level a book about the distinctive traditions and practices of American law, but at another about a basic problem in liberal, democratic, multicultural polities: When people of different political beliefs, of varying religious faiths, of clashing worldviews disagree, how can we arbitrate among them in a way acceptable to all? In other words, how can a pluralistic society be ruled legitimately? These questions can be raised in the context of the American legal system, but they go much further, as we hope instructors who use this book will recognize.

Reason in Law has been graced over the years by some very astute readers. Lief and I want to thank those who commented on the fifth edition and so guided our work on the sixth: Christopher P. Banks, University of Akron; Robert A. Carp, University of Houston; Paul Lermack, Bradley University; and C. Scott Peters, University of Louisville. We also want to acknowledge the hard work of all the production staff at Longman Publishers and the Clarinda Company, especially Anita Castro and Trish Finley.

Additionally, I want to thank all the great teachers who have professed law to me over my years in academia. At the University of Minnesota, this would include Sam Krislov, Don Gillmor, and Ted Glasser (since moved on to Stanford); at Berkeley, Robert Kagan, Sandy Muir, Martin Shapiro, and Robert Post; and during my time at Wellesley, Susan Silbey, Alan Schechter, and Sally Merry. I also want to thank those patient and resourceful souls at Wellesley who assisted me in this project, Cortney Harding, Lydia Chan, Jane Choi, Jenny Randall, Christine Ho, Amy Delamaide, and especially the administrators of the political science department, Sue Lindsey and Cyndy Northgraves.

Tom Burke
Wellesley College
January 22, 2001

Tom Burke says it all, or nearly. I want to add my thanks to Jane Stark, who has managed the academic affairs of eleven diverse political scientists at Colorado College virtually single-handedly, and Robin Satterwhite, Colorado College's research librarian extraordinaire. She is the finest research associate imaginable. Although Tom did the lion's share of work on this new edition, we both take full and equal responsibility for all its imperfections. Fortunately, neither judges nor professors need to achieve perfection in order to do their jobs well.

Lief Carter
The Colorado College
January 22, 2001

About the Authors

Lief Carter grew up in the Seattle area in the age of "innocent" rock 'n roll (the 1950s). He earned his AB from Harvard College (1962) and his law degree from Harvard Law School (1965). The Vietnam War ended his career as a legal practitioner just as it started. He served in the Peace Corps (Bolivia) as an alternative form of service in 1966–1967 and then returned to graduate school at the University of California, Berkeley, where he earned his PhD in political science (1972). His dissertation received the Corwin Award of the American Political Science Association. He taught at the University of Georgia from 1973 until 1995, when he became the McHugh Family Distinguished Professor at The Colorado College. In addition to *Reason in Law*, he has published books on criminal prosecution, administrative law, and theories of constitutional interpretation. Lief is currently working on a writing project that he calls "liberal politics as play" and lives in Manitou Springs, Colorado.

Tom Burke is proud to have been born and raised in the city of Minneapolis, Minnesota, during the years when it was famous for great politicians like Hubert Humphrey and Walter Mondale, as well as for fabulous entertainers such as the Replacements and Prince. (Alas, Jesse "The Body" Ventura, who combined both pursuits, came later.) Tom earned a BA from the University of Minnesota in 1988, then abandoned his home state for the University of California, Berkeley, where he received his PhD in 1996. There he studied with many of the professors who two decades earlier had taught Lief Carter, and, like Lief, he received the Corwin Award of the American Political Science Association for his dissertation. He has taught for the past five years at Wellesley College, just outside of Boston, Massachusetts, and has written articles on disability, campaign finance, and the place of rights in American politics. Look for his book *Litigation and Its Discontents* in finer bookstores around early 2002.

Reason in Law

I was much troubled in spirit, in my first years upon the bench, to find how trackless was the ocean on which I had embarked. I sought for certainty. I was oppressed and disheartened when I found that the quest for it was futile. I was trying to reach land, the solid land of fixed and settled rules, the paradise of a justice that would declare itself by tokens plainer and more commanding than its pale and glimmering reflections in my own vacillating mind and conscience. . . . As the years have gone by, and as I have reflected more and more upon the nature of the judicial process, I have become reconciled to the uncertainty, because I have grown to see it as inevitable. I have grown to see that the process in its highest reaches is not discovery, but creation; and that the doubts and misgivings, the hopes and fears, are part of the travail of mind, the pangs of death and the pangs of birth, in which principles that have served their day expire, and new principles are born.

What is that I do when I decide a case? To what sources of information do I appeal for guidance? In what proportions do I permit them to contribute to the result? In what proportions ought they to contribute? If a precedent is applicable, when do I refuse to follow it? If no precedent is applicable, how do I reach the rule that will make a precedent for the future? If I am seeking logical consistency, the symmetry of the legal structure, how far shall I seek it? At what point shall the quest be halted by some discrepant custom, by some consideration of the social welfare, by my own or the common standards of justice and morals? Into that strange compound which is brewed daily in the caldron of the courts, all these ingredients enter in varying proportions. I am not concerned to inquire whether judges ought to be allowed to brew such a compound at all. I take judge-made law as one of the existing realities of life. There, before us, is the brew. Not a judge on the bench but had a hand in the making.

—JUDGE BENJAMIN N. CARDOZO,
THE NATURE OF THE JUDICIAL PROCESS (1921)

Chapter
1

What Legal Reasoning Is, and Why It Matters

I have grown to see that the [legal] process in its highest reaches is not discovery, but creation.

—Benjamin N. Cardozo

They ain't nuthin' *until I calls 'em.*

—Attributed to umpire Bill Klem

AN OVERVIEW OF LAW AND POLITICS

*R*eaders who use this book to explore legal reasoning for the first time deserve some signposts at the start of their journey, for this book does not take some roads you might expect it to travel. First, this is not a "prelaw" book. We have not written it to teach people how to be lawyers, how to pass law school admissions tests or bar exams, or how to get rich. Second, this book does not exhaustively review all the scholarship on its subject, much of which is technical and geared toward a professional audience of jurisprudents. Instead, underneath this exploration of legal reasoning lies a study of politics and power. Legal reasoning serves simultaneously as the velvet glove covering the fist of judicial power and as the sincerest expression of our ideals of justice and of community.[1]

Because readers need to know what legal reasoning is in order to see clearly its political significance, we leave our main analysis of the political character of law and legal reasoning until the end of the book. But readers should know now that the legal reasoning road goes there. *Politics* refers to those things people do in communities in order to minimize threats to their well-being. Political behavior sometimes tries to conserve what is and sometimes tries to change what is. People who thrive

---

[1] *Community* can mean many different things, depending on the context in which people use this (or any) word. We can speak of a community of Napster users or of Britney Spears fans. For our purposes here, *community* means the physical space that courts rule. California courts, for example, speak on matters of California law to the community of everyone in California, including prisoners, infants, and illegal aliens, because the California courts have power over all of them. Federal courts speak to the community of all people in the United States.

because their communities support them tend to do political things that preserve their communities. When people do not experience community support, they either give up or do political things to try to change their community.

Like other forms of politics, law can either preserve communities or change them. By the end of the book you will have encountered many examples of legal actions that resulted in both change and preservation. Law is also like other forms of politics because it affects the quality of communities. When people believe that judges cynically manipulate legal language to reach partisan and self-interested political ends, faith in fairness and equity ebbs, motives for social cooperation falter, and communal life becomes more nasty and brutish. The sense of injustice can cause explosive social damage, as the riots in Los Angeles following the Rodney King verdict in early 1992 suggest.

Less dramatically, but just as significant, distrust in the impartiality of judges creates disrespect for legal institutions and ultimately the rule of law. The U.S. Supreme Court's ruling in *Bush v. Gore,* the 2000 presidential election case, may have had this effect, because it seemed to many people animated by partisan conservative political passions that favored Governor Bush. In his dissent in this case, Supreme Court Justice Stephen Breyer warned that by interjecting itself so forcefully on one side of a political dispute, the Supreme Court risked creating "a self inflicted wound—a wound that may harm not just the Court, but the Nation." Yet law can also strengthen our trust in the virtue of those who govern. The Supreme Court's 1992 *Casey* decision reaffirming the right to choose an abortion was applauded by many precisely because it hinged on the votes of conservative judges who seemed to lay their political ideologies aside.

All judicial rulings create losers, so there is always the potential for discontent with the decisions judges make. The only weapon judges have against this discontent is the persuasiveness with which they explain their reasoning. Thus judges should take legal reasoning seriously because the political stakes are high. It is the way judges exert their political power.

The legal reasoning in the presidential election cases in 2000 became a matter of great public scrutiny, with opinions ranging widely. We present many of the issues which that case raised in Appendix B of this book. But people on both sides of the case agreed that poor legal reasoning put the Supreme Court at risk. Professor Richard J. Pierce Jr., of George Washington University Law School, an open supporter of Governor Bush, said in an interview: "I would have hoped [the Justices] would have found a way not to be perceived as acting on their own political preferences. When very sophisticated, knowledgeable people, not rabid people, believe that's what happened, it's tragic. I am very, very concerned for the court."[2]

Judges, much more than other politicians, take legal reasoning seriously, because it is their language for preserving their authority and trustworthiness.[3] Richard John Neuhaus has written:

---

[2] See "Divining the Consequences of a Court Divided," *New York Times,* 17 December 2000, sec. 4, pp. 1 and 4. See also, Jeffrey Rosen, "Disgrace: The Supreme Court Commits Suicide," *New Republic,* 25 December 2000, pp. 18–21. "[T]hese four vain men and one vain woman have not only cast a cloud over the presidency of George W. Bush. They have, far more importantly, made it impossible for citizens of the United States to sustain any kind of faith in the rule of law as something larger than the self-interested political preferences of William Rehnquist, Antonin Scalia, Clarence Thomas, Anthony Kennedy, and Sandra Day O'Connor." (p. 18)

[3] Thirty years ago academics thought and taught about law "not as a body of rules to be learned, but as man's chief means of political and social control." Charles Howard and Robert Summers, *Law: Its Nature, Function, and Limits* (Englewood Cliffs, N.J.: Prentice-Hall, 1965), p. iii. Today's metaphors for exploring law are very different. We instinctively resist the technocratic and mechanistic implications of "social control."

[T]he law calls life to account. That is to say, the law possesses authority. Without such authority the law is merely a bundle of rules backed up by force; with such authority the law is a power we are bound to acknowledge.[4]

Legal reasoning is a language through which we can debate the rightness and wrongness of what our community is and what we want it to become. Both the best and worst elements of politics pervade all elements of law. We return to this theme at the end of the book.

Many paths connect law and politics. The politics of selecting judges routinely screens out certain marginal voices and interests from the legal process. Protecting either personal or group interests via the legal process costs so much money that the law does not consistently hear the voices of the poor. The law favors those who know from experience how to manipulate the system—landlords, corporate managers, and experienced felons, perhaps—against their more naive or inexperienced opponents.[5] The adversary system, in which British and American courts (unlike those of most nations) leave the task of presenting facts and shaping arguments up to the contending parties, can screen out important social issues. The "rich and famous"—Sean "Puffy" Combs is the most prominent recent example—frequently seem to escape the clutches of the law.

These and many more political issues can and do fill many worthy books on legal politics. However, to avoid confusion or frustrated expectations, let us alert students here that legal reasoning, the subject matter of *this* book, does not address these questions directly. We are looking at one part of a much larger picture: Judges, and usually appellate judges, give reasons explaining why they reach a decision, why they conclude that one side should win and the other lose. When we examine judges' legal reasoning, we ask questions like these: Do we trust the integrity of the decision? Do we trust that judges have used their power with integrity? These questions differ from questions about whether we, if we were in their shoes, would decide the same way. If you don't see this distinction clearly now, you should by the end of this book, which is at its deepest level a book about political morality. We know we can't always have it our way, and having it our way isn't always just.[6]

Legal reasoning confronts the root problem of all forms of politics: People disagree with one another about what their communities should do. This fact of human life is sometimes labeled "plurality," or "pluralism," though the trendy term today is "diversity." In a "multicultural," "globalized" world we are increasingly aware of the ways in which many attributes—race, class, gender, sexual orientation, and religion, to name the most prominent—contribute to human plurality.[7] These attributes can profoundly shape the way we see the world. When, for example, the Brooklyn Museum exhibited a painting of the Virgin Mary that was decorated with elephant dung, New York mayor Rudolf Giuliani denounced it as "sick stuff" that amounted to an attack on religion. Many Roman Catholics agreed. Others saw the painting as a meditation on the "sad, plain facts of life and death" that, far from attacking Roman Catholicism, reflected its earthy, humane qualities. When Giuliani threatened to

---

[4] "Law and the Rightness (and Wrongness) of Things," 22 *Worldview* 40 (1979).

[5] Marc Galanter, "Why the Haves Come Out Ahead," 9 *Law and Society Review* 95–160 (1974).

[6] For example, in the 1996 film *Dead Man Walking*, Matthew Poncelet made callow excuses for the brutal murders he committed.

[7] The scholars who have contributed to "critical race theory" specialize in thinking about how one dividing line, race, is established and maintained, and how it is used by both the powerful and the powerless in legal controversies. See *Critical Race Theory: The Cutting Edge*, Richard Delgado, ed. (Philadelphia: Temple University Press, 1995) and *Critical Race Theory: The Key Writings That Formed the Movement*, Kimberle Crenshaw, ed. (New York: The New Press, 1995).

eliminate the city's financial support of the museum, arguing that Roman Catholic taxpayers should not be forced to subsidize art that demeaned their religion, defenders of the museum argued that a cutoff would violate artistic freedom.[8]

How can a diverse society deal with such conflicts? Some can be settled by "agreeing to disagree," a common resolution in liberal societies. Those who liked the painting could go see it; those who were offended could avoid it. But we cannot finesse all conflicts in this way. In the Virgin Mary controversy, for example, someone had to decide whether the museum should continue to receive government funding. Sometimes legislators, bureaucrats, and executives like Mayor Giuliani make these controversial decisions. Sometimes nongovernmental parties make them. But frequently in the United States they are made by judges. Writing back in the 1830s, the great French observer of American society Alexis de Tocqueville concluded that "there is hardly a political question in the United States that does not sooner or later turn into a judicial one."[9] This propensity of Americans to turn to courts when they disagree is hard to miss today, when judges are deciding matters as varied as whether Napster is unfair to rock bands, or whether Elian Gonzales should go back to Cuba, or whether colleges should continue affirmative action policies.

Judges in a pluralistic society like the United States have a tough task: They must convince communities, including those who lose because of their decisions, that they are not simply choosing sides, but instead acting impartially. The many dividing lines in American society make this especially difficult. A judge appointed to decide whether New York City could legally cut off funding of the Brooklyn Museum because of the Virgin Mary painting would necessarily displease either many devout Roman Catholics or many supporters of the arts.[10] Those on the less powerful side of society's dividing lines—racial, religious and sexual minorities, for example—are particularly likely to distrust the motives of judges who decide against them, especially when the judges are drawn from the more powerful side. Many members of the Cuban-American community did not believe that the judges in the Elian Gonzales case had decided it fairly, just as many racial minorities were unconvinced that the all-white jury that acquitted the police officers who beat Rodney King was acting without prejudice.

Judges can't transcend social dividing lines, and they can't make decisions that please all groups and individuals. This book argues, however, that, even in highly controversial cases like *Bush v. Gore*, judges can still convince communities of their fairness and impartiality. One can disagree with a decision, but still respect the decision maker. At bottom, then, this book explores a classic political question: By what standards can we say that someone we disagree with nevertheless argues with integrity? Our answer is that judges can convince others of their integrity when they use "good legal reasoning." This book is an account of what exactly that involves. Other good books describe what law is; this book explores what law ought to be.

A DEFINITION OF LAW

Law is a language, not simply a collection of rules. What distinguishes law from other ways of making sense of life? Lawyers and judges attempt to prevent and solve other people's problems, but so do physicians, priests, professors, and plumbers.

---

[8] Natalie Angier, "The Shock of the Natural; Works in Brooklyn Have a Long Tradition," *New York Times,* 5 October 1999, p. E1; Ralph Blumenthal and Carol Vogel, "Museum Says Giuliani Knew of Show in July and Was Silent," *New York Times,* 5 October 1999, p. B1.

[9] Alexis de Tocqueville, *Democracy in America,* J.P. Mayer, tr. (New York: Harper and Row, 1969), p. 270.

[10] In reality Mayor Giuliani never followed through on his initial threat to defund the museum.

The term *problem solving* therefore includes too much. Lawyers and judges work with certain kinds of problems, problems that can lead to conflicts, even physical fights, among people. It is the *kind* of problem judges and lawyers work with that helps define law.

Contrary to the impression that television drama gives, with its emphasis on courtroom battles, most lawyers generally practice "preventive law." They help people discover ways to reduce their taxes or write valid wills and contracts. They study complex insurance policies and bank loan agreements. Such efforts reduce the probability of conflict. Most lawyers usually play a planning role. They help people create their own "private laws," laws governing their personal affairs and no more.

But, of course, some conflicts start anyway. Why? Sometimes they start because a lawyer did the planning and preventing poorly, or because the client did not follow a lawyer's good advice. Sometimes lawyers cannot find in rules of law a safe plan with which to prevent a conflict. Many conflicts, however, such as the auto collision, the dispute with a neighbor over a property line, or the angry firing of an employee, begin without lawyers. Then people may call them in after the fact, not for an ounce of prevention but for the pounding of a cure.

If a battle erupts spontaneously, lawyers may find a solution in the rules of law, though once people get angry with each other they may refuse the solution lawyers offer. If a struggle arises, however, and if the lawyers don't find a solution or negotiate a compromise, then either one side gives up or the opponents go to court; they call in the judges to give their solution.

You may now think you have a solid definition of law: Law is the process of preventing or resolving conflicts between people. Lawyers and judges do this; professors, plumbers, and physicians, at least routinely, do not. But parents prevent or resolve conflicts among their children daily. And parents, perhaps exasperated from coping with family fights, may turn to a family counselor to deal with their own conflicts. Many ministers no doubt define one of their goals as reducing conflict. Lawyers, then, aren't the only people who try to resolve conflicts.

Law, like the priesthood and professional counseling, encounters an immense variety of problems. Law requires the ability to see specifics and to avoid premature generalizing and jumping to conclusions. So do good counseling, good "ministration," and good parenting. But what distinguishes the conflict solving of lawyers and judges from the conflict solving of parents, counselors, or ministers? Consider these three cases. What makes them distinctively *legal* problems?

- A Massachusetts supermarket chain's order of a carload of cantaloupe from Arizona arrives two weeks late and partially rotten. The supermarket chain refuses to take delivery of the melons and refuses to pay for them. Did the seller in the contract of sale guarantee their safe arrival? Did the delay cause the decay, or had some spore infected the melons before shipment? Did the railroad act negligently in causing the delay, thus making it liable for the loss? Should the supermarket chain try to recover the profit it didn't make because it had no melons to sell, and if so, from whom? Do any regulations made by the Department of Agriculture or the Interstate Commerce Commission speak to the problem?[11]

---

[11] Real life offers us a much more complicated version of this case of the rotten cantaloupe. See *L. Gillarde Co. v. Joseph Martinelli and Co., Inc.,* 168 F.2d 276 (1st Cir. 1948) and 169 F.2d 60 (1948, rehearing). The case has introduced three generations of students at Harvard Law School, Lief Carter among them, to the complexities of the legal process in Henry M. Hart Jr. and Albert M. Sacks, *The Legal Process* (Cambridge: Harvard Law School, 1958), pp. 10–75. These materials were published in 1994 in William N. Eskridge Jr., *The Legal Process: Problems in the Making and Application of Law* (Westbury, Conn.: Foundation Press).

- A young man, entranced by the thought of flying, steals a Cessna from an airstrip in Rhode Island and manages to survive a landing in a Connecticut corn patch. He is prosecuted under the National Motor Vehicle Theft Act, which prohibits transportation "in interstate or foreign commerce [of] a motor vehicle, knowing the same to have been stolen. . . ." The statute defines *motor vehicle* to "include an automobile, automobile truck, automobile wagon, motorcycle, or any other self-propelled vehicle not designed for running on rails." Does the pilot's brief flight amount to transportation of the plane "in interstate . . . commerce?" Is an airplane a "vehicle" within the meaning of the act?[12]

- Some University of Wisconsin students object to the student fees they are required to pay with their tuition. These mandatory fees fund more than 600 student organizations, from the "Future Financial Gurus of America" and the College Republicans to campus chapters of the International Socialist Organization and the American Civil Liberties Union. The students argue that by forcing them to pay the fees to groups whose message they find offensive, the university has violated their freedom of speech. Do these fees violate the First Amendment by compelling the students to pay for speech they despise? Or is the university *supporting* freedom of speech by funding a diverse array of student organizations?[13]

These are legal problems, not counseling or psychological or parental problems, because we define their nature and limits—but not necessarily their solution—in terms of rules that the state, the government, has made. The laws of contract and of negligence help define the problem or the quarrel between the melon seller and the melon buyer. So, as it turns out, do Department of Agriculture shipping regulations for farm produce. Criminal statutes passed by legislatures define, among many concepts, how the government may deal with thieves. The First Amendment and other provisions in the U.S. Constitution create rights that public agencies like the University of Wisconsin must respect. Governments have made these rules; they are laws. The process of resolving human conflicts through law begins when one person or several persons decide to take advantage of the fact that the government has made rules to prevent or resolve such conflicts. When people convert a problem into a legal conflict by taking it to court, the court's resolution of the problem has the force of the government behind it. Even in a noncriminal case, if the loser or losers don't pay up, the judge may order jail terms.

The law, then, is a language that lawyers and judges use when they try to prevent or resolve problems—human conflicts—using official rules made by the state as their starting point. To study reason in this process is to study how lawyers and judges justify the choices they inevitably make among alternative legal solutions. For example, legal reasoning studies how they justify saying an airplane is or is not a "vehicle" in the context of the National Motor Vehicle Theft Act. Throughout this book we shall study the legal process by asking the central questions lawyers and judges ask themselves as they do their work: What does the law mean as applied to the problem before me? What different and sometimes contradictory solutions to the problem does the law permit?

[12] Cf. *McBoyle v. United States*, 283 U.S. 25 (1931). The letter abbreviations following the names of cases identify the series of books that contains the judicial opinion deciding the case. The first number indicates the volume in the series that contains the opinion, and the second number is the starting page of the opinion. Appendix A discusses *McBoyle* further.

[13] *Board of Regents of University of Wisconsin v. Southworth*, 120 S.Ct. 1346 (2000).

Now stop and compare this definition of law and legal reasoning with your own intuitive conception of law, with the definition of the legal process you may have developed from television, movies, and other daily experiences. Do the two overlap? Probably not very much. The average layperson usually thinks of law as trials, and criminal trials at that. But trials, by our definition, are one of the less legal, or "law-filled," parts of the legal process because much of the conflict-settling work of lawyers and judges involves deciding not what law means but what happened. Devotees of the O. J. Simpson affair do not question the law that governed the case. They seek the facts. Trials, like Simpson's criminal and civil trials, are not so much legal reasoning as they are a microscopic kind of historical research: Did the deceased pull a knife on the defendant before the defendant shot him, or didn't he? Did that witness really see the defendant run the red light just before the defendant hit the police car? We are confident enough that these historical problems do not require legal reasoning that we often turn the job of solving them over to groups of amateur historians, better known as juries.

Rules do tell juries what facts to seek. Pulling the knife *could* excuse the shooting through the law of self-defense, though if the deceased were a child of three it would almost surely not. Running the red light could establish legal negligence, though it might not if the defendant were driving his car in a funeral procession at the time.

We cannot totally separate law and facts; but the heart of the reasoning part of law, and the subject of this book, lies not in figuring out what happened but in analyzing what facts the rules allow us to seek and what to do with these facts once we "know" them. Turning to the eager flyer, the historical problem we must solve is whether that particular defendant at some specified point in the past actually flew someone else's airplane to another state without permission. The legal reasoning problem, on the other hand, requires deciding whether we ought to call the plane a "vehicle" in this statute's context.

The illustrative case at the end of this chapter sets out the distinction between trial and appellate decisions. In that case a trial court had decided that a certain Mr. Prochnow was the father of his wife's baby. The facts—which included a suspicious liaison between the wife and another man, the physical separation of the husband and wife except for one encounter eight months before the birth of a full-term baby, and the incompatibility of the husband's blood type with that of the child—seemed to point conclusively in the other direction. Nevertheless, certain official rules of law, as interpreted by the appellate court, seemed to prevent the trial judge from treating all this evidence as conclusive. This case also provides our first full-length example of a court trying (and in our judgment failing) to do legal reasoning well.

A DEFINITION OF LEGAL REASONING

A fundamental political expectation in the United States holds that people who exercise power and authority over others must *justify* how and why they use their power as they do. We expect, both in private and in public life, that people whose decisions directly affect our lives will give reasons why they deserve to hold their power and show how their decisions serve common rather than purely selfish ends. We expect teachers to have and articulate grading standards. We expect elected politicians to respond to the needs of voters. In all such cases we reject the authoritarian notion that power justifies itself, that those with money or political office can therefore do whatever they please. Holding judges responsible for justifying their power may seem obvious to us, but this practice is actually a fairly recent development in Western political philosophy. The alternatives—governing through greater physical strength and brute force, or governing through pure tradition and authoritarian right (as did kings when they proclaimed "divine right" to rule)—may have seemed acceptable theories when people believed that God willed everything. However, religious theories of government, still prevalent in many parts of the world, tend to produce so much religious warfare and bloodshed that liberal philosophers from John Locke forward have tried to substitute reason and justification for force and authority.[14] The most common criticism of Robert Bork's theory of constitutional interpretation—a theory that requires faithful adherence today to the intentions and purposes of the men who originally wrote the Constitution—points out that Bork speaks in the religious language of preliberal authoritarian government. Bork in effect turns the framers of our Constitution into religious authorities whose dictates we must obey. The title of Bork's book—*The Tempting of America: The Political Seduction of the Law*—gives you the idea.[15]

Courts in the United States hold and exercise political power. Judicial outcomes in lawsuits can literally kill and bankrupt people. Courts, like the other branches of government, possess and use power to make law. Whether appellate judges meet or fail to meet our fundamental expectation about the use of judicial power depends on the quality of their legal reasoning. Appellate judges in most nontrivial cases write opinions explaining and thereby justifying the results they reach.[16] Just as elections hold legislators, governors, presidents, and many other politicians accountable, so their opinions hold appellate judges accountable.[17]

Our culture encourages some misunderstanding about legal reasoning. Perhaps because, starting in the Renaissance, a stream of discoveries about the physical world has continuously bombarded Western civilization, we too often assume that legal reasoning is good when it discovers the law's "right answer," the correct legal solution to a problem. The idea that we live under a government of laws, not men, seems based on the assumption that correct legal results exist, like undiscovered planets or subatomic particles, quite independent of man's knowledge.

Of course if law (and science) actually worked that way, a book on legal reasoning would be absurd. To see whether a judge settled a contract dispute correctly, we would simply study the law of contract. To determine the correctness of the U.S. Supreme Court's 1954 decision banning official public school segregation, we would study the Constitution. In all cases trained lawyers and legal scholars would, like priests in olden days, have special access to correct answers that laypeople—most readers of this book—could not hope to match. The layperson would either defer to the conclusion of the expert or, if they didn't like the legal result, rebel.

Appellate judges do justify their power through the quality of the opinions they write. The quality of their opinions, however, depends on something other than proving that they got the law right. After all, when the law is clear enough that people on

---

[14] Lief Carter develops this theme further in his first chapter of *An Introduction to Constitutional Interpretation: Cases in Law and Religion* (White Plains, N.Y.: Longman, 1991).

[15] (New York: The Free Press, 1990). See also Bork's *Slouching Towards Gomorrah* (New York: HarperCollins, 1996). Bruce Ackerman's "Robert Bork's Grand Inquisition," 99 *Yale Law Journal* 1419 (1990) dissects Bork's religious rhetoric particularly well.

[16] For an introduction to the legal procedures and terms by which cases reach the appellate level, see Appendix A, beginning at p. 158.

[17] All federal judges are appointed for life. Impeachment and removal from office are very rare. Most state judges are elected; but election challenges, especially at the appellate level, are also rare. The defeat of California Chief Justice Rose Bird and Associate Justices Cruz Reynoso and Joseph Grodin in November 1986 was an exception. See Henry J. Abraham, *The Judicial Process*, 6th ed. (New York: Oxford University Press, 1993), pp. 21–39.

opposite sides of a case can agree on what it commands, people usually don't spend the many thousands of dollars that contesting a case in an appellate court requires. Legal reasoning, in other words, describes what judges do to justify their decision when they *cannot* demonstrate or prove that they have reached the "right answer." As Benjamin Cardozo pointed out the better part of a century ago, appellate judges *create* law. The uncertainties and imperfections in law force judges to choose what the law ought to mean, not merely report on what it does mean.

To persuade us that the law ought to mean what the judge has decided, the judicial opinion ought to persuade us to share the judge's beliefs about four kinds of things:

1. The *case facts* established in the trial and preserved in the record of the evidence produced at the trial
2. The facts, events, and other conditions that we observe in the world, quite apart from the case at hand, which we call *social background facts*
3. What the *rules of law*, that is, the official legal texts created by the state, say about cases like this
4. Widely shared moral *values* and social principles

These four elements are the main building blocks of all legal reasoning. Sometimes judges hide them, but the elements are always there. And thus we arrive at our definition of legal reasoning:

> *Legal reasoning describes how a legal opinion combines the four elements: the facts established at trial, the rules that bear on the case, social background facts, and widely shared values. When a judge reasons well, the opinion harmonizes or "fits together" these four elements.*

This definition, no doubt, seems abstract and fuzzy at first. We hope that by the time you finish this book you will understand this definition and see that it is not simply an academic theory of law. These four building blocks are so essential to legal reasoning that we should practice learning how to identify and distinguish them in concrete cases. Here is a bit more explanation and an example of each of the four.

CASE FACTS

Case facts are perhaps the easiest of the four building blocks to understand. These are facts about the dispute between the parties in the case as developed in a trial. In a jury trial, the judge usually charges the jury that it must find certain things to be true in order to find for the plaintiff, or to find a defendant guilty; a jury verdict of guilt or liability necessarily finds such facts to be true. In a trial where a judge sits, the judge will usually read into the court record his findings of fact. In either case, the only way an appellate court can overturn a trial court's factual conclusions is to hold that they have no substantial basis in the evidence and are therefore "clearly erroneous,"[18] a rare event.

A host of case facts were mustered in the flurry of lawsuits filed over the 2000 presidential election. For example, courts heard evidence about the number of "undercounted" ballots (those in which no vote for president had been recorded by machines), the number of "overvotes" (ballots not counted because they contained two votes for president), and about how older balloting technologies, like those that required voters to punch out a "chad" in a card to record their vote, produced higher rates of undercounted votes than did newer technologies such as optical scanning.

---

[18] See Rule 52A, Federal Rules of Civil Procedure.

SOCIAL BACKGROUND FACTS

Every lawsuit reflects both a particular case and a more general social problem. Lawsuits give courts the opportunity to rethink the sorts of policies that might best remedy the social problem illustrated by the case. Judges resolving cases must think about the best way to solve not only the immediate conflict, but the larger social problem it reflects. To do so they must make decisions about the facts of the larger problem as well as facts about the case. These are social background facts. Such facts can be contested, as for example when two sides in a lawsuit over purportedly defective tires disagree about how often "normal" tires fail, or in a medical malpractice case about what the standard treatment for a particular illness would be. But often, social background facts are uncontroversial. For example, in *Prochnow v. Prochnow*, the child support case presented at the end of this chapter, both sides acknowledged that babies do not arise spontaneously in the womb but must be created through insemination. As this example suggests, the disputants don't have to debate social background facts in order for them to play a role in the case. Moreover, even when the social background facts in a case aren't clear, judges and juries nonetheless often rely on hunches about them, something Judge Learned Hand does openly in a case you will read in Chapter 2, *United States v. Repouille*.

A plethora of social background facts about the Internet colored *Reno v. The American Civil Liberties Union*. This case concerned the Communications Decency Act (CDA), enacted into law in 1996, which made it a crime to knowingly transmit "obscene or indecent" material over the Internet to minors. The Supreme Court ruled that the CDA violated the First Amendment. In his opinion for the Court, Justice John Paul Stevens rested his decision on several social background facts about the Internet. He concluded, for example, that Internet users seldom encounter sexually explicit material "by accident," that the Internet is less invasive to the home than radio or television, and that there is no "effective method for a sender to prevent minors from obtaining access to its communications . . . without also denying access to adults."[19]

RULES OF LAW

Judges must take account of all the rules of law that are relevant to a case. Rules of law can come from statutes or constitutions, but they can also come from precedents—previously decided cases. The justices in the majority in *Casey*, the case that reaffirmed the right to an abortion, rested their decision largely on rules of law created by *Roe v. Wade*, the Supreme Court's initial decision holding that the Constitution gave women such a right.

The 2000 presidential election litigation debated many rules of law. Indeed, as you will see clearly when you review the case in Appendix B, the case turned primarily on the meaning of statutory and constitutional rules. Florida judges had to make sense of somewhat contradictory state statutes governing "protests" and "contests" of election results. Gore and Bush attorneys argued whether the federal "safe harbor" statute, which guarantees that Congress will recognize duly selected state electors in presidential elections, applied to the case. Some members of the U.S. Supreme Court believed that Florida judges, by ordering election officials to count "undervotes," had violated Article II of the U.S. Constitution, which requires presidential electors be chosen "in such manner as the *legislature* . . . may direct." Finally, the U.S. Supreme Court ultimately halted the recount by interpreting the "equal protection clause" of the Fourteenth Amendment to the Constitution. The Court ruled that the recount procedures violated the Fourteenth Amendment because they allowed election officials to use varying standards in counting votes from county to county.

---

[19] *Reno v. ACLU*, 117 S.Ct. 2139 (1997).

WIDELY SHARED VALUES

To be convincing, judges must also take account of social values. This is not an invitation for judges to recite their own values, nor to pick the values they deem most worthy. Instead, judges must try to persuade communities they have considered widely shared values that are most relevant to a dispute.

Two widely shared values, freedom and privacy, were cited in *A.Z. v. B.Z.*, a dispute between a woman who wanted to implant frozen embryos in her womb and her ex-husband, who didn't want any more children with her. The frozen embryos were left over from fertility treatments the couple had taken while married. The ex-husband had signed seven consent forms saying that if the couple separated, the wife would retain the choice of whether to implant them. Nonetheless, the Supreme Judicial Court of Massachusetts ruled in the husband's favor, concluding that "respect for liberty and privacy requires that individuals be accorded the freedom to decide whether to enter into a family relationship."[20]

You can imagine how all four building blocks of legal reasoning play some role in each of these cases: *Rules of law* about when contracts can be disregarded also shaped the ruling in the frozen embryos case. The widely shared values of freedom of speech and the protection of children from injurious influences both were part of the Internet indecency case. And it is a *social background fact* that fathers usually feel responsible for their offspring. All cases have each of the four building blocks in them, though sometimes the opinion in the case attempts to hide them.

Several immensely important corollaries follow from our definition of legal reasoning. First, two judges may reach different results in the same case, yet each may reason equally well or badly. Like two excellent debaters, two opposing opinions may still persuade us that each judge has fit together the four elements into a vision of justice that we trust.

Second, to repeat, legal reasoning is ultimately political, not technically legal. Laypeople who read judicial opinions can and should react to them and decide whether the opinion actually persuades them. No one opinion will persuade everyone. Reactions for and against judicial decisions about such volatile issues as abortion inevitably shape the development of law in the future.

Third, legal reasoning does *not* refer to the specific calculations that go on in a judge's head. In 1929, U.S. District Judge Joseph Hutcheson confessed that the actual decision-making process revolved around the judicial "hunch."[21] Professor Warren Lehman in 1986 agreed: "What we call the capacity for judgment . . . is an intellectualized account of the capacity for decision making and action, whose nature is not known to us."[22] Legal reasoning justifies the decision but does not explain how the judge arrived at it. In theory a devilishly partisan judge could decide cases solely to advance her political agenda, yet write masterful opinions that appear fair and impartial. (And a truly apathetic judge could flip a coin to make a decision, then write a brilliant opinion that convincingly justified it.) We will never know with certainty why a judge decided as he did, and it would be foolish to assume that the judge's opinion is some kind of record of the decision process. That is

---

[20] *A.Z. v. B.Z.*, 431 Mass. 150; 725 N.E.2d 105 (2000).

[21] Joseph C. Hutcheson, Jr., "The Judgment Intuitive: The Function of the 'hunch' in Judicial Decision," 14 *Cornell Law Quarterly* 274 (1929). Hutcheson defined *hunch* as "a strong intuitive impression that something is about to happen."

[22] Warren Lehman, *How We Make Decisions* (Madison: Institute for Legal Studies of the University of Wisconsin Law School, 1986), p. 12. For an analysis of the subconscious influences on a judge, see Richard Danzig, "Justice Frankfurter's Opinions in the Flag Salute Cases," 36 *Stanford Law Review* 675 (1984).

not to say that there is no relationship between the quality of a judge's reason-giving and the quality of her decision-making. The discipline of writing thoughtful, well-considered opinions is likely to make the judge's decision-making more thoughtful and well-considered as well. Psychologists have found that when people learn to think in new ways they can literally reshape their brains, and thus improve the way they make decisions.[23] It is no stretch, then, to believe that judges who write well-reasoned opinions are also likely to make good decisions. Yet even so, there is always a gap between the decision and the reasoning that explains it. A judge's opinion is her public justification of the choice she has made, not a window into her soul.

Finally, the process by which judges seek to fit the four elements of legal reasoning together inevitably requires them to simplify and distort each element to some degree. Therefore, most opinions will fail to meet the requirements of formal logic. (The Supreme Court's rulings about establishment of religion—which allow churches and church schools many tax advantages, yet prohibit the government from providing certain forms of financial aid to church schools—are notoriously incoherent by purely logical standards.) So, too, opinions will simplify the moral and empirical issues in them. Simplification and alteration are a fact of life. We always must reshape raw materials if we want to fit them together smoothly.

Thus we return to the point made previously, that law does not provide a technique for generating "right answers." This book's analysis assumes that nothing, including science and technology, can ever be correct in an absolute demonstrable sense. It is a commonplace belief in the philosophy of science today that, as the dust jacket for a noted physics book puts it:

> Physicists do not discover the physical world, they invent *a* physical world—they invent a story that fits as closely as possible the facts they create in their experimental apparatus. In the words of Einstein, "Physical concepts are free creations of the human mind. . . ." Physicists do not always agree on the same theories, or even on the same facts, but they agree on the procedures to be followed in testing theories and establishing facts. . . . The physical world is made up of leptons and quarks because physicists *talk* about the world in terms of leptons and quarks. This is the vocabulary that gives them the power to predict the outcome of their experiments. The word *real* is not descriptive. *Real* is an honorific term we bestow on our most cherished beliefs—our most treasured ways of speaking.[24]

For the same reasons, pitches in baseball become balls and strikes, for all practical purposes, because the umpire calls them that way—even when we may see the pitch differently. Just so with judges and lawyers, who agree to follow certain procedures and to use a common vocabulary of legal reasoning but who do not automatically agree on legal outcomes—or even on which techniques of legal reasoning to use and when to use them.

SOURCES OF OFFICIAL LEGAL TEXTS

The range of legal problems and conflicts is practically infinite, but lawyers and judges will, one way or another, resolve the issues by referring to and reasoning about official legal texts created by the state ("rules of law" or just "legal rules" for

---

[23] Susan C. Vaughn argues that successful psychotherapy creates this structural transformation. See Vaughn, *The Talking Cure: The Science Behind Psychotherapy* (New York: Henry Holt, 1998).
[24] Bruce Gregory, *Inventing Reality: Physics as Language* (New York: John Wiley and Sons, 1988). And Geoffrey Joseph wrote, "What one finds [in the physical sciences] is a succession of theories, each of which resolutely ignores certain fundamental questions." "Interpretation in the Physical Sciences," 58 *Southern California Law Review* 9 (1985), p. 12.

short). Despite the endless variety of legal problems, lawyers and judges usually resort to four categories of official texts: *statutes, common law, constitutional law,* and *administrative regulations.*

The easiest category to understand is what we often call "laws"—the *statutes* passed by legislatures. Laypeople tend to think of statutes as the rules defining types of behavior that society wishes to condemn: crimes. However, legislatures enact statutes governing (and sometimes creating!) many problems without enacting criminal statutes—civil rights, income tax rates, and social security benefit levels, for example. For our purposes this statutory category also includes the local ordinances passed by the elected bodies of cities and counties.

But there is a problem here: Legislatures do not enact statutes to cover everything. And when lawyers and judges face a problem without a statute, they normally turn to that older set of legal texts called *common law.*

Judges, not legislators, make common-law rules, but not by calling together a judicial convention to argue, log-roll, draft, and finally vote on (or bury) proposed laws. Common-law rules have emerged through a process introduced in England before the discovery of the New World. The process began essentially because the king of England chose to assert national authority by sending judges throughout the country to act, to decide cases, in the name of the Crown. The king did not write rules to govern all judges' decisions. It was because the judges acted in the name of the central government, certainly a shaky government by our standards, that their decisions became law common to all the king's domain. Many common-law rules originated in local custom or in the minds of the judges themselves.

The process by which these decisions became "law" took a surprisingly long time. In the beginning, the reasons for judicial decisions were murky, and judges applied them inconsistently. But observers of the courts wrote descriptions of the cases, often just the facts and the result, and judges began to look to these descriptions for past examples to guide current judicial action. The formal practice whereby judges write opinions explaining their choices, which other judges in turn treat as legal authority called *precedents,* is only a few hundred years old, but it is a powerful and stabilizing force in legal reasoning today. Precedents, the official legal texts created by courts themselves, receive much attention in this book because the facts and values embedded in the examples of precedents are fundamental tools of legal reasoning.

Chapters 3 and 4 examine legal reasoning in common and statutory law, and Chapter 5 explores the third category of official legal texts, *constitutional law.* The Constitution of the United States and the 50 state constitutions set out the structure and powers of government. They also place legal limits on the way those who govern can use their power. While statutes (and common law, where statutory law is silent) can govern anybody, constitutions govern the government.[25] The U.S. Constitution even governs presidents, although most constitutional cases involve an alleged conflict between the national or state constitutions and a decision made and enforced by lesser public administrators who claim to act under statutory authority.

Administrative regulations—of the Internal Revenue Service, or the San Francisco Zoning Board, or any of the thousands of national, state, and local administrative agencies—make up the fourth category of legal texts. Executives and nonelected administrators can make rules only when a constitution or a statute gives

---

[25] If I, as a private citizen, don't like a speech of yours and forcibly remove you from your podium, I will probably violate a principle of common or statutory law. And I would violate the value favoring free exchange of ideas. But I will not violate the First Amendment of the Constitution. If, however, I did this to you while working as a government official, such as an FBI agent, that could be a constitutional violation.

them the authority to do so. Problems in administrative law can fascinate and perplex as much as any. Because the length of this book and your time have limits, we shall examine reasoning about administrative regulations only indirectly. Do not, however, let this deliberate neglect mislead you into thinking the subject is unimportant. One of the cases you will read in Chapter 4, in which the Supreme Court ruled that the Food and Drug Administration did not have the authority to regulate tobacco, was a major loss for antismoking crusaders, since the FDA was prepared to impose stringent regulations on sales of cigarettes. Administrative regulations are shaping law and our lives more and more.[26] The scope of this book, however, is mainly confined to historically more developed official legal texts: *statutes, common law,* and *constitutional law.*

THE CHOICES THAT LEGAL REASONING CONFRONTS

While official legal texts are the starting point for legal reasoning, they are rarely the endpoint. If judges could resolve disputes simply by reciting the words of a legal text, disputes would not come to court in the first place. Anybody can read. Lawsuits over the presidential election of 2000, for example, debated contradictions in Florida election laws. While one provision said that voting returns submitted more than seven days after the election "shall be ignored," a more recent statute said that such returns "may be counted." Even where official legal texts are not so strikingly contradictory, people can usually find ways to dispute their meaning: Witness President Clinton's quibbling over the meaning of the word "is" during the Monica Lewinsky scandal. For better or worse, it takes judicial reasoning and judgment to say what legal texts actually mean in the context of specific cases. In most cases, judges must reconcile the potential inconsistencies and contradictions among widespread values, the actual words of legal rules and prior judicial opinions, and their own views of the case facts and the social background facts in the cases before them. Judges must make difficult choices such as these:

- Does the case before me call for continued adherence to the historical meaning of legal words? Must I do what the framers of statutory or constitutional language hoped their language would accomplish? How can I discover what they hoped? When do social, political, and technological changes permit or require a different or revised interpretation?
- Does this case call for judicial deference to the literal meaning of the words themselves? In what circumstances do I decide more wisely by ignoring the actual dictionary definitions of the words in a statute or constitution?
- Does this case obligate me to follow a judicial precedent the wisdom of which I doubt? When am I free to ignore a relevant precedent?

Throughout the following chapters we shall see that choices like these—the choice of change or stability and of literal or flexible interpretation of words and precedents, for example—have no "right answer." Judges inevitably have discretion to decide.

There exists a second reason why judges will continuously create law. The moral values that claim to govern a case collide. Thus, the Constitution contains language protecting the freedom of the press. It also contains language ensuring the

---

[26] See Lief Carter and Christine Harrington, *Administrative Law and Politics,* 3rd ed. (New York: HarperCollins, 2000). The Congress of the United States generally enacts a few hundred statutes per year, but the federal bureaucracy issues 3,000 to 5,000 rules per year.

fairness of criminal trials. But an unrestrained press can do much to prejudice the fairness of a trial.

In this instance, perhaps judges can do justice by reaching a fair compromise between these interests. A more difficult problem arises not when two interests collide but when two ideas of justice itself collide. One such collision pits *general* justice against *particular* justice. Is it just for bus drivers and train engineers to pull away from the station always exactly on time, even though someone racing down the platform to get home for Christmas will miss it? Is it not true in the long run, to paraphrase the late Professor Zechariah Chafee, that fewer people will miss buses and trains if everyone knows that buses and trains always leave on the dot, that more people will miss if they assume that they can dally and still find the vehicle at the station? While it is often possible to engineer compromises among competing interests, it is often impossible to compromise between different visions of justice itself. Unless she is corrupt or lazy, a judge will *strive* to do justice, but whether she succeeds often remains debatable.

A particularly poignant example of sacrificing particular justice to general justice occurred on June 22, 1992, when the United States Supreme Court struck down the conviction of a White teenager who burned a crudely made cross in the yard of a neighboring African American family. All nine justices struck down the conviction, which was based on the St. Paul, Minnesota, Bias-Motivated Crime ordinance. The ordinance read in part:

> Whoever places on public or private property a symbol, object, appellation, characterization or graffiti, including, but not limited to, a burning cross or Nazi swastika, which one knows or has reasonable grounds to know arouses anger, alarm, or resentment in others on the basis of race, color, creed, religion, or gender commits disorderly conduct and is guilty of a misdemeanor.

All nine justices condemned the placement of the burning cross. However, Justice Scalia found the ordinance violated First Amendment principles of free expression because it punished some expressions but not others based on the political acceptability of the contents. While Scalia found the ordinance too narrow, other justices found it unconstitutional because it was too broad. Legitimate political expression often arouses alarm or resentment, they reasoned, and this ordinance would punish desirable as well as obnoxious expression.[27] For the sake of both these general principles of justice, the injured family lost because the vandal went unpunished.

The ways of making legal choices described here do not make judges or anyone else completely "objective," because legal decisions require choices from among competing values. The problem of general versus particular justice is a good illustration. A value, a preference, or a moral "feeling" is not a concept we can prove to be right or wrong. Those who adopt values that conflict with yours will call you biased, and you may feel the same way about them. A discussion of legal reasoning can stress that some values are better than others, but arguments on both sides will remain. If the argument gets heated, each side will accuse the other of being biased. In the final chapter, we will examine more fully the nature of bias and impartiality in law. If "biases" and "values" are identical psychological feelings or beliefs about right and wrong, then legal reasoning cannot eliminate them; but we will see that judges can act impartially nevertheless. You can guess, from our definition of legal reasoning, that the impartial judge will persuasively harmonize, or coherently fit together, the four elements described in this chapter. We trust that with the next four

---

[27] See *R. A. V., Petitioner v. City of St. Paul,* 112 S.Ct. 2538 (1992).

chapters under your belt, you will follow easily the more complete development of this idea in the final chapter.

Impartiality, however, does not eliminate the tragic element in law. In Martha Nussbaum's great book, *The Fragility of Goodness,* we learn that tragic situations exist whenever circumstances pull people in two inconsistent but equally good directions at once. Imagine yourself having to decide the hate-speech case or the frozen embryo case mentioned earlier, and you will feel their inherently tragic nature. Nussbaum (and most contemporary moral philosophers) rejects Kant's claim, as Nussbaum puts it, "that objective practical rules be in every situation consistent, forming a harmonious system like a system of true beliefs. . . . It appears that our duties may conflict. But this cannot be so, since the very concepts of duty and practical law rule out inconsistencies." Impartiality requires a judge to persuade us that she has reached the better result. But if a judge fakes reaching a mechanically correct result and denies the tragic choices in a case, she will not persuade us to trust her exercise of power over us. We will know better because we know, from Greek mythology and from our own experience, that we often cannot do right without doing wrong. Legal reasoning matters because, done well, it helps communities survive and transcend life's tragic side. As Nussbaum writes, "If we were such that we could in a crisis dissociate ourselves from one commitment because it clashed with another, we would be less good."[28]

Illustrative Case

Each chapter gives you a chance to apply what you have learned to an example of legal reasoning. After presenting the Prochnow case, we pose questions that will help you identify the four legal reasoning elements in its majority and dissenting opinions.

Prochnow v. Prochnow
Supreme Court of Wisconsin
274 Wisconsin 491 (1957)

A husband appeals from that part of a decree of divorce which adjudged him to be the father of his wife's child and ordered him to pay support money. The actual paternity is the only fact which is in dispute.

Joyce, plaintiff, and Robert, defendant, were married September 2, 1950, and have no children other than the one whose paternity is now in question. In February 1953, Robert began his military service. When he came home on furloughs, which he took frequently in 1953, he found his wife notably lacking in appreciation of his presence. Although he was home on furlough for eight days in October and ten in December, after August 1953, the parties had no sexual intercourse except for one time, to be mentioned later. In Robert's absence Joyce had dates with a man known as Andy, with whom she danced in a tavern and went to a movie, behaving in a manner which the one witness who testified on the subject thought unduly affectionate. This witness also testified that Joyce told her that Robert was dull but that she and Andy had fun. She also said that a few days before Friday, March 12, 1954, Joyce told her she had to see her husband who was then stationed in Texas but must be back to her work in Milwaukee by Monday.

On March 12, 1954, Joyce flew to San Antonio and met Robert there. They spent the night of the 13th in a hotel where they had sex relations. The next day, before returning to

[28] Martha C. Nussbaum, *The Fragility of Goodness: Luck and Ethics in Greek Tragedy and Philosophy* (New York: Cambridge University Press, 1986), pp. 31 and 50.

Milwaukee, she told him that she did not love him and was going to divorce him. Her complaint, alleging cruel and inhuman treatment as her cause of action, was served on him April 8, 1954. On September 16, 1954, she amended the complaint to include an allegation that she was pregnant by Robert and demanded support money.

The child was born November 21, 1954. Robert's letters to Joyce are in evidence in which he refers to the child as his own. He returned to civilian life February 13, 1955, and on February 18, 1955, answered the amended complaint, among other things denying that he is the father of the child born to Joyce; and he counterclaimed for divorce alleging cruel and inhuman conduct on the part of the wife.

Before trial two blood grouping tests were made of Mr. and Mrs. Prochnow and of the child. The first was not made by court order but was ratified by the courts and accepted in evidence as though so made. This test was conducted in Milwaukee on March 21, 1955. The second was had in Waukesha September 29, 1955, under court order. The experts by whom or under whose supervision the tests were conducted testified that each test eliminated Robert as a possible parent of the child. An obstetrician, called by Robert, testified that it was possible for the parties' conduct on March 13, 1954, to produce the full-term child which Mrs. Prochnow bore the next November 21st. Mrs. Prochnow testified that between December 1953 and May 1954, both inclusive, she had no sexual intercourse with any man but her husband. . . .

BROWN, Justice.

The trial judge found the fact to be that Robert is the father of Joyce's child. The question is not whether, on this evidence, we would have so found: we must determine whether that finding constituted reversible error.

Section 328.39 (1) (a), Stats., commands:

> Whenever it is established in an action or proceeding that a child was born to a woman while she was the lawful wife of a specified man, any party asserting the illegitimacy of the child in such action or proceeding shall have the burden of proving beyond all reasonable doubt that the husband was not the father of the child. . . .

Ignoring for the moment the evidence of the blood tests and the effect claimed for them, the record shows intercourse between married people at a time appropriate to the conception of this baby. The husband's letters after the child's birth acknowledge it is his own. The wife denies intercourse with any other man during the entire period when she could have conceived this child. Unless we accept the illegitimacy of the baby as a fact while still to be proved, there is no evidence that then, or ever, did she have intercourse with anyone else. The wife's conduct with Andy on the few occasions when the witness saw them together can justly be called indiscreet for a married woman whose husband is absent, but falls far short of indicating adultery. Indeed, appellant did not assert that Andy is the real father but left that to the imagination of the court whose imagination, as it turned out, was not sufficiently lively to draw the inference. Cynics, *among whom on this occasion we must reluctantly number ourselves* [emphasis supplied], might reasonably conclude that Joyce, finding herself pregnant in February or early March, made a hasty excursion to her husband's bed and an equally abrupt withdrawal when her mission was accomplished. The subsequent birth of a full-term child a month sooner than it would usually be expected if caused by this copulation does nothing to dispel uncharitable doubts. But we must acknowledge that a trial judge, less inclined to suspect the worst, might with reason recall that at least as early as the preceding August, Joyce had lost her taste for her husband's embraces. Divorce offered her freedom from them, but magnanimously she might determine to try once more to save the marriage: hence her trip to Texas. But when the night spent in Robert's arms proved no more agreeable than such nights used to be she made up her mind that they could live together no more, frankly told him so and took her departure. The medical testimony concerning the early arrival of the infant does no more than to recognize eight months of gestation as unusual. It admits the possibility that Robert begat the child that night in that San Antonio hotel. Thus, the mother swears the child is Robert's and she knew, in the Biblical sense, no other man. Robert, perforce, acknowledges that it may be his. Everything else depends on such reasonable inferences as one chooses to draw from the other admitted facts and circumstances. And such inferences are for the trier of the fact. Particularly, in view of Sec. 328.39 (1) (a), Stats., supra, we cannot agree with appellant that even with the blood tests left out of consideration, the record here proves beyond a reasonable doubt that Joyce's husband was not the father of her child.

Accordingly we turn to the tests. The expert witnesses agree that the tests excluded Mr. Prochnow from all possibility of this fatherhood. Appellant argues that this testimony is conclusive; that with the tests in evidence Joyce's testimony that she had no union except with her husband is insufficient to support a finding that her husband is the father. . . . But the Wisconsin statute authorizing blood tests in paternity cases pointedly refrains from directing courts to accept them as final even when they exclude the man sought to be held as father. In its material parts it reads:

> Sec. 325.23 *Blood tests in civil actions.* Whenever it shall be relevant in a civil action to determine the parentage or identity of any child, . . . the court . . . may direct any party to the action and the person involved in the controversy to submit to one or more blood tests, to be made by duly qualified physicians. Whenever such test is ordered and made the results thereof shall be receivable in evidence, but only in cases where definite exclusion is established. . . .

This statute does no more than to admit the test and its results in evidence—there to be given weight and credibility in competition with other evidence as the trier of the fact considers it deserves. No doubt in this enactment the legislature recognized that whatever infallibility is accorded to science, scientists and laboratory technicians by whom the tests must be conducted, interpreted, and reported retain the human fallibilities of other witnesses. It had been contended before this that a report on the analysis of blood is a physical fact which controls a finding of fact in opposition to lay testimony on the subject, and the contention was rejected. . . . When the trial judge admitted the Prochnow tests in evidence and weighed them against the testimony of Mrs. Prochnow he went as far in giving effect to them as our statute required him to do. Our opinions say too often that trial courts and juries are the judges of the credibility of witnesses and the weight to be given testimony which conflicts with the testimony of others for us to say that in this case the trial court does not have that function. . . .

The conclusion seems inescapable that the trial court's finding must stand when the blood-test statute does not make the result of the test conclusive but only directs its receipt in evidence there to be weighed, as other evidence is, by the court or jury. We hold, then, that the credibility of witnesses and the weight of all the evidence in this action was for the trial court, and error cannot be predicated upon the court's acceptance of Joyce's testimony as more convincing than that of the expert witnesses.

Judgment affirmed.

WINGERT, Justice (dissenting). With all respect for the views of the majority, Mr. Chief Justice FAIRCHILD, Mr. Justice CURRIE, and the writer must dissent.

In our opinion the appellant, Robert Prochnow, sustained the burden placed upon him by Sec. 328.39 (1) (a), Stats., of proving beyond all reasonable doubt that he was not the father of the child born to the plaintiff.

To meet the burden, appellant produced two classes of evidence, (1) testimony of facts and circumstances, other than blood tests, which create grave doubt that appellant is the father, and (2) the evidence of blood tests and their significance, hereinafter discussed. In our opinion the blood test evidence should have been treated as conclusive in the circumstances of this case.

Among the numerous scientific achievements of recent decades is the development of a method by which it can be definitely established in many cases, with complete accuracy, that one of two persons cannot possibly be the parent of the other. The nature and significance of this discovery are summarized by the National Conference of Commissioners on Uniform State Laws, a highly responsible body, in the prefatory note to the Uniform Act on Blood Tests to Determine Paternity, as follows:

> In paternity proceedings, divorce actions and other types of cases in which the legitimacy of a child is in issue, the modern developments of science have made it possible

to determine with certainty in a large number of cases that one charged with being the father of a child could not be. Scientific methods may determine that one is not the father of the child by the analysis of blood samples taken from the mother, the child, and the alleged father in many cases, but it cannot be shown that a man is the father of the child. If the negative fact is established it is evident that there is a great miscarriage of justice to permit juries to hold on the basis of oral testimony, passion, or sympathy, that the person charged is the father and is responsible for the support of the child and other incidents of paternity. . . . There is no need for a dispute among the experts, and true experts will not disagree. Every test will show the same results. . . .

[T]his is one of the few cases in which judgment of court may be absolutely right by use of science. In this kind of a situation it seems intolerable for a court to permit an opposite result to be reached when the judgment may scientifically be one of complete accuracy. For a court to permit the establishment of paternity in cases where it is scientifically impossible to arrive at that result would seem to be a great travesty on justice. (Uniform Laws Annotated, 9 Miscellaneous Acts, 1955 Pocket Part, p. 13.)

In the present case the evidence showed without dispute that the pertinent type of tests were made of the blood of the husband, the wife, and the child on two separate occasions by different qualified pathologists, at separate laboratories, and that such tests yielded identical results, as follows:

	3/17/55	9/29/55
	Blood types	
Robert Prochnow (Husband)	AB	AB
Joyce Prochnow (Wife)	O	O
David Prochnow (Child)	O	O

There is no evidence whatever that the persons who made these tests were not fully qualified experts in the field of blood testing, nor that the tests were not made properly, nor that the results were not correctly reported to the court. . . .

Two qualified experts in the field also testified that it is a physical impossibility for a man with type AB blood to be the father of a child with type O blood, and that therefore appellant is not and could not be that father of the child David. Both testified that there are no exceptions to the rule. One stated "There is no difference of opinion regarding these factors amongst the authorities doing this particular work. None whatsoever." The evidence thus summarized was not discredited in any way and stands undisputed in the record. Indeed, there was no attempt to discredit it except by the wife's own self-serving statement that she had not had sexual relations with any other man during the period when the child might have been conceived. . . .

Questions about the Case

1. This case requires the court to interpret several statutes. Which are they? The case also involves a procedural rule that differentiates the work of appellate courts from that of trial courts. What is that rule?
2. What factual assertions about this dispute did the trial court accept as proved? What factual assertions did it reject?
3. What social background facts are at issue here? What choice did the appellate court have to make about social background facts in order to decide this case?[29]

[29] *Hint:* Don't discount the social background fact that medical practitioners make mistakes. In 1995 a Harvard School of Public Health research team studying two well-regarded Boston hospitals found 334 errors in drug delivery to patients over a six-month period. ("Hundreds of Drug Errors Are Found at Two Hospitals," *New York Times*, 6 July 1995, p. A8.) Doesn't the possibility of error help explain why the statute uses the phrase "receivable in evidence"?

4. Did not the majority's decision to reject the conclusive proof of the blood tests rest on some value choices? Does the court articulate these choices? If not, what might they have been? Does this decision necessarily depend on a fundamentalist religious conviction that God can always alter nature if He wishes? Or might the court have believed that, in the interest of giving David any father at all, it was best to assign paternity to Robert despite science?
5. Why was the law ambiguous in this case?
6. Do you find that the majority or the dissenting opinion does a better job of legal reasoning? Why?
7. How does this opinion change the law? That is, if the dissent had prevailed in this case, how would the reading of the rules of law at issue in this case change?

Chapter 2

Change and Stability in Legal Reasoning

The mystery of life is not a problem to be solved, but a reality to be experienced.

—AART VAN DER LEEUW

*T*he first chapter began to narrow this book's scope of inquiry. We do not in this book put ourselves in the shoes of legislators, nor do we examine how elections or lobbying efforts or presidential leadership produce new law. While this book does not explore many important political issues, it does inevitably steer us into political waters in three critical ways.

First, studying legal reasoning shows us that "the law" does not substitute for politics, it *is* politics. Unless the parties agree that "the law" automatically resolves a case (and when this happens they usually don't go to court in the first place), the judge will make and defend choices. That is, the judge will use his or her political power to change people's lives—to send them to jail or the death chamber, to bankrupt them, to humiliate them or vindicate them. Legal reasoning, as explained in the first chapter, becomes the language we use for analyzing whether the judge has used this political power fairly and persuasively.

Second, once we learn from studying legal reasoning that the most impartial and fair judges inevitably make political choices when they decide cases, we learn that we must take other questions about legal politics very seriously. Whom we elect as president, for example, will affect the selection of people to sit on the federal courts, and that, in turn, will inevitably affect who wins and who loses in the judicial system. At a hearing on his nomination to the Supreme Court, Clarence Thomas once asserted that he would "strip down like a runner" and leave a life's worth of beliefs and political attitudes behind him when he ascended to the bench. If Thomas was simply promising that he would not allow his attitudes to *predetermine* his decisions, his statement was unremarkable. If instead Thomas's pledge was to become an attitudeless judge, his promise was not simply unrealistic but absurd.[1] A long line of political science research demonstrates that the worldviews and experiences of

---

[1]David Broder, "A Justice with No Agenda," *Washington Post*, 15 September 1991, p. C7. Martha Minow makes Justice Thomas's comments the starting point of her analysis in her article "Stripped Down Like a Runner or Enriched by Experience," in G. Larry Mays and Peter R. Gregware, eds., *Courts and Justice: A Reader* (Prospect Heights, Ill.: Waveland Press, 1995), pp. 366–382.

judges affect the decisions they make.[2] This fact does not reflect some monstrous failure by judges to achieve objective, and hence "correct," legal judgments. There is, remember, no single "right answer" to legal questions, so it is nonsensical to condemn a judge for making an "incorrect" or "biased" decision. Judges can, however, be evaluated based on how well they explain their decisions. Judges, then, don't find right answers to legal questions, but they do create "good" and "bad" answers. This book shows you how to tell the good from the bad. Judges who use good legal reasoning bolster a community's confidence in the legal system by demonstrating they have thought carefully about the factors that are relevant to a decision. That—not attitudelessness—is all we can expect of judges. Invariably, then, judges bring their attitudes with them when they ascend to the bench, and controversy over judicial appointments like Thomas's is to be expected.

Thirdly, as our emphasis on good reasoning suggests, the legal process, for all its political characteristics, is still a distinctive kind of politics. The practices and customs and norms that go with being a U.S. congressperson or senator inevitably shape how that kind of politician thinks. Judges, because they have been trained in the law and are constantly exposed to legal arguments, think differently about politics than do legislators. Moreover, the audience for legal opinions expects a different set of justifications for political action than does the audience for legislative decisions. It is, for example, perfectly acceptable for a senator to explain that she made a particular decision because it benefitted her home state, or some interest group she supports; a judge who explained his vote in this way would be considered corrupt or incompetent. Law, like any language practice, limits the horizons of what becomes thinkable within that framework. What counts as good evidence, or an appropriate case to hear, or a recognizable social background fact or legitimate social value, all depends on the tradition of legal practices that make such things thinkable in the first place. So, as you grapple with legal reasoning issues throughout this book, please keep in the back of your mind that you are simultaneously studying the political language by which the law creates and perpetuates its power.[3]

The first section of this chapter explores why legal language does not generate "correct" answers to contested legal questions. The second section asserts that this uncertainty and ambiguity benefits us more than it harms us, at least as a general rule. The third section examines the other side of the uncertainty coin, the general philosophical conditions in which judges should choose legal clarity and stability at the expense of other values. The concluding section reviews some general and inevitable characteristics of law that make it forever changing, never perfected.

---

[2] For a wide-ranging treatment of why language and logic do not yield objectively "correct" interpretations of the world, see Stanley Fish's essays collected in *There's No Such Thing as Free Speech* (New York: Oxford University Press, 1994). Recent empirical studies of judicial decision making support the approach we take here. See, for example, Jeffrey A. Segal and Harold J. Spaeth, *Majority Rule or Minority Will: Adherence to Precedent on the U.S. Supreme Court* (New York: Cambridge University Press, 1999); *The Supreme Court and the Attitudinal Model* (Cambridge: Cambridge University Press, 1993); Saul Brenner and Harold Spaeth, *Stare Indecisis* (Cambridge: Cambridge University Press, 1995); Lawrence Baum, *The Puzzle of Judicial Behavior* (Ann Arbor: University of Michigan, 1997); and Lee Epstein and Jack Knight, *The Choices Judges Make* (Washington, D. C.: Congressional Quarterly Press, 1997).

[3] Stanley Fish's essay, "The Law Wishes to Have a Formal Existence," in *There's No Such Thing as Free Speech*, pp. 141–179 (cited in note 2), describes this phenomenon particularly well. We're particularly grateful to Michael McCann for showing us why specifying this point is so essential to this book's larger argument. For a thorough description of how law helps constitute the hopes and expectations of laypersons outside the judical system, see McCann's *Rights at Work* (Chicago: University of Chicago Press, 1994).

SOURCES OF UNPREDICTABILITY IN LAW

The Disorderly Conduct of Words

Cases often go to courts (and particularly appellate courts) because the law does not determine the outcome. Both sides believe they have a chance to win. The legal process is in these cases *unpredictable*. Legal rules are made with words, and we can begin to understand why law is unpredictable by examining the ambiguity of words, the "disorderly conduct of words," as Professor Chafee put it.[4] Sometimes our language fails to give us precise definitions. There is, for example, no way to define the concept of *table* so as to exclude some items we call "benches," and the reverse.[5] More often, words and statements that seem clear enough in the abstract may nevertheless have different meanings to each of us, because we have all had different experiences with the objects or events in the world that the word has come to represent. The experiences of each of us are unique in many respects, so no one word or set of words necessarily means the same thing to all of us. Bill Clinton insisted during his impeachment trial that he spoke truthfully when he denied in a deposition that he had ever had sex with Monica Lewinsky, since to him *sex* meant intercourse. Clinton's claim was widely ridiculed, but a study in the *Journal of the American Medical Association* showed that most college students considered oral sex not to be "sex."[6]

As this example indicates, words are malleable, and people can shape them to suit their own interests. Here's another example: In 1962 Congress, to encourage new business investment, allowed businesspeople up to a 10 percent tax credit for investing in new personal property for their business. Investments like new machinery would qualify, but new buildings and permanent building fixtures would not. In 1982 the Justice Department sued the accounting firm of Ernst and Whinney for using words to disguise real property as personal property. What the accountants called "movable partitions," "equipment accesses," and "decorative fixtures" were in reality doors, manholes, and windows—all real property unqualified for the tax deduction. A "freezer" was in reality an entire refrigerated warehouse, "cedar decoration" was a wood-paneled wall, and "movable partitions—privacy" described toilet stalls.[7]

Words are slippery because their meaning always depends on their context: John Train has developed lists of what he calls "antilogies," words that can have opposite meanings in different contexts.[8] Thus the infinitive *to dust* can refer to removing dust or to laying down dust, as in crop dusting. *To continue* can mean to proceed

---

[4]Zechariah Chafee, "The Disorderly Conduct of Words," 41 *Columbia Law Review* 381 (1941). The perfecting of computer enhancement of visual images threatens to make seemingly objective photographs and video records, offered as physical evidence in trials, as uncertain as verbal testimony. The technique, called *morphing*—as seen in movies like *Star Trek VI* and *Terminator II*—can change one image into an imaginary one as realistic as the original.

[5]Thanks to Professor Martin Landau, University of California, Berkeley, for this example. If you don't believe it, try creating this definitional distinction—paying attention to coffee tables and tool benches. Further suppose a state enacts a statute exempting from its sales tax all "food and foodstuffs." What is *food*? Is chewing gum food? Is coffee? Is beer?

[6]Stephanie A. Sanders and June Machover Reinisch, "Would You Say You 'Had Sex' If . . . ?" *Journal of the American Medical Association* 281 (1999):275–276.

[7]Jim Drinkhall, "Turnabout has IRS Accusing Taxpayers of Gobbledygook," *Wall Street Journal*, 12 November 1982, p. 1.

[8]See "Antilogies," *Harvard Magazine*, November–December 1985, p. 18, and "More Antilogies," *Harvard Magazine*, March–April 1986, p. 17.

or to delay a proceeding. *To sanction* both authorizes and condemns. *To buckle* can mean to fasten together or fall apart. Or consider a great old computer joke. The experts had invented a machine that would translate from English to Russian and back. To test it they programmed in the phrase, "The spirit is willing but the flesh is weak," then took the Russian translation and programmed it to come back in English. Lacking the specific biblical context for the original, the computer did the best it could with the Russian context, but the English retranslation came back, "The vodka is agreeable but the meat is rotten." This sudden confusion of contexts is a primary source of humor, as revealed in the story where the city lawyer asked a witness if "you, too, were shot in the fracas?" He got this answer from a less sophisticated witness: "No, sir, I was shot midway between the fracas and the navel."

The disorderly conduct of words affects legal reasoning most immediately when a judge faces the task of interpreting a statute for the first time, when no judicial precedent interpreting the statute helps the judge to find its meaning. Therefore, we shall refine the problem of disorderly words in Chapter 4, which examines judicial choices in statutory interpretation "in the first instance."

The Unpredictability of Precedents

The previous paragraph suggests that precedents help narrow the range of legal choices judges face when they justify a decision. Indeed, precedents do just that, but they never provide complete certainty. Reasoning by example also perpetuates a degree of unpredictability in law. To see why, we proceed through six analytical stages.

Stage One: Reasoning by Example in General   Reasoning by example, in its simplest form, means accepting one choice and rejecting another because the past provides an example that the accepted choice somehow "worked." Robert, for example, wants to climb a tree but wonders if its branches will hold. He chooses to attempt the climb because his older sister has just climbed the tree without mishap. Robert reasons by example. His reasoning hardly guarantees success: His older sister may still be skinnier and lighter than he. Robert may regret a choice based on a bad example, but he still reasons that way. If he falls and survives, he will possess a much better example from which to reason in the future.

The most important characteristic of reasoning by example in any area of life is that no rules tell the decider *how* to decide which facts are similar and which are different. Let us therefore see how this indeterminacy occurs in legal reasoning.

Stage Two: Examples in Law   In law, decisions in prior cases provide examples for legal reasoning. For starters, a precedent contains the analysis and the conclusion reached in an earlier case in which the facts and the legal question(s) resemble the current conflict a judge has to resolve. Even when a statute or a constitutional rule is involved, a judge will look at what other judges have said about the meaning of that rule when they applied it to similar facts and answered similar legal questions. A judge hearing the case of the airplane thief would not simply read the National Motor Vehicle Act; a judge hearing the dispute over the University of Wisconsin's mandatory student fees wouldn't simply stare at the words of the First Amendment. Both would primarily look at previous cases in which judges had interpreted these rules.

To understand more fully how precedents create examples, we must return to the distinction between law and history. How does a judge know whether facts of a prior case really do resemble those in the case now before the court?

Trials themselves do *not* normally produce precedents. As we have seen, trials seek primarily to find the immediate facts of the dispute, to discover who is lying, whose memory has failed, and who can reliably speak to the truth of the matter. When a jury hears the case, the judge acts as an umpire, making sure the lawyers present the evidence properly to the jury so that it decides the "right" question. Often judges do the jury's job as well. The law does not allow jury trials in some disputes, and even where it does, sometimes both parties prefer to use a judge. The parties may feel the issues are too complex for laypeople or that a "bench trial" will take less time and cost less money.

Whether or not a jury participates in a trial, it is up to the trial judge to decide the issues of law that the lawyers raise. The conscientious trial judge will explain to the parties orally for the record why and how she resolves the key legal issues in their case. In some instances she will give them a written opinion explaining her legal choices, and this may be published. But since at trial the judge pays most attention to the historical part of the case, deciding what happened, she usually keeps her explanations at the relatively informal oral level. As a result, other judges will not find these opinions reported anywhere; they cannot discover them even if they try. Hence few trial judges create precedents even though they resolve legal issues.

Thus the masses of legal precedents that fill the shelves of law libraries mostly emerge from the appellate process. You should not, however, lose sight of the fact that lawyers use many of the same legal reasoning techniques when formulating their arguments and advising their clients.

Stage Three: The Three-Step Process of Reasoning by Example   Legal reasoning often involves reasoning from the examples of precedents. Powerful legal traditions impel judges to solve problems by using solutions to similar problems reached by judges in the past. Thus a judge seeks to resolve conflicts by discovering a statement about the law in a prior case—the example—and then applying this statement or conclusion to the current case. Lawyers who seek to anticipate problems and prevent conflicts follow much the same procedure. Professor Levi calls this a three-step process in which the judge sees a factual similarity between the current case and one or more prior cases, announces the rule of law on which the earlier case or cases rested, and applies the rule to the current case.[9]

Stage Four: How Reasoning by Example Perpetuates Unpredictability in Law   To understand this stage we must return to the first step in the three-step description of reasoning by example, the step in which the judge decides which precedent governs. The judge must *choose* the facts in the current case that resemble or differ from the facts in the case, or line of cases, in which prior judicial decisions first announced the rule. The judge no doubt accepts the obligation, made powerful by legal tradition, to "follow precedent," but the judge is under no obligation to follow any particular precedent. He completes step one *by deciding for himself* which of the many precedents are similar to the facts of the case before him and *by deciding for himself* what they mean.

No judicial opinion in a prior case can require that a judge sift the facts of the present case one way or another. She is always free to do this herself. A judge writing an opinion can influence a future user of the precedent she creates by refusing to

---

[9]Edward Levi, *An Introduction to Legal Reasoning* (Chicago: University of Chicago Press, 1949), p. 2. Please do not confuse the six analytical stages we use in this chapter with the three-step reasoning process inherent in our legal system itself.

report or consider some potentially important facts revealed in the trial transcript. But once she reports them, judges in later similar cases can use the facts in their own way. They can call a fact critical that a prior judge reported but deemed irrelevant; they can make a legal molehill out of what a prior judge called a mountain. Thus the present judge, the precedent user, retains the freedom to choose the example from which the legal conclusion follows.

We call judicial freedom to choose the governing precedent by selectively sifting the facts *fact freedom*. This is a major source of uncertainty in law, because it is impossible to predict with total accuracy how a judge will use fact freedom. Thus we cannot say that "the law" applies known or given rules to diverse factual situations, because we don't know the applicable rules until after the judge uses fact freedom to choose the precedent.

Stage Five: An Illustration of Unpredictability in Law   Consider the following example from the rather notorious history of the Mann Act. The Mann Act, passed by Congress in 1910, provides in part that "Any person who shall knowingly transport or cause to be transported . . . in interstate or foreign commerce . . . any woman or girl for the purpose of prostitution or debauchery, or for any other immoral purpose . . . shall be deemed guilty of a felony." Think about these words for a minute. Do they say that if I take my wife to Tennessee for the purpose of drinking illegal moonshine whiskey with her I have violated the Mann Act? What if I take her to Tennessee to rob a bank? Certainly robbing a bank is an "immoral purpose." Is it "interstate commerce"? But we are jumping prematurely to Chapter 4. For the moment, you should see only that the Congress has chosen some rather ambiguous words, and then turn your attention to the main problem: deciding how best to read the facts of the precedent cases so as to reach a decision in the following case.

Mr. and Mrs. Mortensen, owners and operators of a house of prostitution in Grand Island, Nebraska, went with two employees on a well-earned vacation to Yellowstone and Salt Lake City. The girls did lay off their occupation completely for the duration of the trip, and they paid for much of the trip themselves. Upon their return they resumed their calling. More than a year later, federal agents arrested the Mortensens and, on the basis of the vacation trip, charged them with violation of the Mann Act. The jury convicted the Mortensens. Their lawyer appealed to an appellate court judge.

Unpredictability in law arises when the judge cannot automatically say that a given precedent is or isn't factually similar. To simplify matters here, let us now assume that only one precedent exists, the decision of the U.S. Supreme Court in *Caminetti v. United States*, announced in 1917.[10] How does this example determine the result in *Mortensen?* Assume that in *Caminetti* two married men took two young women (ages 19 and 20) who were not their wives from Sacramento, California, to a cabin near Reno, Nevada, where they had sexual relations. The girls went voluntarily; they were neither prostitutes nor known to be "fast." By traveling to Reno, the men may have hoped to avoid prosecution by California state officials. On these

---

[10]*Caminetti v. United States*, 242 U. S. 470 (1917). *Caminetti*'s facts and holding cover noncommercial as well as commercial sexual immorality. For a much fuller discussion of *Caminetti*, which in fact was a headline-making national scandal involving, among many players, a U.S. attorney general who went on to sit on the U.S. Supreme Court, see this book's final chapter, pp. 139–143.

facts the Supreme Court in *Caminetti* upheld the conviction under the Mann Act. Does this case seal the Mortensens' fate? Does this precedent require the courts to find Mr. and Mrs. Mortensen guilty under the Mann Act? To answer these questions the judge must decide whether this case is factually similar to *Mortensen.* Is it?

In one sense, of course it is. In each case the defendants transported women across state lines, after which sex out of wedlock occurred. In another sense, it isn't. Without going to Reno the girlfriends might not have slept with the defendants. But if the Mortensens had not sponsored the vacation, the women would have continued their work. The Mortensens's transportation *reduced* the frequency of prostitution. The two boyfriends maintained or increased "illicit sex." Should this difference matter? The judge is free to select one interpretation of the facts or the other in order to answer this question. Either decision will create a new legal precedent. It is precisely this freedom to decide either way that increases unpredictability in law.

Stage Six: Reasoning by Example Facilitates Legal Change   Why does judicial fact freedom make law change constantly? Legal rules change every time they are applied because no two cases ever have exactly the same facts. Although judges treat cases as if they were legally the same whenever they apply the rule of one case to another, deciding the new case in terms of the rule adds to the list of cases a new and unique factual situation. To rule in the Mortensens' favor, as the Supreme Court did in 1944, gave judges new ways of looking at the Mann Act.[11] With those facts, judges after 1944 could, if they wished, read the Mann Act more narrowly than they did in *Caminetti. Mortensen* thus potentially changed the meaning of the Mann Act, thereby changing the law.

But as the situation turned out, the change did not endure. In 1946 the Court upheld the conviction, under the Mann Act, of certain Mormons, members of a branch known as Fundamentalists, who took "secondary" wives across state lines. No prostitution at all was involved here, but the evidence did suggest that some of the women did not travel voluntarily. Fact freedom worked its way again.[12] The Court extended *Caminetti* and by implication isolated *Mortensen.* The content of the Mann Act, then, has changed with each new decision and each new set of facts.

Is law always as confusing and unclear as these examples make it seem? In one sense certainly not. To the practicing lawyer, most legal questions the client asks possess clear and predictable answers. But in such cases—and here we return to the definition of legal conflicts in Chapter 1—the problems probably do not get to court at all. Uncertainty helps convert a human problem into a legal conflict. We focus on uncertainty in law because that is where reason in law takes over.

In another sense, however, law never entirely frees itself from uncertainty. Lawyers always cope with uncertainties about what happened, uncertainties that arise in the historical part of law. If they go to trial on the facts, even if they think the law is clear, the introduction of new evidence or the unexpected testimony of a witness may raise new and uncertain legal issues the lawyers didn't consider before the trial. Lawyers know they can never fully predict the outcome of a client's case, even though much of the law is clear to them most of the time.

[11]*Mortensen v. United States,* 322 U.S. 369 (1944).
[12]*Cleveland v. United States,* 329 U.S. 14 (1946).

IS UNPREDICTABILITY IN LAW DESIRABLE?

Is it desirable that legal rules do not always produce clear and unambiguous answers to legal conflicts? Should the legal system strive to reach the point where legal rules solve problems in the way, for example, that the formula for finding square roots of numbers provides automatic answers to all square root problems?

Despite the human animal's natural discomfort in the presence of uncertainty, some unpredictability in law is desirable. Indeed, if a rule had to provide an automatic and completely predictable outcome before courts could resolve conflicts, society would become intolerably repressive, if not altogether impossible. There are two reasons why.[13]

First, since no two cases ever raise entirely identical facts, society must have some way of convincing litigants that treating different cases *as if they were the same* is fair. But if the legal system resolved all conflicts automatically, people would have little incentive to *participate* in the process that resolves their disputes. If the loser knew in advance he would surely lose, he would not waste time and money on litigation. He would not have the opportunity to try to persuade the judge that his case, always factually unique, *ought* to be treated by a different rule. Citizens who lose will perceive a system that allows them to "make their best case" as fairer than a system that tells them they lose while they sit helplessly.

Only in unpredictable circumstances will each side have an incentive to present its best case. Because the law is ambiguous, each side thinks it might win.[14] This produces an even more important consequence for society as a whole, not just for the losers. The needs of society change over time. The words of common law, statutes, and constitutions must take on new meanings. The participation that ambiguity encourages constantly bombards judges with new ideas. The ambiguity inherent in reasoning by example gives the attorney the opportunity to persuade the judge that the law *ought* to say one thing rather than another. Lawyers thus keep pushing judges to make their interpretation of "the law" fit new circumstances and changes in social values.

We are not encouraging legislators and judges to applaud legal uncertainty, much less to maximize it by crafting vague statutes and ambiguous opinions. Rather, we argue that uncertainty in law is unavoidable. This uncertainty is, however, more a blessing than a curse. The participation that uncertainty in law encourages gives the legal process and society itself a vital capacity to change its formal rules as less formal and official human needs and values change.

THE OTHER SIDE OF THE COIN: STARE DECISIS AS A STABILIZING AND CLARIFYING ELEMENT IN LAW

This discussion of unpredictability in law should not lead you to believe that law is never clear. Government by law cannot function without some consensus on the meaning of laws. If society is to work, most law must be clear much of the time. We must be able to make wills and contracts, to insure ourselves against disasters, and to plan hundreds of other decisions with the confidence that courts will back our decisions if the people we trust with our freedom and our property fail us.

---

[13]Levi, *An Introduction to Legal Reasoning*, pp. 1–6.

[14]The process also has the desirable effect of encouraging negotiation and compromise. Each side has an incentive to settle because each side knows it could lose.

There is indeed a force pushing toward stability within reasoning by example it-self: Once judges determine that a given precedent is factually similar enough to de-termine the outcome in the case before them, then in normal circumstances they fol-low the precedent. We call this the doctrine of *stare decisis*, meaning "we let the prior decision stand."

Stare decisis operates in two dimensions. Stare decisis in the first, or *vertical*, dimension acts as a marching order in the chain of judicial command. Courts in both the state and federal systems are organized in a hierarchy within their jurisdictions. Thus the supreme courts of Georgia and of the United States each sit at the top of an "organization chart" of courts. The rulings of the highest court in any jurisdiction legally control all the courts beneath it. Stare decisis stabilizes law vertically be-cause no court should ignore a higher authoritative decision on a legal point. As long as the U.S. Supreme Court holds that airplanes are not "vehicles" within the National Motor Vehicle Theft Act (NMVTA), all courts beneath it must legally honor that ruling in any future airplane theft case that may arise under the act.

There is, however, a more interesting *horizontal* dimension to stare decisis. Horizontal stare decisis is the binding force of a precedent *on the court that created it* over time. But what if a supreme court makes a decision that, either a few years or many decades later, it decides has become "bad" law and policy? When should a court follow its own "bad" precedent? The U.S. Supreme Court's decision in June of 1992 to continue to follow *Roe v. Wade*—and to reaffirm that the Constitution implic-itly grants a female a right to choose whether to continue a pregnancy prior to viabil-ity—amounted to a debate on this very question. The *New York Times* quoted on its front page the essence of the Court's horizontal stare decisis reasoning. Justice O'Connor extolled the importance of keeping law clear and stable. "Liberty finds no refuge in a jurisprudence of doubt . . . ," her opinion began. Justice Kennedy wrote of the importance of respecting the interest in relying on the law: "An entire genera-tion has come of age free to assume Roe's concept of liberty in defining the capacity of women to act in society, and to make reproductive decisions." And Justice Souter spoke eloquently of preserving the Court's image: "A decision to overturn . . . would address error, if error there was, at the cost of both profound and unnecessary damage to the Court's legitimacy, and to the Nation's commitment to the rule of law."[15]

As the abortion opinions suggest, stare decisis becomes significant only when a judge has reason to doubt the policy or wisdom of a precedent. If Souter, Kennedy, and O'Connor had thought the Roe precedent unproblematic, they would not have emphasized the importance of stare decisis in their opinions. An emphasis on stare decisis also presupposes that a past "bad" or "troublesome" decision really does ap-ply to the case at hand. If Souter, Kennedy, and O'Connor had not agreed the *Roe* case was controlling, stare decisis would have played no role in their opinions. So stare decisis becomes crucial only when judges doubt the wisdom of an applicable precedent.

Professor Thomas S. Currier has stated well the values justifying the principle of horizontal stare decisis. He suggests five values that should lead judges toward continuing to follow otherwise "bad" precedents:

> 1. *Stability.* It is clearly socially desirable that social relations should have a reasonable degree of continuity and cohesion, held together by a framework of rea-sonably stable institutional arrangements. Continuity and cohesion in the judicial

---

[15]*New York Times*, 30 June 1992, p. A1; and *Planned Parenthood v. Casey*, 112 S.Ct. 2791 (1992).

application of rules [are] important to the stability of these institutional arrangements, and society places great value on the stability of some of them. Social institutions in which stability is recognized as particularly important include the operation of government, the family, ownership of land, commercial arrangements, and judicially created relations. . . .

2. *Protection of Reliance.* [T]he value here is the protection of persons who have ordered their affairs in reliance upon contemporaneously announced law. It is obviously desirable that official declarations of the principles and attitudes upon which official administration of the law will be based should be capable of being taken as determinate and reliable indications of the course that such administration will in fact take in the future. . . . This value might be regarded as a personalized variation on the value of stability; but it is broader in that it is recognized even where no social institution is involved, and stability as such is unimportant.

3. *Efficiency in the Administration of Justice.* If every case coming before the courts had to be decided as an original proposition, without reference to precedent, the judicial workload would obviously be intolerable. Judges must be able to ease this burden by seeking guidance from what other judges have done in similar cases.

4. *Equality.* By this is meant the equal treatment of persons similarly situated. It is a fundamental ethical requirement that like cases should receive like treatment, that there should be no discrimination between one litigant and another except by reference to some relevant differentiating factor. This appears to be the same value that requires rationality in judicial decision-making, which in turn necessitates that the law applied by a court be consistently stated from case to case. The same value is recognized in the idea that what should govern judicial decisions are rules, or at least standards. The value of equality, in any event, appears to be at the heart of our received notions of justice.

5. *The Image of Justice.* This phrase does not mean that any judicial decision ought to be made on the basis of its likely impact upon the court's public relations, in the Madison Avenue sense, but merely that it is important not only that the court provide equal treatment to persons similarly situated, but that, insofar as possible, the court should appear to do so. Adherence to precedent generally tends not only to assure equality in the administration of justice, but also to project to the public the impression that courts do administer justice equally.[16]

The next chapters will describe more precisely the circumstances in which Currier's reasons for horizontal stare decisis should and should not compel a judge to follow rather than depart from a precedent. Here you should simply note that, in fact, most law is clear enough to prevent litigation most of the time. Lawyers can advise us on how to make valid wills and binding contracts. We know that if someone steals our car and takes it to another state, federal officials, under the authority of the National Motor Vehicle Theft Act, can try to track down the car and the criminal. Without a system of precedents it would be harder for us to predict judicial decisions and therefore more difficult for us to plan to avoid legal conflicts.

These forces in law pushing toward predictability and stability should not, however, obscure this chapter's main conclusion. Cases routinely arise where the best possible legal reasoning *cannot* provide a "right answer." New mixes of facts and legal rules pop up literally every day. This book discusses many socially important legal issues, but let us make the point here with a deliberately minor example: Some years ago a federal appellate court had to wrestle with the legal definition of "doll",

---

[16]Thomas S. Currier, "Time and Change in Judge-Made Law: Prospective Overruling," 51 *Virginia Law Review* 201 (1965), pp. 235–238. See also James Hardisty, "Reflections on Stare Decisis," 55 *Indiana Law Journal* 41 (1979).

because the new tariff laws imposed a 12 percent import tariff on "dolls" but allowed importing "toy soldiers" duty free. Question: Is the item made in Hong Kong and known as "G.I. Joe" a doll, like Barbie, or a toy soldier? The lawyers for Joe's seller, Hasbro, pointed out that like the clothes of older metal toy soldiers—but unlike those of most dolls—Joe's clothes were painted on. Hasbro lost. Just as in politically heated areas like abortion, so in little cases like this one, we and the parties want to know *why*. Only through legal reasoning can judges justify their answers.

Illustrative Cases

In the federal judicial system it is common for the intermediate appellate courts to hear cases in panels of three judges, with the outcome determined by majority vote. Here are two opinions written by Learned Hand sitting on two separate panels. The first is a precedent for the second. Notice that they were decided just a month apart. You should read the second case to see how Judge Hand uses his fact freedom to distinguish *Repouille* from the first case, *Francioso*, then to see how Judge Frank uses fact freedom a different way, and finally to explore the possibility that both judges in *Repouille* have used their fact freedom foolishly.

United States v. Francioso
164 F.2d 163 (Nov. 5, 1947)

L. HAND, Circuit Judge.

This is an appeal from an order admitting the appellee, Francioso, to citizenship. At the hearing the "naturalization examiner" objected to his admission upon the ground that he had married his niece and had been living incestuously with her during the five years before he filed his petition. Upon the following facts the judge held that Francioso had been "a person of good moral character" and naturalized him. Francioso was born in Italy in 1905, immigrated into the United States in 1923, and declared his intention of becoming a citizen in 1924. His wife was born in Italy in 1906, immigrated in 1911, and has remained here since then. They were married in Connecticut on February 13, 1925, and have four children, born in 1926, 1927, 1930, and 1933. Francioso was the uncle of his wife, and knew when he married her that the marriage was unlawful in Connecticut and that the magistrate would have not married them, had they not suppressed their relationship. They have always lived together in apparent concord, and at some time which the record leaves indefinite, a priest of the Catholic Church—of which both spouses are communicants—"solemnized" the marriage with the consent of his bishop.

In United States ex rel. *Iorio v. Day*, in speaking of crimes involving "moral turpitude" we held that the standard was, not what we personally might set, but "the commonly accepted mores": i.e., the generally accepted moral conventions current at the time, so far as we could ascertain them. The majority opinion in the United States ex rel. *Berlandi v. Reimer* perhaps looked a little askance at that decision; but it did not overrule it, and we think that the same test applies to the statutory standard of "good moral character" in the naturalization statute. Would the moral feelings, now prevalent generally in this country, be outraged because Francioso continued to live with his wife and four children between 1938 and 1943? Anything he had done before that time does not count; for the statute does not search further back into the past.

In 1938 Francioso's children were five, eight, eleven and twelve years old, and his wife was 31; he was morally and legally responsible for their nurture and at least morally responsible for hers. Cato himself would not have demanded that he should turn all five adrift. True, he might have left the home and supported them out of his earnings; but to do so would deprive his children of the protection, guidance and solace of a father. We can think of no course open to him which would not have been regarded as more immoral than that which he followed, unless it be that he should live at home, but as a celibate. There may be purists who would insist that this alone was consistent with "good moral conduct"; but we do not believe that the conscience of the ordinary man demands that degree of ascesis; and we have for warrant the fact that the Church—least of all complaisant with sexual lapses—saw fit to sanction the continuance of this union. Indeed, such a marriage would have been lawful in New York until 1893, as it was at common law. To be sure its legality does not determine its morality; but it helps to do so, for the fact that disapproval of such marriages was so long in taking the form of law, shows that it is condemned in no such sense as marriages forbidden by "God's law." It stands between those and the marriage of first cousins which is ordinarily, though not universally, regarded as permissible.

It is especially relevant, we think, that the relationship of these spouses did not involve those factors which particularly make such marriages abhorrent. It was not as though they had earlier had those close and continuous family contacts which are usual between uncle and niece. Francioso had lived in Italy until he was eighteen years of age; his wife immigrated when she was a child of four; they could have had no acquaintance until he came here in August, 1923, only eighteen months before they married. It is to the highest degree improbable that in that short time there should have arisen between them the familial intimacy common between uncle and niece, which is properly thought to be inimical to marriage. . . .

Order affirmed.

Repouille v. United States
165 F.2d 152 (Dec. 5, 1947)

L. HAND, Circuit Judge.

The District Attorney, on behalf of the Immigration and Naturalization Service, has appealed from an order, naturalizing the appellee, Repouille. The ground of the objection in the district court and here is that he did not show himself to have been a person of "good moral character" for the five years which preceded the filing of his petition. The facts are as follows. The petition was filed on September 22, 1944, and on October 12, 1939, he had deliberately put to death his son, a boy of thirteen, by means of chloroform. His reason for this tragic deed was that the child had "suffered from birth from a brain injury which destined him to be an idiot and a physical monstrosity malformed in all four limbs. The child was blind, mute, and deformed. He had to be fed; the movements of his bladder and bowels were involuntary, and his entire life was spent in a small crib." Repouille had four other children at the time towards whom he has always been a dutiful and responsible parent; it may be assumed that his act was to help him in their nurture, which was being compromised by the burden imposed upon him in the care of the fifth. The family was altogether dependent upon his industry for its support. He was indicted for manslaughter in the first degree; but the jury brought in a verdict of manslaughter in the second degree with a recommendation of the "utmost clemency"; and the judge sentenced him to not less than five years nor more than ten, execution to be stayed, and the defendant to be placed on probation, from which he was discharged in December 1945. Concededly, except for this act he conducted himself as a person of "good moral character" during the five years before he filed his petition. Indeed, if he had waited before filing his petition from September 22, to October 14, 1944, he would have had a clear record for the necessary period, and would have been admitted without question.

Very recently we had to pass upon the phrase "good moral character" in the Nationality Act; and we said that it set as a test, not those standards which we might ourselves approve, but whether "the moral feelings, now prevalent generally in this country" would "be outraged" by the conduct in question: that is, whether it conformed to "the generally accepted moral conventions current at the time."[a] In the absence of some national inquisition, like a Gallup poll,

---

[a]*United States v. Francioso,* 164 F.2d 163, (2d Cir., 1947). [Footnote in original.]

that is indeed a difficult test to apply; often questions will arise to which the answer is not ascertainable, and where the petitioner must fail only because he has the affirmative. Indeed, in the case at bar itself the answer is not wholly certain; for we all know that there are great numbers of people of the most unimpeachable virtue, who think it morally justifiable to put an end to a life so inexorably destined to be a burden on others, and—so far as any possible interest of its own is concerned—condemned to a brutish existence, lower indeed than all but the lowest forms of sentient life. Nor is it inevitably an answer to say that it must be immoral to do this, until the law provides security against the abuses which would inevitably follow, unless the practice were regulated. Many people—probably most people—do not make it a final ethical test of conduct that it shall not violate law; few of us exact of ourselves or of others the unflinching obedience of a Socrates. There being no lawful means of accomplishing an end, which they believe to be righteous in itself, there have always been conscientious persons who feel no scruple in acting in defiance of a law which is repugnant to their personal convictions, and who even regard as martyrs those who suffer by doing so. In our own history it is only necessary to recall the Abolitionists. It is reasonably clear that the jury which tried Repouille did not feel any moral repulsion at his crime. Although it was inescapably murder in the first degree, not only did they bring in a verdict that was flatly in the face of the facts and utterly absurd—for manslaughter in the second degree presupposes that the killing has not been deliberate—but they coupled even that with a recommendation which showed that in the substance they wished to exculpate the offender. Moreover, it is also plain, from the sentence which he imposed, that the judge could not have seriously disagreed with their recommendation.

One might be tempted to seize upon all this as a reliable measure of current morals; and no doubt it should have its place in the scale; but we should hesitate to accept it as decisive, when, for example, we compare it with the fate of a similar offender in Massachusetts, who, although he was not executed, was imprisoned for life. Left at large as we are, without means of verifying our conclusion, and without authority to substitute our individual beliefs, the outcome must needs be tentative; and not much is gained by discussion. We can say no more than that, quite independently of what may be the current moral feeling as to legally administered euthanasia, we feel reasonably secure in holding that only a minority of virtuous persons would deem the practise morally justifiable, while it remains in private hands, even when the provocation is as overwhelming as it was in this instance.

However, we wish to make it plain that a new petition would not be open to this objection; and that the pitiable event, now long passed, will not prevent Repouille from taking his place among us as a citizen. The assertion in his brief that he did not "intend" the petition to be filed until 1945, unhappily is irrelevant; the statute makes crucial the actual date of filing.

Order reversed; petition dismissed without prejudice to the filing of a second petition.

FRANK, Circuit Judge (dissenting).

This decision may be of small practical import to this petitioner for citizenship, since perhaps, on filing a new petition, he will promptly become a citizen. But the method used by my colleagues in disposing of this case may, as a precedent, have a very serious significance for many another future petitioner whose "good moral character" may be questioned (for any one of a variety of reasons which may be unrelated to a "mercy killing") in circumstances where the necessity of filing a new petition may cause a long and injurious delay. Accordingly, I think it desirable to dissent.

The district judge found that Repouille was a person of "good moral character." Presumably, in so finding, the judge attempted to employ that statutory standard in accordance with our decisions, i.e., as measured by conduct in conformity with "the generally accepted moral conventions at the time." My colleagues, although their sources of information concerning the pertinent mores are not shown to be superior to those of the district judge, reject his finding. And they do so, too, while conceding that their own conclusion is uncertain, and (as they put it) "tentative." I incline to think that the correct statutory test (the test Congress intended) is the attitude of our ethical leaders. That attitude would not be too difficult to learn; indeed, my colleagues indicate that they think such leaders would agree with the district judge. But the precedents in this circuit constrain us to be guided by contemporary public opinion about which, cloistered as judges are, we have but vague notions. (One recalls Gibbon's remark that usually a person who talks of "the opinion of the world at large" is really referring to "the few people with whom I happened to converse.")

Seeking to apply a standard of this type, courts usually do not rely on evidence but utilize what is often called the doctrine of "judicial notice," which, in matters of this sort, properly permits informal inquiries by the judges. However, for such a purpose (as in the discharge of many other judicial duties), the courts are inadequately staffed, so that sometimes "judicial notice" actually means judicial ignorance.

But the courts are not helpless; such judicial impotence has its limits. Especially when an issue importantly affecting a man's life is involved, it seems to me that we need not, and ought not, resort to our mere unchecked surmises, remaining wholly (to quote my colleagues' words) "without means of verifying our conclusions." Because court judgments are the most solemn kind of governmental acts—backed up as they are, if necessary, by the armed force of the government—they should, I think, have a more solid foundation. I see no good reason why a man's rights should be jeopardized by judges' needless lack of knowledge.

I think, therefore, that, in any case such as this, where we lack the means of determining present-day public reactions, we should remand to the district judge with these directions: The judge should give the petitioner and the government the opportunity to bring to the judge's attention reliable information on the subject, which he may supplement in any appropriate way. All the data so obtained should be put of record. On the basis thereof, the judge should reconsider his decision and arrive at a conclusion. Then, if there is another appeal, we can avoid sheer guessing, which alone is now available to us, and can reach something like an informed judgment.[b]

Questions About the Cases

1. What legal questions does Judge Hand ask about Mr. Francioso's behavior? How does he answer them?
2. What facts about the *Repouille* case make *Francioso* factually similar enough to serve as a precedent?
3. The problem in both cases is how a court should determine whether an applicant for naturalization has the required good moral character. In *Francioso* Judge Hand uses a method that permits him to conclude that Mr. Francioso should become a citizen. How does he do so?
4. Does Judge Hand use the same method in *Repouille*? If so, what facts distinguish the two cases so that, even though Mr. Francioso won, Mr. Repouille lost?
5. What method would Judge Frank use? How, if at all, does it differ from Hand's method? Which of these two do you prefer? Why?

[b]Of course, we cannot thus expect to attain certainty, for certainty on such a subject as public opinion is unattainable. [Footnote in original.]

<table>
<tr><td>

Chapter
3
</td><td>

Common Law
</td></tr>
</table>

> *The life of the law has not been logic; it has been experience. The felt*
> *necessities of the time, the prevalent moral and political theories, intuitions*
> *of public policy, avowed or unconscious, even the prejudices which judges*
> *share with their fellow-men, have had a good deal more to do than the*
> *syllogism in determining the rules by which men should be governed.*
> —OLIVER WENDELL HOLMES JR.

C ommon law at first may seem a bizarre creature. You are probably somewhat familiar with statutory law, in which judges interpret laws passed by legislatures, and constitutional law, in which judges interpret the Constitution. (We will examine each of these more familiar forms of law in Chapters 4 and 5.) In common-law cases judges receive no guidance from either legislatures or constitution-makers. They refer instead only to cases other judges decided in the past and the doctrines that have emerged from them. But, you might ask, if judges in common-law cases are reasoning solely from precedents, what were *those* precedents based on? The surprising answer is that they too were based on precedents, in fact a chain of precedents that stretches back hundreds of years—and all the way across the Atlantic Ocean, to England. To get to the beginning of this chain and understand the origins of the common law, then, we must travel back to medieval England, where you are invited to try a bit of role-playing.[1]

ORIGINS OF COMMON LAW

Put yourself in the position of William the Conqueror. You are, like many of your Norman kin, a shrewd politician. You have just managed the remarkable political feat, at least for the eleventh century, of assembling thousands of men and the necessary supporting equipment to cross the English Channel and to win title to England in battle. In these feudal days, title means ownership, and in a real sense you own England as a result of the Battle of Hastings.

However, your administrative headaches have just begun. On the one hand you must reward your supporters—and your supporters must reward their supporters—with grants of your land. On the other hand, you don't want to give up any of the land completely. You deserve to and shall collect rents—taxes are the modern

---

[1]Plucknett's "concise" history of the subject is over 700 pages long. Theodore F. T. Plucknett, *A Concise History of the Common Law*, 5th ed. (Boston: Little, Brown, 1956). For real conciseness try Frederick G. Kempin, *Historical Introduction to Anglo-American Law in a Nutshell*, 2nd ed. (St. Paul: West, 1973). To contrast common-law systems with the deductive or "code-based" systems of law on the European continent, see John Henry Merryman, *The Civil Law Tradition*, 2nd ed. (Stanford: Stanford University Press, 1985).

equivalent—from the landholders beneath you. You must give away with one hand but keep a legal hold with the other.

Furthermore, you must keep the peace, not only among the naturally restless and resentful natives but also among your supporters. As time goes on and their personal loyalty to you dwindles, they will no doubt fight more readily over exactly who owns which lands. And, of course, you have a notion that you and your successors will clash with that other group claiming a sort of sovereignty, the Church.

You must, in short, develop machinery for collecting rents, tracking ownership, and settling disputes.

Fortunately, you have conquered a relatively civilized land. At the local level some degree of government already exists on which you can build. In what we would call counties, but which the natives call shires, a hereditary *shire reeve* (our sheriff) cooperates with a bishop representing the Church to handle many of the problems of daily governance. These shires have courts, as do the smaller villages within them. You hope that, in the next century at least, your successors will be able to take control of them.

Meanwhile you take the action of any good politician. You undertake a survey, a sort of census, of who owns what lands—the *Domesday Book*. You organize into a Great Council all the lords (to whom you granted large amounts of land), church leaders, and many of the major native landlords who swear allegiance to you. They advise you (and you thus co-opt their support) on the important policy questions before you. You start appointing the local sheriffs yourself. You also create a permanent staff of bureaucrats—personal advisors who handle and resolve smaller problems as they arise.

You succeed in creating a new political reality, one in which it soon becomes somehow right to govern in the name of the ultimate landlord, the king.

So much for the role-playing.

William in no sense developed the contemporary common-law system, but he did create the political reality in which that development had to happen: Governing in the king's name—settling land disputes, collecting rents, and keeping the peace—meant rendering justice in the king's name. William's personal advisors (his staff) often traveled about the country administering *ad hoc* justice in the king's name. Additionally, many of the more serious offenses, what we would today call *crimes*, came directly to the Great Council for decision because they were offenses against the king's peace.

One hundred years later, Henry II began the actual takeover of the lower local courts. Initially, the king insisted on giving permission to the local courts before they could hear any case involving title to his land. A litigant would have to obtain from London a *writ of right* and then produce it in court before the court could hear the case. Shortly thereafter the king's council began to bypass the local courts altogether on matters of land title. Certain council members heard these cases at first; but, as they became more and more specialized and experienced, they split off from the council to form the king's Court of Common Pleas.

Similarly, the council members assigned to criminal matters developed into the Court of the King's Bench. The Court of the Exchequer, which handled rent and tax collections, evolved in similar fashion.

Only three problems remained. The first concerned the rules of law these judges should use. One solution, ultimately adopted in many continental jurisdictions, was simply to use the old Roman codes. In England, however—partly because it was easy and partly because it possessed considerable local political appeal—the king's judges adopted the practice of the pre-Conquest local courts. This practice of the lower courts consisted of adopting the local customs of the place and time and applying to daily events what people felt was fair. We might call this the custom of following custom.

The custom of following custom, however, produced the second problem. In a sparsely populated area—a primitive area by today's standards of commerce and transportation—customs about crimes, land use, debts, and so forth varied considerably from shire to shire, village to village, and manor to manor. But the king's judges could hardly decide each case on the basis of whatever local custom or belief happened to capture the fancy of those living where the dispute arose. To judge that way would amount to judging on shifting and inconsistent grounds. Judging would not occur in the name of the king but in the name of the location where the dispute arose. Following local custom would undercut William's long-range political objectives.

Hence the royal courts slowly adopted some customs and rejected others in an attempt to rule consistently in the king's name. Because justice in England rested on the custom of customs, the customs that the royal courts adopted and attempted to apply uniformly became the customs *common* to all the King's land. Thus the royal courts did not just follow custom; they created new common customs by following some, rejecting others, and combining yet others into new customs.

Of course, by doing this the courts no longer ruled by custom, strictly speaking. Because they sought to rule in the king's name, they sought to rule consistently. In doing so, the courts rejected some customs. Although judges no doubt felt that what they decided was right because it had its roots in some customs, it would be wiser to say they created not common custom but common law—law common throughout England.

With the solution of the third problem as follows, the story of the origins of common law ends. If judges adopt today a custom by which to govern other similar cases before the royal courts tomorrow, then tomorrow the judges must have some way of remembering what they said today. By the year 1250, the problem of faulty judicial memory so bothered one judge, Henri de Bracton, that he wrote a huge treatise attempting to solve it. Plucknett describes the work this way:

> [Bracton] procured, for his own private use, complete transcripts of the pleadings in selected cases, and even referred to the cases in the course of his treatise. This great innovation gives to his work in several places a curiously modern air, for like modern law writers he sometimes praises and sometimes criticises his cases. At the beginning of his book he explains, however, that the contemporary bench is not distinguished by ability or learning, and that his treatise is, to some extent, a protest against modern tendencies. He endeavours to set forth the sound principles laid down by those whom he calls "his masters" who were on the bench nearly a generation ago; hence it is that his cases are on the average about twenty years older than his book. Of really recent cases he used very few. It must not, therefore, be assumed that we have in Bracton the modern conception of case law. He never gives us any discussion of the authority of cases and clearly would not understand the modern implications of *stare decisis*. Indeed, his cases are carefully selected because they illustrate what he believes the law ought to be, and not because they have any binding authority; he freely admits that at the present moment decisions are apt to be on different lines. Bracton's use of cases, therefore, is not based upon their authority as sources of law, but upon his personal respect for the judges who decided them, and his belief that they raise and discuss questions upon lines which he considers sound. Although it is true that the use of cases as a source of law in the modern sense was still far in the future, nevertheless Bracton's use of cases is very significant. He accustomed lawyers of the thirteenth and early fourteenth centuries to read and to

discuss the cases which he put in his book, and this was a great step towards the modern point of view.[2]

Bracton's great work, together with smaller pamphlets of other judges and lawyers, were followed within half a century by "year-books," annual reports of court proceedings and decisions that heavily emphasized procedure. Procedure in England, the correct way and the incorrect way to proceed in court, had rapidly become rigid, and lawyers who could not master it and who could not remember all the strict technicalities lost their cases. They needed to write the technicalities down to remember them. Out of necessity, Bracton and his successors began the tradition—very much expanded today—of writing down the essential conclusions of the courts and using these writings as guides for future judicial choices.

As Plucknett reminds us, however, Bracton and his followers did not create the practices of reasoning by example and stare decisis as we now know them. Indeed, until the American Revolution, men actively rejected the notion that judges actually made law as they decided cases. Men believed rather in natural law, if not God's law at least nature's own. To them the proper judicial decision rested on true law. The decision that rested elsewhere was in a sense unlawful. This was, after all, the problem facing Bracton. Prior to and throughout most of the eighteenth century, lawyers and judges thought of common law as a collected body of correct legal doctrine, not the process of growth and change that reasoning by example—to say nothing of the changes and compromises in political life—makes inevitable.

Additional reasons explain why common law only rather recently began to emphasize reasoning from precedents. Bracton's treatise and the many that followed it did not reliably report the factual details of each and every case. These were unofficial, incomplete, and often critical commentaries. Not even a judge who wanted to follow the examples of precedents could use them with confidence. Only the radical and recent change in viewpoint and the recognition that law comes from politicians and not from God or nature, coupled with accurate court reporting, permitted reasoning by example and stare decisis to flourish.[3]

It is time to close this historical circle. In calling the common law judge-made law, we mean that for a variety of historical reasons, a large body of legal rules and principles exist because judges without legislative help have created them. As long as judges continue to apply them, they continue to re-create them with each application. The fact that judges for most of this history thought they simply restated divine or natural law matters relatively little to us today. What matters is that the twentieth-century United States has inherited a political system in which, despite legislative supremacy, judges constantly and inevitably make law. How they do so—how they reason, in other words—thus becomes an important question in the study of politics and government. The central question in this book is not *whether* courts should make law but *what* law to make, and *how*.

[2]Plucknett, pp. 259–260. For a recent and particularly concise review of how slowly and fitfully common-law judges came to appreciate that they inevitably make law as they decide each case, see Roger Cotterrell, *The Politics of Jurisprudence* (London: Butterworth and Co., 1989), Chapter 2.

[3]Kempin, p. 85, suggests that as late as 1825 in the United States and 1865 in England stare decisis rested on very shaky ground. Anthropologists are quite comfortable with the conclusion that rules of law, in contrast to imperfectly articulated customs and interpersonal understandings, play a relatively insignificant role in many if not most of the world's justice systems. See Stanley Diamond, "The Rule of Law vs. the Order of Custom," 51 *Social Research* 387 (1984).

REASONING BY EXAMPLE IN COMMON LAW

Much of the everyday law around us falls into the category of common law. Although modern statutes have supplanted some of it, particularly in the important area of commercial transactions, even these statutes for the most part preserve basic definitions, principles, and values articulated first in common law. One of the most important common-law categories, also probably the one least touched by statute today, concerns the law of tort. Tort law wrestles with these problems: What defines and limits a person's liability to compensate those he hurts? What counts as a hurt serious enough to merit compensation? Breaking someone's leg? Embarrassing someone? When does law impose liability on me if I threaten someone with a blow (assault)? If I strike the blow (battery)? If I publicly insult another (libel and slander)? If I do careless things that injure other people (negligence)? These questions may sound like questions of criminal law to you, but they are not, for the law of torts does not expose the lawbreaker to punishment by the state. The law of torts—while much of it overlaps criminal law—defines at what times people who hurt other people's bodies, their property, their reputations, or their freedom must compensate them for their hurt. Today tort law is constantly in the news, in lawsuits over the harms caused by guns, cigarettes, breast implants, asbestos, even hot coffee at McDonald's. And as always, tort law is evolving in response to, as Justice Holmes put it in the epigraph for this chapter, the "felt necessities of the time" and the "prevalent moral and political theories" of the day.

In this section, indeed for the bulk of the chapter, we illustrate common law in action with problems of tort law, mostly of negligence. We do not discuss tort law in its entirety, for it would take a book triple the size of this one to review all the subtleties and uncertainties in this body of law. We shall instead focus in some detail on an important and perennial question in the law of tort: At what point do the rights and privileges of owning property stop and at what point does our legal obligation not to hurt others begin?

Because the common law of tort has continuously evolved for more than a century, we begin with some old cases that may seem fairly irrelevant today. In the nineteenth and early twentieth centuries the legal question often took the following form: To what extent may we hurt other people without incurring a legal liability to compensate those we hurt *because we hurt them on our own land*? By the end of this chapter, you will see that the common-law process has transformed that question about property into this one: Where do the rights and privileges of being private and free stop and our legal obligation to help others begin? For example, does a therapist have a duty to warn potential targets of a patient who is threatening violence? Or, as in the case at the end of this chapter, does a gun manufacturer bear responsibility when its product is used in a crime? No doubt, fifty years from now the question will have modulated yet again. Common law is a process of continual incremental adjustment, a story always to be continued.

Let us begin with a review of some basic rules of common law that seemed to govern in the middle of the last century. First, the common law of negligence required one to act in a way a reasonable and prudent person would act and to refrain from acting in a way a reasonable and prudent person would refrain from acting. Lawyers would say that a "standard of care" existed. Second, the law defined the classes of persons to whom a "duty" to act carefully was and was not owed. Third, law imposed liability upon those who in fact carelessly violated the "reasonable man" standard. Whether a person in fact acted negligently in a specific case is one of those legal history questions juries often decide. Fourth, someone to whom a duty is owed must actually suffer an injury as a result of the hurt. Juries often make this factual decision also. Thus the critical legal questions in negligence cases involve the definition of the standard and the duty.

Similarly, the law of battery commands us not to strike another deliberately unless a reasonable person would do so, as in self-defense. If we strike another unreasonably, then we become liable as long as we owe a duty to the injured person not to strike.

As you may already suspect, the requirement of a duty before liability attaches can make a great difference. One of the common-law principles of the last century quite plainly said that people do not owe a duty to avoid injuring, carelessly or deliberately, people who *trespass* (encroach without express or implied permission) on their property.

We shall examine three common-law cases to illustrate some of the main features of reasoning in common law. These cases provide evidence, or clues, that support some basic truths about the common-law process:

- General principles, including the rules of negligence and battery just described, do not neatly resolve legal problems.
- Precedents do not neatly resolve legal problems, either.
- In reasoning from precedents, judges do make choices and do exercise fact freedom; it is this exercise that best describes how and why they decide as they do.
- Social background facts often influence case outcomes more powerfully than the facts in the litigation itself.
- The beliefs and values of individual judges do influence law.
- The precise meaning of common-law rules—here of trespass and of duty—changes as judges decide each new case.
- Over time, as fundamental social values change, common law also changes in a fundamental way to reflect these changes in social values.
- Judges have shifted their conception of their role from a belief that they are required to apply divine or natural law toward a recognition of the inevitability of judicial lawmaking and its consequences.
- Judges have also shifted the way they explain their decisions, moving from mechanical jurisprudence to "realism," a style that acknowledges the role of social background facts and changing values (the"felt necessities" and "prevalent moral and political theories" that Justice Holmes described) in their judgments.

Here are the three cases.

The Cherry Tree

It is summer in rural New York. The year is 1865. The heat of midday has passed. Sarah Hoffman, an unmarried woman living with her brother, a country doctor, sets out at her brother's request to pick ripe cherries for dinner.

A cherry tree stands on her brother's land about two feet from the fence separating his land from that of his neighbor, Abner Armstrong. Sarah's previous cullings have left few cherries on Hoffman's side of the fence. Hence, nimbly enough for her age, Sarah climbs the fence and from her perch upon it begins to take cherries from the untouched branches overhanging Abner's yard.

Angered by this intrusion, Abner runs from his house and orders her to stop picking his cherries. She persists. Enraged, he grabs her wrist and strongarms her

down from the fence. Ligaments in the wrist tear. She cries from the pain and humil-
iation. She sues at common law for battery. The trial jury awards her $1000 damages.

Abner appealed. He claimed that *he,* not Sarah nor her brother, owned the cherries overhanging his land. Because he owned the cherries, he had every right to protect them, just as he could prevent Sarah from pulling onions in his garden with a
long-handled picker from her perch. In other words, Sarah was not a person to whom
Abner owed a duty. By her trespassing and her interference with Abner's property,
Sarah exposed herself to Abner's legal battery committed in defense of his property.

Abner's lawyer cited many legal sources in support of his argument. He began
with the maxim, *cujus est solum, ejus est usque ad coelum et ad inferos,* sometimes
translated as "he who has the soil, has it even to the sky and the lowest depths." He
then referred the appellate judge to the great English commentator, Blackstone,
quoting: "Upwards, therefore, no man may erect any building, or the like to over-
hang another's land." He also cited *Kent's Commentaries,* the Bouvier Institutes,
Crabbe's Text on Real Property, and seven cases in support of his position. One of
these, an English case titled *Waterman v. Soper,* held "that if A plants a tree upon
the extremest limits of his land and the tree growing extends its roots into the land of
B next adjoining," then A and B jointly own the tree.[4]

Sarah's lawyer responded that, in law, title to the tree depends on who owns title
to the land from which the tree grows. Sarah did not trespass; therefore, Abner owed
her the duty not to batter her. In support he cited several commentaries, Hilliard's
treatise on real property, and four cases. Sarah's lawyer relied especially on a case,
Lyman v. Hale, decided in Connecticut in 1836.[5] In *Lyman* the defendant picked
and refused to return pears from branches overhanging his yard from a tree the
plaintiff had planted four feet from the line. The *Lyman* opinion explicitly rejected
the reasoning of the English precedent, *Waterman.* Despite the antiquated language,
Lyman is a remarkably sensible, unlegalistic opinion. The court held that
Waterman's "roots" principle is unsound because of the practical difficulties in applying it:

> How, it may be asked, is the principle to be reduced to practice? And here, it should
> be remembered, that nothing depends on the question whether the branches do or do
> not overhang the lands of the adjoining proprietor. All is made to depend solely on
> the enquiry, whether any portion of the roots extend into his land. It is this fact alone,
> which creates the [joint ownership]. And how is the fact to be ascertained?
>
> Again; if such [joint ownership] exist, it is diffused over the whole tree. Each
> owns a certain proportion of the whole. In what proportion do the respective parties
> hold? And how are these proportions to be determined? How is it to be ascertained
> what part of its nourishment the tree derives from the soil of the adjoining proprietor?
> If one joint owner appropriates . . . all the products, on what principle is the ac-
> count to be settled between the parties?
>
> Again; suppose the line between adjoining proprietors to run through a forest or
> grove. Is a new rule of property to be introduced, in regard to those trees growing so
> near the line as to extend some portions of their roots across it? How is a man to
> know whether he is the exclusive owner of trees, growing, indeed, on his own land,
> but near the line; and whether he can safely cut them, without subjecting himself to
> an action?
>
> And again; on the principle claimed, a man may be the exclusive owner of a
> tree, one year, and the next, a [joint owner] with another; and the proportion in which
> he owns may be varying from year to year, as the tree progresses in its growth.

[4]*Waterman v. Soper,* 1 Ld Raymond 737 (opinion undated).
[5]*Lyman v. Hale,* 11 *Conn. Rep.* 177 (1836).

> It is not seen how these consequences are to be obviated, if the principle con-
> tended for be once admitted. We think they are such as to furnish the most conclu-
> sive objections against the adoption of the principle. We are not prepared to adopt it,
> unless compelled to do so, by the controuling [sic] force of authority. The cases relied
> upon for its support, have been examined. We do not think them decisive.[6]

In effect the *Lyman* opinion says property titles must be clear to help us plan our affairs, to help us know whether we can or can't cut down a tree for winter firewood, for
example. Given the inescapable background facts about trees, the roots rule introduces inevitable uncertainty. We must therefore reject it.

The appellate court in New York found *Lyman* most persuasive and followed it.
Sarah won.[7]

Abner appealed again, to the state's highest court of appeals. In 1872 (court de-
lays are not a uniquely modern phenomenon) Abner lost again. The attorneys presented the same arguments. Perhaps surprisingly, however, the highest court did not
mention *Lyman*. Instead it seemed to say that *Waterman* does correctly state the law,
but Abner's lawyer forgot to prove that the cherry tree's roots actually extended
across the property line:

> We have not been referred to any case showing that where no part of a tree stood on
> the land of a party, and it did not receive any nourishment therefrom, that he had any
> right therein, and it is laid down in Bouvier's Institutes . . . that if the branches of
> a tree only overshadow the adjoining land and the roots do not enter into it, the tree
> wholly belongs to the estate where the roots grow.[8]

Therefore Abner lost.

This simple case, occupying only a few pages in the reports of the two New York
appellate courts, richly illustrates many essential features of common law:

1. Note first that none of the judges either in *Hoffman* or in *Lyman* questioned
their authority to decide these cases without reference to statutes. The laws, both of
assault and battery and of the more fundamental problem of ownership, come from
the common-law heritage of cases, commentaries, and treatises. The judges automatically assumed the power to make law governing a very common human conflict—overlapping claims to physical space on this planet. Surely a legislature could
legislate on the subject, but judges have no guilt about doing so themselves in the
face of legislative silence.

In this connection, recall that legislatures pass statutes addressing general
problems. How likely is it that a legislature would ever pass a statute regulating tree
ownership on or near property lines? Is it not better that our government contains a
mechanism, the courts, that must create some law on this subject once the problem
turns out to be a real one?

2. The general common-law definitions of battery and of property ownership do
not resolve this case. Neither do specific precedents. Instead, both sides cite conflicting principles and inconsistent precedents and urge from them contradictory
conclusions. The judge must find some justification or reason for choosing, but nothing in either side's argument, at least in this case, compels the judge to choose one
way rather than another. Judges possess the freedom to say that either *Lyman* or
Waterman expresses the right law for resolving this problem.

---

[6]*Lyman v. Hale*, pp. 183–184.

[7]*Hoffman v. Armstrong*, 46 Barbour 337 (1866).

[8]*Hoffman v. Armstrong*, 48 N.Y. 201 (1872), pp. 203–204.

Consider specifically the matter of the Connecticut precedent, *Lyman*. Judges possess the freedom to say, as the first appellate court said, "We find the facts of *Lyman* much like those in Abner's conflict with Sarah. We also find *Lyman*'s reasoning persuasive; therefore we apply the rule of *Lyman* to this case and rule for Sarah." But judges also possess the freedom to say, as did the second court, "Connecticut precedents do not govern New York. Older common law precedents and principles from England conflict with Connecticut's law. We choose the older tradition. Abner would win if only he could show that the roots really grew on his property."

The New York courts in *Hoffman* had other options. The second court could have easily assumed that—since roots underground grow about the same distances as do branches above ground—the roots did cross the line, and that their nourishment probably supported the cherries Sarah tried to pick. Or the court could have taken judicial notice of the fact that any reasonably sized tree grows roots in all directions more than two feet from its base. But it didn't.

Judges must decide which facts in the case before them matter, and what they mean. They must simultaneously decide what the facts in the often inconsistent precedents mean in order to reach their legal conclusion. The two appellate courts reached the same conclusion but by emphasizing different facts. The first court found that roots shouldn't matter. Even though legal authorities sometimes mention them, the court believed the location of roots should have no legal significance. To give root location legal significance suddenly makes our knowledge of what we own more uncertain. Before we can cut down a tree we must trespass on our neighbor's land and dig a series of holes in his yard looking for roots. And what if the neighbor has flowers growing in a bed that he doesn't want dug up? The root rule leaves us out on a limb.

3. To understand how these two courts choose differently to reach the same result, examine the difference in their basic approach to the problem. The first appellate court seems eager to assume the responsibility to shape law, to acknowledge relevant background facts, and hence to make laws that promote human cooperation in daily affairs. The second court approaches the problem much more cautiously. It seems to say: "We admit the precedents conflict. Fortunately we do not really need to choose between them. As long as Abner failed to prove the roots grow on his side of the fence, he loses either way. Therefore we choose the path that disturbs common law the least. The lower appellate court explicitly chose to reject *Waterman*, but we don't have to do that, so we won't."

This judicial caution is very common, but it is not particularly wise. Without realizing it, the highest New York court (whose opinion therefore overrides the precedential value of the better opinion of the court below) has made new law. Now we have New York precedent endorsing *Waterman*. Future courts will have to wrestle with the problem of overruling it, or blindly follow it and produce all the practical problems against which *Lyman* rightly warned.

The reason these two sets of judges ruled differently, therefore, rests precisely on the fact that they are different people with different values and beliefs about what judges ought to do. Their values help determine the law they create.

4. At a deeper level, the difference reflects much more than a difference in judicial beliefs. These two approaches illustrate two contrasting common-law styles. The final higher court opinion in *Hoffman* views common law as fixed, stable, and true. It wants to avoid upsetting Bouvier's *Institutes* and Blackstone's maxims if it possibly can. The court thinks these are the common law. In contrast, the lower court's *Lyman* approach, while predating *Hoffman* by nearly 40 years, observes the spirit rather than the letter of common law. It views common

law as a tradition in which judges seek to adapt law so that it improves our capacity to live together peacefully and to plan our affairs more effectively. It retains the capacity to change with changing conditions. This more modern style comes closer to helping law foster social cooperation—our legal system's most fundamental goal.

5. Finally, the case of the cherry tree illustrates a fundamental difference between common law and statutory interpretation. In statutory interpretation, as we will explain in Chapter 4, judges must think carefully about the purposes behind the laws they're interpreting. Once the court determines a statute's purpose, it has no need to second-guess the wisdom of that purpose.

In common law, on the other hand, the judge who reasons from a precedent does not care about what the prior judge intended or about the purpose of the announced rule of law. In common law, the judge is always free to decide on his own what the law ought to say. The prior judge's intent or purpose does not dictate how his opinion will bind as precedent. Put another way, the legislature's classification of what does and does not belong in its legal category, a classification created by the words of the statute, does bind the judge. In common law, the judge deciding the case creates the classification. He sets his own goals.

This goal-setting occurred in both the first and second *Hoffman* opinions. The first court wanted to make workable and practical law, not because *Lyman* or any other precedent commanded it to but because the court wanted to achieve that goal. The second court ruled as it did not because Bouvier's *Institutes* or *Waterman* commanded it to do so, but because that court preferred the goal of changing past formal statements of law as little as possible.[9]

The Pit

Five years after Sarah Hoffman's final victory, New York's highest court faced a related common-law problem. A Mr. Carter, along with several other citizens of the town of Bath, maintained an alley running between their properties: "Exchange Alley," people called it. The public had used the alley for 20 years as a convenient way to travel from one long block to another, but the town never acknowledged Exchange Alley as a public street nor attempted to maintain it. In May 1872, Carter began excavating to erect a building on his land. The construction went slowly, so slowly in fact that on a gloomy night the next November an open pit still remained on Carter's property. That night a Mr. Beck passed through the alley on his customary way to supper when, rather suddenly, a carriage turned down the alley and rushed toward him. Beck stepped rapidly to his left to avoid the carriage, tripped, and fell headlong into the pit, injuring himself. Although the evidence was never completely clear, since the alley had no marked border, it appeared that the pit began no less than 7 feet away from the outermost possible edge of the "public" alley.

The lawsuit that followed brought much the same kind of issue to the court as had Sarah's problem. Lawyers for Carter cited the common-law rule that landowners have the right to use their property as they please. They have no duty to avoid harming trespassers negligently. The lawyers cited English cases to show that travelers who were hurt falling into pits 5, 20, and 30 feet from a public way could not recover damages because the danger must "adjoin" the public way.

---

[9]Judges do not have this discretion in statutory cases. The statutory language of the Mann Act, for example, commands the courts to consider at least the transportation of willing prostitutes a crime, and the courts should not ignore that command.

Despite these arguments the court held for Beck. It had no difficulty whatsoever determining that, even though Carter and others together privately owned Exchange Alley, allowing the public to use the property over time created a duty to the users not to hurt them negligently.[10]

But the pit excavated truly private property. Is a 7-foot distance from a public alley sufficient to exempt the owner from liability to the public, or does the pit legally "adjoin" the alley, thereby creating a duty of care?

The court ruled that the alley did adjoin. It held Carter negligently responsible for Beck's injuries. It approved the idea that if the hole was "so situated that a person lawfully using the thoroughfare, and, in a reasonable manner, was liable to fall into it, the defendant was liable."[11]

The court did not have to rule this way. It could have defined adjoining pits as pits that literally border on public land. Or it could have said that 7 feet was simply too far away to make a landowner liable. But the court offered a better decision. As in *Lyman,* it produced a workable distinction between injuries to deliberate trespassers and to those who reasonably attempt to use either their own space or the public's space. Just as in the *Lyman* and *Hoffman* decisions, the judges in *Beck v. Carter* chose as they did because their values—their beliefs about desirable and undesirable social relations—led them to this conclusion. If they deeply believed in the absolute sanctity of private property, ambiguity in common law would certainly have given them freedom to say, "Landowners must be free to do what they wish with their land. Carter's pit was entirely on his private land, separated from the thoroughfare. Therefore Carter owed Beck no duty of care."

The Diving Board

Before you proceed, note how these two principal cases, reduced to their simplest terms, combine to form a seemingly comprehensive statement of law: When the plaintiff's deliberate act is not proved a trespass on the defendant's property, then the defendant owes the plaintiff a duty of care *(Hoffman).* Furthermore, when the plaintiff accidentally but conclusively does trespass on the defendant's property, but the defendant should have foreseen the injury from such accidental trespass, the defendant is also liable *(Beck).* Thus arises the final question: What result should a court reach when the plaintiff deliberately and unambiguously trespasses on the defendant's property and is injured?

On another summer day in New York—July 8, 1916—Harvey Hynes and two friends had gone swimming at a favorite spot along the Bronx bank of the then relatively unpolluted Harlem River. For five years they and other swimmers had dived from a makeshift plank nailed to the wooden bulkhead along the river.

The electrified line of the New York Central Railroad ran along the river. The power line was suspended over the track between poles, half of which ran between

[10]As an aside, you might try at this point to define *property*. You should observe from this example that, legally speaking, property is not so much what people hold title to as it is what the law says they can and cannot do with a thing, whether they hold title to it or not.

[11]*Beck v. Carter*, 68 N.Y. 283 (1876), p. 293. If you are dubious, measure off 7 feet from your standing place in a very dark room and mark the spot. Then imagine you suddenly must get out of the way of a carriage by moving toward your mark in the dark. If you pass the mark, you've fallen in the pit. In 1996, in a case evaluating the free speech rights of antiabortion protesters at abortion clinics, the Supereme Court debated during oral argument the "meaning" of 15 feet. See "Court Hears Challenge to Anti-Abortion Curb," *New York Times*, 17 October 1996, p. A8.

the track and the river. Legally the railroad owned the strip of riverbank containing track, poles, wires, and bulkhead. Hence, about half of the 16-foot diving board touched or extended over the railroad's land while the rest reached out, at a height of about 3 feet, over the surface of the public river.

As Harvey prepared to dive, one of the railroad's overhead supports for the power line suddenly broke loose from the pole, bringing down with it the writhing electric line that powered the trains. The wires struck Harvey, throwing him from the board. His friends pulled him dead from the waters of the Harlem River.

Harvey's mother sued the railroad for the damages caused by its alleged negligence in maintaining the supports for the wire. Conceding that New York Central's maintenance of the supports failed to meet the "reasonable man" standard of care, the trial court and the intermediate appellate court nevertheless denied her claim. Harvey was a trespasser, a deliberate trespasser, and property owners have no duty to protect such trespassers from harm.

Before proceeding further, reflect on the cases of the cherry tree and the pit. You are about to see these rather distantly related cases, two cases among thousands that had tried to thrash out the borderline between property and tort, merge as key precedents in the final *Hynes* decision.

The lawyers for the railroad presented a battery of cases in their favor. They cited *Hoffman* to show that while perched on the board—even if he was over the river—Harvey trespassed, because the board was attached to the railroad's land. They also cited cases, *Beck* among them, to establish the point that the trespass was not a temporary and involuntary move from a public space but a sustained series of deliberate trespasses onto the defendant's land.

Three of the justices on New York's highest court agreed. The railroad had no duty of care to this trespasser. But a majority of four, led by Cardozo, supported Harvey's mother and reversed.

Cardozo cited relatively few precedents. He did, however, cite *Hoffman* and *Beck,* but not in the way the railroad's lawyers had hoped. The lawyers tried to convince the judges that a mechanical rule commanded a decision for the railroad. Anything, a cherry tree or a diving board, belongs to the railroad if it is affixed to the railroad's land, regardless of what it overhangs. Therefore, Harvey, at the time the wires struck him, trespassed. Since the trespass was deliberate, *Beck* commands a decision for the railroad.

Cardozo, however, appealed to the deeper spirit of these cases, a spirit that rejects mechanical rules like the root rule for determining ownership of cherry trees. He cited *Hoffman* not for its reasoning but for its result: There was no real trespass. The spirit requires enunciating policy—law—that corresponds to a deeper sense of how society ought to regulate rights and responsibilities in this legal, as well as physical, borderland. He wrote:

> This case is a striking instance of the dangers of "a jurisprudence of conceptions" (Pound, "Mechanical Jurisprudence," 8 *Columbia Law Review,* 605, 608, 610), the extension of a maxim or a definition with relentless disregard of consequences to . . . "a dryly logical extreme." The approximate and relative become the definite and absolute. Landowners are not bound to regulate their conduct in contemplation of the presence of trespassers intruding upon private structures. Landowners *are* bound to regulate their conduct in contemplation of the presence of travelers upon the adjacent public ways. There are times when there is little trouble in marking off the field of exemption and immunity from that of liability and duty. Here structures and ways are so united and commingled, superimposed upon each other, that the fields are

brought together. In such circumstances, there is little help in pursuing general maxims to ultimate conclusions. They have been framed *alio intuitu*. They must be reformulated and readapted to meet exceptional conditions. Rules appropriate to spheres which are conceived of as separate and distinct cannot, both, be enforced when the spheres become concentric. There must then be readjustment or collision. In one sense, and that a highly technical and artificial one, the diver at the end of the springboard is an intruder on the adjoining lands. In another sense, and one that realists will accept more readily, he is still on public waters in the exercise of public rights. The law must say whether it will subject him to the rule of the one field or of the other, of this sphere or of that. We think that considerations of analogy, of convenience, of policy, and of justice, exclude him from the field of the defendant's immunity and exemption, and place him in the field of liability and duty. . . .[12]

Note again the effect of fact freedom on judicial choices. Although they wrote no dissenting opinion, we can make an intelligent guess that the dissenters in *Hynes* reasoned from *Hoffman* this way: "The fact is that the diving board grew from the railroad's land. If the cherry tree growing from *Hoffman*'s land belongs to him, then the board belongs to the railroad. Therefore Harvey trespassed." But Cardozo refuses to rest his opinion on the simple analogy between a diving board that hangs over a river and a cherry tree that projects into an adjoining yard. Cardozo in effect responds, "The important fact is that Sarah didn't really trespass. Just as she used what didn't clearly belong to Abner, so these boys diving into the river from a board over the river didn't really interfere with the railroad's property." Cardozo uses his fact freedom to draw on what he considers to be the most important aspect of the precedents. Reason in law does not allow us to say that his choice legally is right and the other legally wrong. After all, with a switch of one vote, *Hynes* would produce a very different legal precedent. However, by recognizing that judges have the freedom to choose among different ways of interpreting precedents, we free ourselves to say we favor one choice over another, and to justify why we feel that way.

Cardozo's opinion reflects the rise of "realism," an approach to law that rejects the view that legal conflicts can be solved just like mathematical problems, through formal logic. Instead, realism recognizes that, as Justice Holmes says in the epigraph to this chapter, "the life of the law has not been logic, but experience." Experience—changes in social background facts, and changes in social values—is central to Cardozo's justification of his decision. For example, Cardozo's opinion stresses the value of social cooperation over the values of private property and individual autonomy. In this respect the *Hynes* case foreshadowed one of the most dramatic changes that our legal system has ever experienced, the shift in the twentieth century from a legal philosophy whose principles emphasize property rights and individualism to a system that promotes social caring and cooperation. In tort law, for example, judges have greatly expanded the duty of manufacturers to take care that the goods they make are safe. Lawsuits against manufacturers for injuries caused by unsafe cars, faulty tires, dangerous drugs, toxic chemicals, even "non-defective" products like cigarettes and guns, would not have been possible without these changes in tort doctrine.[13]

---

[12]*Hynes v. New York Central R.R.*, 231 N.Y. 229 (1921), pp. 235–236. How should a judge, following *Hynes*, rule in a case identical to *Hoffman* except that Abner picks cherries from the branches overhanging his yard and that, to stop him, Sarah shoots him in the leg with a .22 pistol?

[13]For a careful analysis of the impact of realism on tort law, see G. Edward White, *Tort Law in America: An Intellectual History* (New York: Oxford University Press, 1980).

As the example of product liability indicates, realism has deeply influenced judging, so that judges today are more conscious of the importance of social background facts and changes in social values. They are less likely to hide behind a formal statement of law in a treatise, a commentary, or a common-law principle. Judges today are more self-conscious too about their ability—one might even say their duty—to make good public policy. These changes, have, however, created controversy. As we'll see, judicial policymaking in tort law has become particularly controversial.

KEEPING THE COMMON-LAW TRADITION ALIVE

The preceding section introduces the most typical common-law judicial problem, one in which precedents provide some guidance but do not automatically resolve problems. In the typical situation, the judge faces an array of precedents—some of which may seem inconsistent, some imaginative, and others wedded to past "truths" in common law. None of them automatically controls, so the judge must make a choice. Sometimes the precedent or principle gives the judge no more than a point of departure from which to justify the unexpressed beliefs and values that determine the result. Precedents in many cases are vehicles for rationalizations.

Sometimes, however, a genuinely new problem arises, one to which precedents prove so remote, so factually different, that the judge cannot build his rationalizations on them. He must then realize that a decision for either party in the case will create not a new variation on older law but a new and different law—a new and different definition of how people should relate to one another. In other situations, the reverse happens. The judge faces a precedent so factually similar to the one before him that he cannot distinguish or ignore it. If he chooses to reach a new result, he must overrule the precedent.

This section answers questions involving these less typical judicial problems: How should judges proceed when they cannot find common-law cases that seem to apply to the case before them? When should they make common law from whole cloth? Conversely, in what circumstances should courts choose deliberately to reject a case or principle that controls the case before it? How, in other words, does stare decisis operate in common law?

Answers to these questions depend in part on what we think about the proper balance between judicial and legislative lawmaking. What kinds of problems require the kind of fact-gathering and value-balancing techniques available to legislatures but not courts? What types of problems require, for their solution, the creation of complex administrative planning and enforcement apparatus that only legislatures can create, fund, and supervise?

You may have already discerned our general approach to the problem of judicial-legislative balance. Let us make it explicit here. Courts and legislatures have much in common. They both gather evidence in a systematic way, courts through witnesses at trial and through the briefs of the parties on appeal, and legislatures through committee hearings and the many other efforts of lobbyists. Both institutions gather evidence, at least formally, in an open-minded way. Courts hear both sides. Our adversary system requires it. Legislatures also hear competing arguments in committee hearings and through the efforts of lobbies. Furthermore, both courts and legislatures possess lawmaking power. People who look to law to plan their affairs know they should look to both institutions for legal guidance. Finally, politics influences both branches of government. Many state judges win office by election.

Politicians appoint federal judges as well as state judges in nonelective posts, so political restraints affect both.

In Chapter 5 we will address some important political differences between judges and legislators. Nevertheless, *judges should always presume themselves competent to take the lawmaking initiative when the legislature has not spoken clearly to them.* In other words, because as a general matter courts and legislatures have a similar authority and competence, the burden of proof always rests on the party that argues for the court to remain silent on the theory that the legislature is better qualified to speak.

Making Common Law without Close Precedents

In early March 1928, two seagoing tugboats towing barges of coal set out in good weather from Norfolk, Virginia, bound for New York. About midnight on March 8, under fair skies but with the barometer falling slightly, the tugs passed the Delaware Breakwater, a safe haven for tugs and barges caught in bad weather. The next morning, however, the wind began to freshen. By noon, gale-force winds blew up heavy seas. Early in the afternoon two barges sprung leaks. Their crews signaled the tugs that they would proceed to anchor the barges and ride out the storm. They did so, but conditions steadily worsened. The Coast Guard heroically rescued the crews of both barges late in the day. The dawn light on March 10 revealed no trace of the barges. By then, both the barges and their cargoes rested on the ocean floor.

The coal owners sued the barge company, alleging both that the company had breached its contract of carriage and that the unseaworthiness of the barges made it liable for the loss of the coal. The barge company in turn sued the tugboat owners for the loss of both the coal and the two barges. The barge owners claimed that the two tugs had not properly handled the cargo. More precisely, they claimed that the tug owners should bear the total loss because they had not provided their tugs with conventional AM radio receivers.

At trial, the barge owners established several critical facts. On March 8 the Arlington weather bureau broadcast a 10:00 A.M. prediction calling for shifting and increasing winds the following day. Another ship in the vicinity of the tugs and barges had received this report on its AM radio. At 10:00 P.M. on the same day, the Arlington bureau predicted "increasing east and southeast winds, becoming fresh to strong Friday night and increasing cloudiness followed by rain on Friday." On the basis of the morning report, one tug owner towing cargo in the vicinity had anchored at the Delaware Breakwater. Even the captain of the defendant tug conceded at trial that, had he heard the evening report, he would have done the same.

Place yourself in the position of a judge resolving this case. In your first step, aided by the arguments of the lawyers, you try to discover how much, if any, of this problem the law already makes clear. You soon find that the law of admiralty—a branch of common law for our purposes—imposes an absolute liability on shipowners for the loss of cargoes in their ships if unseaworthiness of the ship caused the loss. Note that this unseaworthiness doctrine does not simply extend the law of negligence to the sea. The shipowner may have no knowledge of the faulty condition. It may have been impossible even for a reasonable and prudent man to prevent the unseaworthy condition—hidden rot in some of a hull's wooden planking, for example. The rule creates a guarantee of seaworthiness.

But is a ship that does not carry a radio in 1928 therefore unseaworthy because it won't receive weather reports? On this point the law gives no help. You find that Congress has passed a statute requiring steamers carrying more than 50 passengers to carry two-way radios so that they can call for help and receive information, but the statute does not include tugs and barges. You find no precedents whatsoever linking seaworthiness with possession of radios or any other new invention. At this point you have several choices. You might say:

Choice One

Congress in its wisdom chose not to require two-way shortwave radios of tugs and barges. Furthermore, Congress has made no law requiring AM radios. Therefore, Congress has intended that tugs without AM radios are seaworthy and the tug owners are not liable for the loss.

Choice Two

I find no law requiring receiving sets. Since legislatures, not the courts, are the lawmakers in our democratic nation, I have no legal authority to find the tug owners liable. Therefore they are not liable.

You can, we trust, reject both these choices immediately. We have no evidence whatsoever that Congress thought about AM receivers, much less intended or decided to pass a statute calling tugs without them nevertheless seaworthy. We could just as easily conclude that the statute recognizes the general importance of radios in improving navigation safety. Therefore, the statute gives shipowners a positive signal that they should seriously examine whether radios can help them navigate better. If you have any further doubts about the weakness of the first choice, consider the fact that no congressional statute required tugs to carry compasses.

The second choice conflicts with the common-law tradition. Courts do continue to make law as conditions change; over the years, courts have specifically fashioned the principles of admiralty and of seaworthiness within admiralty law. So you might instead say:

Choice Three

I admit that judges retain their general lawmaking power in admiralty. In this case, however, only a legislature can decide whether ships must carry radios. Only through legislative hearings could we learn, for example, how common it was in 1928 for people to own radios. It would hardly be fair to hold the tug owners liable if, in 1928, radios were only novel. Similarly, only legislative hearings can learn whether shipowners themselves carry radios and think it wise or necessary to do so. If they do, then the fact dictates a new policy of seaworthiness, but we can't tell. As in ancient common law, custom may hold the key to justice, but only a legislature today is equipped to find the key.

The third choice may sound like an improvement, but it's not. Its major premise, that courts can't obtain the facts, is false. The actual case, from which this example is derived, shows that the courts were able to make the necessary factual determinations.[14] The brief for the cargo owners documented the phenomenal growth in the sales of radios, over 1,000 percent between 1922 and 1928. It quoted Frederick Lewis Allen's *Only Yesterday* (1931): "At the age of three and a half years, radio broadcasting had attained its majority. Behind those figures of radio sales lies a whole chapter of the life of the Postwar Decade: radio penetrating every third home

[14]*The T. J. Hooper*, 60 F.2d 737 (2nd Cir. 1932). As is customary in admiralty law, the name of the ship whose seaworthiness is questioned provides the name of the case.

in the country; giant broadcasting stations with nation-wide hook-ups."[15] The cargo owners also elicited testimony on the witness stand from one tug captain to the effect that, although only one tug line required radios, at least 90 percent of the tugs had them, if only for entertainment

The lesson here is critically important. As a rule, courts can find background facts as effectively as can legislatures. We applaud the adversary system in courts precisely because we believe it gives lawyers the incentive to present the fullest possible range of facts to support their position. Legislatures may be superior law-makers where complex problems require a simultaneous set of solutions and the means to coordinate them, but well-established judicial practices allow courts in cases like this one to establish the background facts that determine whether a given legal choice is wise and fair.

Choices Four and Five

Custom is a time-honored source of common law. In this case it has been convinc-ingly shown that tugs customarily carry radios. Radio has become a part of our every-day lives. The absence of the radios in this case caused the loss.

Custom is a time-honored source of common law. In this case it has been convinc-ingly shown that a majority of tug owners do not customarily require radios. Since we cannot say that the customs of the sea require radios, we cannot conclude that the absence of a radio in this case caused the loss.

Choices four and five are improvements over earlier choices; they are better judi-cial choices because they do not shrink from judicial responsibility for lawmaking. They succeed where the other choices failed in that they create a clear rule to guide fu-ture conduct. But, of course, you should still feel unsatisfied, for custom appears to pro-duce two contradictory results. How should you choose between them? Better to say:

Choice Six

Is it then a final answer that the business had not yet generally adopted receiving sets? There are, no doubt, cases where courts seem to make the general practice of the calling the standard of proper diligence. . . . Indeed, in most cases reasonable prudence is in fact common prudence; but strictly it is never its measure; a whole calling may have unduly lagged in the adoption of new and available devices. It may never set its own tests, however persuasive be its usages. Courts must in the end say what is required; there are precautions so imperative that even their universal disre-gard will not excuse their omission. . . . We hold the tugs . . . had they been properly equipped . . . would have got the Arlington reports. The injury was a di-rect consequence of this unseaworthiness.

The language of choice six speaks with a power and persuasiveness the other choices lack because it is Judge Learned Hand's own, taken from his opinion finally disposing of the case.[16] Hand's choice sets a clear standard, one that, anticipating the certain further growth of the radio industry, would occur sooner or later. Note, however, that with the exception of choice four, any other choice could well have created a precedent that would delay considerably any judicial decision requiring

---

[15]Quoted in Henry M. Hart and Albert M. Sacks, *The Legal Process* (Cambridge: Harvard Law School, 1958), pp. 432–433. Our selection of illustrative cases in this section draws heavily upon the much larger variety of cases that Hart and Sacks provide. Although we use these cases for somewhat different purposes, we cannot improve upon their choice of working materials; here, as elsewhere, we are much indebted to them.

[16]*The T. J. Hooper,* p. 740.

tugs to carry radios. These choices say tugs don't need to carry radios. Judicial change would require overruling any of these alternative decisions. In short, the timid and deferential judge potentially creates a common-law precedent with just as much policy impact as does the assertive judge.

Above all, Hand's choice avoids the problem of lawmaking by default. Judges can never know whether or when or how Congress will act on any but dramatic national issues. Courts that wait for better legislative solutions may wait for a solution that never comes. Do you disagree with Hand's choice? Is it not the court's proven capacity to establish the facts about the use of radios—coupled with Hand's sound ethical judgment that tugs ought to carry radios—that makes his opinion persuasive?

The problem illustrated in this case is a perennial one in law. Consider for example whether, as some have argued, gun makers should be liable for failing to include trigger locks in their design of handguns. Each year many children are killed by playing with guns, often after finding a gun kept by their parents for self-defense. A properly designed trigger lock, some have argued, would save lives while still allowing adults to defend themselves adequately. Similarly, cigarettes that are designed to extinguish if not actively inhaled could save thousands of lives lost in fires started by sleeping smokers. Should the failure of gun and cigarette companies to sell such products be considered a tort?

Horizontal Stare Decisis in Common Law

We now move to the other end of the spectrum, horizontal stare decisis. How should judges respond to precedents that seem to state outdated or "bad" social policy, but at the same time seem to completely cover and control the outcomes of cases before them? Lawyers label these precedents "precisely on point" or "on all fours with the case at bar." The existence of these precedents does not, however, contradict the concept that law remains ambiguous. Judges always choose the results. Some judges, faced with a precedent that produces an unwanted conclusion, will choose to ignore it, much to the anger of the losing lawyer. Other judges will overrule the precedent, or pointedly refuse to follow it. Choices remain. In these circumstances, a judge's concerns about good social policy must be weighed against the purposes of stare decisis, which, as we have seen, are to promote legal stability, to protect honest reliance, to preserve efficient judicial administration, to maintain similar treatment of persons similarly situated, and to promote public confidence in courts. A judge must give weight to stare decisis only when adherence to a precedent accomplishes these goals.

Here are two sample cases, one where stare decisis theory was used persuasively and one where the court mindlessly botched the job.

Rightly Adhering to Precedent Because the Need for Stability and Reliance Is Present   The law of tort, especially the law of negligence, creates enticing moral questions because, almost by definition in the case of negligence, courts apply the law only when it has in fact failed to control how people behave. The negligent driver simply does not plan to have or avoid an accident based on his knowledge of negligence law, even if he has some understanding of it. As a result, negligence law does not, unless the expectations expressed in an insurance contract are thwarted, confront a judge with the problem of upsetting someone's expectations if he changes the law. Negligence law defines when someone owes someone else a remedy for a past wrong, and this focus leads inevitably to the moral question of how we ought to relate to others, be they friends or strangers.

The need for stability in law more often exists with respect to laws that deal with people's business and contractual relations and with their related planning of the use and disposition of their property. Here we may not reach ultimate moral questions so quickly. When plans depend on law, the law's shortcomings may not justify changing it. We therefore temporarily abandon tort law and turn to one very small problem in a very complicated subject—the law of business contracts.

Contracts, among many other items, are agreements among businesspeople that allow them to formalize their buying and selling of each other's goods and services. Plans involving millions or even billions of dollars can rest on such agreements. For example, a construction company specializing in high-rise office buildings may conditionally contract with a supplier of steel to buy steel at a given price in order to know what to bid on a construction project. If the company receives the award, its entire profit margin could disappear if its steel supplier at the last minute insisted on a higher price for the steel.

But what legal rules convert an ordinary agreement—He: "Can you come to dinner at my place at 8:00?" She: "I'd love to! See you then."—into a legally binding contract? In early common law, if a written agreement contained the impression of a promise-making person's seal in wax, then the beneficiary of the promise could hold him to his promise. Men wore signet rings etched with their sign (their seal) with which to impress the wax. The only exception for a time was the king. He sealed the wax on his agreements with the impression of his front teeth. Gradually the use of wax, seals, and front teeth declined, to the point where printing the word *seal* or the letters *L.S.* (for the Latin *locus sigilli*) created the contractual tie.

Today, seals do not make agreements legally binding: Half the American states have passed statutes abolishing the seal. But, in many jurisdictions in the past and in some today, when people have sealed their contract (perhaps simply by adding at the end "Seal" or "L.S."), the law has made it very difficult for the contracting parties to dispute it. The law has rendered it difficult if not impossible to argue that the contract has been made fraudulently or to prove that the promisor has already performed the act he promised.

Long after agreements became enforceable in law without a seal, the law preserved some of the special rigidities for those contracts with seals. In one specific example, unlike an unsealed contract, only the person named in a sealed contract can be held to it. When, for example, a buyer seeks to disguise his interest by having another contract for him, using the agent's name but remaining the interested party, he along with the agent may find himself bound, but only if the contract of sale bears no seal. The sealed purchase contract, on the other hand, would bind only the agent named in it, not the interested party.

Businesspeople regularly transact business through agents. Sometimes, and this is particularly true in commercial real estate transactions, a businessperson will fund another to buy or sell property for him. He will fund the agent but insist that the agent assume all the responsibilities of the contract. The legal name for such a backer is "undisclosed principal." This technique of preserving anonymity is not necessarily unfair to the other side. If someone buys up various lots in an area in order to build a factory in his own name, the owners approached last may insist on a highly inflated price, knowing that if the buyer fails to get the last lot in order to proceed, all his other purchases will become meaningless.

Beginning in the nineteenth century, by both statute and judicial decision, the legal gap between the protections of sealed and unsealed contracts began to narrow. However, in the 1920s, this New York case arose. In a contract under seal, an agent agreed to buy land without naming an undisclosed principal. The seller agreed, but the agent shortly thereafter withdrew from the agreement. The seller, having learned the name of the principal, sued the principal. He asked the judge to order the principal to pay for the land and accept the deed.

The court ruled for the defendant. It noted many New York precedents limiting the significance of a seal on a contract. Nevertheless it concluded:

> We find no authority for the proposition that a contract under seal may be turned into the simple contract of a person not in any way appearing on its face to be a party to or interested in it, . . . and we do not feel at liberty to extend the doctrine applied to simple contracts executed by an agent for an unnamed principal so as to embrace this case. . . .
>
> Neither do we find any authority since 1876 in this court for the proposition. *Briggs v. Partridge*[17] has been cited by us many times with no hint of disapproval. . . .We repeat that we do not feel at liberty to change a rule so well understood and so often enforced. If such a change is to be made it must be by legislative fiat. . . .
>
> . . . Thousands of sealed instruments must have been executed in reliance upon the authority of Briggs v. Partridge. Many times the seal must have been used for the express purpose of relieving the undisclosed principal from personal liability. It may not be unwise to preserve the distinction for this especial purpose. But whether wise or unwise the distinction now exists.[18]

Any doctrine, stare decisis included, has impact only when it leads to action not likely otherwise. Stare decisis affects judicial choices when, because of judges' commitment to it, they reach decisions they might in general terms think to be poor social policy.

In many respects it is inequitable to allow the undisclosed principal to avoid contractual responsibility because of a seal. New York's Justice Crane, who did not participate in the *Crowley* decision, wrote:

> Thus, if an unsealed contract to sell real estate is signed by the agent in his own name, and the fact that he is acting for another and not for himself appears nowhere upon the face of it, the real principal can always sue and be sued upon the instrument. But if it should happen that the printed letters "L.S." appear after the agent's name, all would be different. The principal could neither sue nor be sued. The absurdity of this is apparent upon the face of the statement, and the danger and pitfall of such a doctrine in business transactions is realized when we pause to consider how many printed forms of agreements have the letters "L.S." stamped upon them, or how easy it is to make the scroll.[19]

But another justice who joined the *Crowley* opinion, Benjamin Cardozo, took the opposite view. Although Cardozo admitted that the seal system seemed an anachronism, he concluded that changing the rules about seals would be unfair:

> Men had taken title in the names of "dummies," and through them executed deeds and mortgages with the understanding, shared by the covenantees, that liability on the covenant would be confined to the apparent principal. They had done this honestly and without concealment.

Cardozo also noted that the seal arrangement had some advantages. Like the corporate form, the seal limited liability, facilitating business transctions. Cardozo con-

[17]*Briggs v. Partridge*, 64 N.Y. 357 (1876).
[18]*Crowley v. Lewis*, 239 N.Y. 264 (1925), pp. 265–267.
[19]Frederick E. Crane, "The Magic of the Private Seal," 15 *Columbia Law Review* 24 (1915), pp. 34–35.

cluded that "retrospective change would be unjust. The evil, if it was one, was to be eradicated by statute."[20]

Both Crane and Cardozo are in a sense correct. The rule may work to an unfair advantage, and it is the place of courts, not just legislatures, to minimize unfair advantages in law. However, the court rightly left legal change to the legislature because it understood that many businessmen, without acting unfairly, regularly employed that legal technique in planning their affairs. Judicial action would upset existing plans made by fair men, but the legislature would make law for the future. This difference, not a difference in lawmaking authority, gives the *Crowley* decision its wisdom.

The distinction between retrospective and prospective lawmaking is tricky. Every time a court makes new case law, it creates a winner and a loser in a case that happened under the older law. How can this retrospective lawmaking ever be fair and just? Judges can solve the stare decisis dilemma by asking whether it really makes sense to believe that the parties to the conflict planned their lives around the old law. In tort cases, for example, conflicts usually arise because of unplanned events, like a car crash. In such circumstances there often is no stare decisis dilemma.

Wrongly Adhering to Precedent When Stability Is Unnecessary   It would be a mistake to conclude that courts should always follow precedents in business, contract, and property matters but never in the case of negligence. It is not that simple. Tort law can, for example, influence a person's decision to insure against loss. Precedents in tort, like precedents in contract, create expectations on which people can rely. In this final illustration, however, let us look at a property problem in which a court, in a thoughtless opinion, followed precedent when the reasons for stare decisis did not support adherence. This case involves the laws of wills and of trusts, areas in which stability and reliance normally deserve great respect.

The case involved a section of the will of a New Jersey resident. In it the deceased, Rosa E. Green, stated: "I give and bequeath unto my husband, William L. Green, all of the money which I have on deposit at the Paterson Savings and Trust Company, Paterson, New Jersey, however, any money which is in the said account at the time of my said husband's death, the said sum shall be held by my niece, Catherine King Fox, absolutely and forever." William died without removing the money.

Naturally Ms. Fox attempted to withdraw the money from the bank. However, heirs of William claimed that the conditional gift to Ms. Fox was invalid. Lawyers for the heirs cited many New Jersey precedents stating that an unconditional bequest in a will, like the one to William, gave him unconditional ownership. Any conditional gift of the same property would have to be invalid; otherwise, the first gift would not be absolute. William's heirs won. The court said:

> Appellants ask this Court to explicitly and expressly overrule the long established law of this state. This we decline to do. Such action would be fraught with great danger in this type of case where titles to property, held by bequests and devises, are involved. A change of the established law by judicial decision is retrospective. It makes the law at the time of prior decisions as it is declared in the last decision, as to

[20]Benjamin N. Cardozo, *The Paradoxes of Legal Science* (New York: Columbia University Press, 1928), pp. 70–71.

all transactions that can be reached by it. On the other hand a change in the settled law by statute is prospective only.[21]

Think briefly about this result in terms of the reasons for stare decisis. For whom should this law remain stable? Who could plan on the basis of this rule? Certainly not Rosa. She intended to make a conditional gift to Catherine but failed. William, if he wanted the money, had only to withdraw it. Until the moment of his death (or legal incapacitation), no one but William could make any plans based on what might happen to "Catherine's" money. For William to plan, we must suppose some reasoning like this: "I am going to die. I don't want the money, but I don't want Catherine to obtain the money, either. I could prevent her from receiving it by depositing it in another bank, but, since the clause is invalid, I'll leave it there." Such planning is possible, but is it probable? Is it the sort of planning that the law needs to preserve at the expense of carrying out the wishes of the deceased? Many people do not know rules of law of this kind. Is it not more probable that William also intended the money to go to Catherine? Is it plausible that, once William died leaving the money in the bank, Catherine made plans on the assumption that she did have the money?

Consider the other purposes of stare decisis: Is the image of justice improved by defeating Rosa's wishes? How important is equality of treatment in this kind of situation? How important is it to say that because courts have refused to carry out the wishes of past testators (the creators of wills) they must treat current testators in the same way for equality's sake?

Finally, efficiency in the judicial process does matter. Judges should not have to question the wisdom of every point of law that arises, but that hardly means they can never do so.

One judge disagreed with the majority in *Fox*. Chief Justice Vanderbilt's dissent is one of the finest essays from the bench on stare decisis, and more generally on the nobility of the common-law tradition. It provides a fitting summary of this section:

VANDERBILT, C. J. (dissenting)

I am constrained to dissent from the views of the majority of the court, first, because they apply to the case a technical rule of law to defeat the plain intent of the testatrix without serving any public policy whatever in so doing and, secondly—and this seems to me to be even more important—because their opinion involves a view of the judicial process, which, if it had been followed consistently in the past, would have checked irrevocably centuries ago the growth of the common law to meet changing conditions and which, if pursued now, will spell the ultimate ossification and death of the common law by depriving it of one of its most essential attributes—its inherent capacity constantly to renew its vitality and usefulness by adapting itself gradually and piecemeal to meeting the demonstrated needs of the times. . . .

By the words in the third paragraph, "any money which is in said account at the time of my said husband's death, the said sum shall be held by my niece, Catherine King Fox, absolutely and forever," the testatrix beyond any doubt intended that her husband could use up the bank account but that if he did not, the plaintiff should take what was left of it on his death. To hold otherwise is to proceed on the untenable assumption that the quoted words are meaningless and to ignore the elementary principle that the provisions of a will are not to be construed as meaningless except on the failure of every attempt to render them effective. . . . This principle is an integral part of the most fundamental rule of testamentary construction, *i.e.*, the duty of the court is to ascertain what the intent of the testator was and, then, having ascertained it, to give it effect. . . .

---

[21]*Fox v. Snow*, 6 N.J. 12 (1950), p. 14.

The opinion of the majority of the court, like every other decision in this State on the subject, makes no attempt to justify the rule it perpetuates either in reason or on grounds of public policy. Despite the deleterious effects of the rule and the lack of any sound principle to support it, the majority maintains that it should not be overthrown, because it has been the long established law of this State and because overruling it "would be fraught with great danger in this type of case where titles to property, held by bequests and devises, are involved" by reason of the retroactive effect of all judicial decisions. This view, if it had been consistently applied in the past, would have prevented any change whatever in property law by judicial decisions. . . . Every change in the law by judicial decision necessarily creates rights in one party to the litigation and imposes corresponding duties on the other party. This is the process by which the law grows and adjusts itself to the changing needs of the times.

The process is necessarily used not only to create new rights and corresponding duties but, where necessary, to strike down old ones. . . . "It is revolting," says Mr. Justice Holmes, "to have no better reason for a rule of law than that so it was laid down in the time of Henry IV. It is still more revolting if the grounds upon which it was laid down have vanished long since, and the rule simply persists from blind imitation of the past," and "To rest upon a formula is a slumber that, prolonged, means death." *Collected Legal Papers* (1920) 187, 306. . . .

To hold, as the majority opinion implies, that the only way to overcome the unfortunate rule of law that plagues us here is by legislation, is to put the common law in a self-imposed strait jacket. Such a theory, if followed consistently, would inevitably lead to the ultimate codification of all of our law for sheer lack of capacity in the courts to adapt the law to the needs of the living present. The doctrine of *stare decisis* neither renders the courts impotent to correct their past errors nor requires them to adhere blindly to rules that have lost their reason for being. The common law would be sapped of its life blood if *stare decisis* were to become a god instead of a guide. The doctrine when properly applied operates only to control change, not to prevent it. As Mr. Justice Cardozo has put it, "Few rules in our time are so well established that they may not be called upon any day to justify their existence as means adapted to an end. If they do not function they are diseased, . . . they must not propagate their kind. Sometimes they are cut out and extirpated altogether. Sometimes they are left with the shadow of continued life, but sterilized, truncated, impotent for harm." *Nature of the Judicial Process* (1921) 98. All lawyers as well as laymen have a perfectly natural longing to think of the law as being as steadfast and immutable as the everlasting hills, but when we face the realities, we must agree with Dean Pound when he says. "Law must be stable, and yet it cannot stand still," *Interpretations of Legal History* (1923). . . , and with Professor Williston when he tells us, "Uniform decisions of 300 years on a particular question may, and sometimes have been overthrown in a day, and the single decision at the end of the series may establish a rule of law at variance with all that has gone before." *Some Modern Tendencies in the Law* (1929) 125. . . .

The dangers that the majority fear, it is submitted, are more apparent than real. The doctrine of *stare decisis* tends to produce certainty in our law, but it is important to realize that certainty *per se* is but a means to an end, and not an end in itself. Certainty is desirable only insofar as it operates to produce the maximum good and the minimum harm and thereby to advance justice. The courts have been reluctant to overthrow established rules when property rights are involved for the simple reason that persons in arranging their affairs have relied upon the rules as established, though outmoded or erroneous, and so to abandon them would result sometimes in greater harm than to observe them. The question whether the doctrine of *stare decisis* should be adhered to in such cases is always a choice between relative evils. When it appears that the evil resulting from a continuation of the accepted rule must be productive of greater mischief to the community than can possibly ensue from disregarding the previous adjudications on the subject, courts have frequently and wisely departed from precedent, 14 Am. Jur., Courts, Section 126.

What then, are the relative evils in the instant case? First, we should consider the evils that will result from a perpetuation of the rule here involved. It has already been demonstrated that the rule, in each and every instance in which it is applied, results in a complete frustration of the legitimate intention of the testator. It can only operate to take property from one to whom the testator intended to give it and to bestow it upon another. . . .

Having considered the evils flowing from continuing to follow the rule, let us now inquire into the evils, if any, which might result from its rejection. It is pertinent at this point to recall the words of Mr. Justice Cardozo minimizing the effect of overruling a decision: "The picture of the bewildered litigant lured into a course of action by the false light of a decision, only to meet ruin when the light is extinguished and the decision is overruled, is for the most part a figment of excited brains." *The Nature of the Judicial Process* (1921) 122 [sic.]. The rule in question by its very nature is never relied upon by those who are seeking to make a testamentary disposition of their property, for if the rule were known to a person at the time of the drawing of his will, its operation would and could be guarded against by the choice of words appropriate to accomplish the result desired. This rule is truly subversive of the testator's intent. It is relied upon only after the testator's decease by those who seek, solely on the basis of its technical and arbitrary requirements, to profit from the testator's ignorance and to take his property contrary to his expressed desires. Certainly it is not unjust or inequitable to deny such persons resort to this rule. . . .[22]

THE COMMON-LAW TRADITION TODAY

Chief Justice Vanderbilt's dissent in *Fox* describes the essence of the common-law tradition. Judicial choices continue to change common law today. Indeed, only within the past one hundred years have judges recognized the inevitability and desirability of choice and change. Thus the full political consequences of choice and change have come sharply into focus.

This new self-consciousness on the part of judges about the nature of judicial choice has more than academic consequences in law. Common law has in the past changed even when judges believed they merely chose the one applicable statute or line of precedents that "correctly" resolved the conflict before them. When judges think they solve problems by mechanically finding the one right solution from the past, the law develops in an almost thoughtless way. Judges do not grapple with moral and economic aspects of policy choices when they do not believe they choose policies.

But, when the point of view shifts, when judges begin believing they do make policy choices, this consciousness changes the kind and quality of law that judges make in several ways.

The first of these changes we have already studied and condemned. It occurs when judges throw up their hands and say, "In a democracy only the legislature can make new law, not the courts. We must, therefore, deliberately avoid making changes." These decisions, in spite of themselves, do make changes, of course— just as the *Fox* decision, by rejecting Vanderbilt's powerful arguments, more deeply embedded a mechanical view of stare decisis as well as the rule against conditional gifts in New Jersey's law.

A second modern view of the consequences of acknowledged judicial discretion can avoid this evil. Judges, acknowledging that they can and do make law, pay

[22]*Fox v. Snow*, pp. 14–15, 21–27.

closer attention, as we are about to see, to the facts and values that help them (and us) decide that some policy choices are wiser than others. Modern decisions do tend to be less mechanistic and more concerned with the consequences for the future of various alternative choices of policy. This quality, after all, gave the *Lyman* and *Hynes* cases their modern flavor.

There is, however, a third consequence of this shift in viewpoint. Judges may dramatically increase the speed of change and deliberately broaden the lengths of the legal jumps they take from old law to new. When judges realize they rightly possess authority to remake common law, they may overreact and enact what they believe are ideal legal solutions without properly honoring competing needs for stability. Similarly, they may ignore the possibility that, while both courts and legislatures share authority to make law, they do not necessarily possess identical institutional characteristics for making wise law.

Some critics argue that this is just what has happened in tort law. Proponents of "tort reform" argue that judges have abused their common-law powers by adopting doctrines that allow too many plaintiffs in personal injury lawsuits to collect too much money. The media have responded to the tort reformers' claims sympathetically by publicizing bizzare or particularly controversial tort lawsuits.[23] Tort reformers have successfully lobbied legislatures to reverse judge-made changes in tort policy, and to limit the gains of personal injury lawsuits by, for example, capping the amount of damages a plaintiff can win. (Pro-plaintiff groups, meanwhile, have gone to court to argue that such legislation unconstitutionally interferes with the power of judges in common-law cases.) Tort law has thus become a battleground not just in the courts but in legislatures and popular culture. [24]

The rise of the tort reform movement demonstrates that judicial policymaking can become the object of great controversy. The potential problems posed by judicial policymaking are so central to reasoning in constitutional law that a thorough canvass of the "judicial limits" territory must be postponed until Chapter 5, which deals with reasoning in constitutional interpretation. But as the example of tort reform reminds us, these same concerns are present in common law as well.

In this perspective, consider the next case. It illustrates deliberate lawmaking. It exemplifies a dramatic expansion of common law, and it faces squarely the double problem of determining whether a given policy is wise and whether the courts were the wise place to make it. The case, *Tarasoff v. Regents of the University of California,* represented a substantial jump forward in the law of negligence and duty.[25]

Tatiana Tarasoff spent the summer of 1969 in Brazil. She had, with her parents' consent and assistance, left her home in California, in part to escape the almost fanatical affections of one Prosenjit Poddar. During her absence Poddar kept his contact alive. He persuaded Tatiana's brother to share an apartment with him near Tatiana's home in Berkeley, California.

Tatiana returned from Brazil in October. On October 27, 1969, Poddar killed her.

In due course, Tatiana's parents learned that Poddar had, during the summer, received psychological therapy on an outpatient basis from Cowell Memorial

---

[23]For two thoughtful critiques of the tort reform movement, see Marc Galanter, "News from Nowhere: The Debased Debate on Civil Justice," 71 *Denver University Law Review* 77 (1993); and "Real World Torts: An Antidote to Anecdote" 55 *University of Maryland Law Review* 1093 (1996).

[24]Thomas F. Burke, *Litigation and its Discontents: The Struggle Over Lawsuits, Lawyers and Legal Rights in American Politics* (Berkeley: University of California Press, 2002).

[25]*Tarasoff v. Regents of the University of California,* 551 P.2d 334 (1976).

Hospital at the University of California, Berkeley. Their further investigation uncovered these facts:

- On August 20, 1969, Poddar told his therapist, Dr. Moore, that he planned to kill his girlfriend when she returned from Brazil.
- When Poddar left, Dr. Moore felt Poddar should be committed for psychiatric examination in a mental hospital. He urgently consulted two of his colleagues at Cowell. They concurred.
- Moore then told two campus police officers that he would request commitment of Poddar. He followed up with a letter of request to the campus police chief.
- Three officers, in fact, took Poddar into custody. Poddar promised them he would leave Tatiana alone in the future. The officers believed Poddar was rational and released him.
- After, and presumably in part because the officers released Poddar, Dr. Moore's supervisor, Dr. Powelson, asked the police to return Moore's letter. Dr. Powelson also ordered destroyed all written evidence of the affair and prohibited any further action to commit Poddar for examination or observation.
- At no point did any members of the hospital staff or the campus police attempt to notify Tatiana, her brother, or her parents of Poddar's threat.
- The staff could easily have determined Tatiana's identity as well as her location and that of her family.

The Tarasoffs sued the doctors, the officers, and the university's board of regents, claiming damages for the loss of their daughter. Among other charges, they alleged that "defendants negligently permitted Poddar to be released from police custody without 'notifying the parents of Tatiana Tarasoff that their daughter was in grave danger from Prosenjit Poddar.'"[26] They claimed, in other words, that the defendants had a duty to use reasonable care to protect Tatiana.

The California Supreme Court upheld the legality of this claim, but only against the regents and the doctors. Reasoning by example played a major part in its result. The court cited precedents from California and elsewhere holding a doctor liable for the damage caused by illness contracted by people in contact with his patient if the doctor negligently failed to diagnose the disease as contagious and to isolate the patient. It also cited a case holding a doctor liable for damages where, following his negligent refusal to admit a mental patient to a hospital, the mental patient assaulted the plaintiff.

The directly relevant case law in California, however, imposed a duty only where the defendant already assumed some responsibility for the victim. If, for example, a mental hospital failed negligently to protect one patient from another's violence, the hospital became liable. In California, no law extended the duty further.

Using fact freedom, however, the court ignored the distinction. It said, "[W]e do not think that the duty should logically be constricted to such situations."[27] Let us review the majority's reasons for the conclusion.

The majority first stated a general framework for determining the existence or absence of a duty, a statement amply supported by recent California precedents. Note above all how different this statement is from earlier mechanical statements like "duty to invitees but no duty to trespassers or licensees." The court, quoting precedents, said the existence of a duty depends

---

[26]Ibid., p. 341.
[27]Ibid., p. 344.

only upon the "balancing of a number of considerations"; major ones "are the foreseeability of harm to the plaintiff, the degree of certainty that the plaintiff suffered injury, the closeness of the connection between the defendant's conduct and the injury suffered, the moral blame attached to the defendant's conduct, the policy of preventing future harm, the extent of the burden to the defendant and consequences to the community of imposing a duty to exercise care with resulting liability for breach, and the availability, cost and prevalence of insurance for the risk involved."

The most important of these considerations in establishing duty is foreseeability. As a general principle, a "defendant owes a duty of care to all persons who are foreseeably endangered by his conduct, with respect to all risks which make the conduct unreasonably dangerous."[28]

Having said this much, the majority then noted that at common law a duty to warn of foreseeable harm done by a dangerous person existed only when the defendant had a "special relationship" with either the source of danger or the potential victim. The court admitted that the doctors had no special relationship to Tatiana, but it asserted that because they did have such a relationship to Poddar, they therefore owed Tatiana a duty of care.

The court cited no convincing precedent or other authority for this expansion of law, but that did not seem to bother it. The court did pay attention to the arguments sustaining and attacking the practical wisdom and effect of the new policy.

The court had to deal first with the possibility that the harm was not foreseeable in the first place. The issue was made even more difficult because only a few years earlier, the court had based an important mental health ruling on the fact that psychological and psychiatric predictions of future behavior are notoriously inaccurate.[29] To this the court responded:

> The role of the psychiatrist, who is indeed a practitioner of medicine, and that of the psychologist who performs an allied function, are like that of the physician who must conform to the standards of the profession and who must often make diagnoses and predictions based upon such evaluations. Thus the judgment of the therapist in diagnosing emotional disorders and in predicting whether a patient presents a serious danger of violence is comparable to the judgment which doctors and professionals must regularly render under accepted rules of responsibility.
>
> We recognize the difficulty that a therapist encounters in attempting to forecast whether a patient presents a serious danger of violence. Obviously we do not require that the therapist, in making that determination, render a perfect performance; the therapist need only exercise "that reasonable degree of skill, knowledge, and care ordinarily possessed and exercised by members of [that professional specialty] under similar circumstances." (*Bardessono v. Michels* (1970) 3 Cal.3d 780, 788 . . .) Within the broad range of reasonable practice and treatment in which professional opinion and judgment may differ, the therapist is free to exercise his or her own best judgment without liability; proof, aided by hindsight, that he or she judged wrongly is insufficient to establish negligence.
>
> In the instant case, however, the pleadings do not raise any question as to failure of defendant therapists to predict that Poddar presented a serious danger of violence. On the contrary, the present complaints allege that defendant therapists did in fact predict that Poddar would kill, but were negligent in failing to warn.[30]

---

[28]Ibid., p. 342.

[29]In this particular case, *People v. Burnick*, 14 Cal. 3rd 306 (1975), the court held that a person could be committed to an institution for mentally disturbed sex offenders only after proof at trial beyond reasonable doubt that the defendant was, in fact, likely to repeat the offense.

[30]*Tarasoff v. Regents*, p. 345.

The court then turned to the most complex policy issue of all: Will imposition of the duty to warn discourage patients from seeking the psychiatric help they need, thus preventing not only their own improvement but perhaps increasing the actual incidence of violent harm to others because people don't get help? The court insisted that such a prediction is entirely speculative. It noted that both the California code of evidence and the Principles of Medical Ethics of the American Medical Association permit a doctor to reveal information about a dangerous person if doing so could protect the patient, other individuals, or the community. The court concluded that

> the public policy favoring protection of the confidential character of patient-psychotherapist communications must yield to the extent to which disclosure is essential to avert danger to others. The protective privilege ends where the public peril begins.
>
> Our current crowded and computerized society compels the interdependence of its members. In this risk-infested society we can hardly tolerate the further exposure to danger that would result from a concealed knowledge of the therapist that his patient was lethal. If the exercise of reasonable care to protect the threatened victim requires the therapist to warn the endangered party or those who can reasonably be expected to notify him, we see no sufficient societal interest that would protect and justify concealment. The containment of such risks lies in the public interest.[31]

Backed by powerful opposition communicated to the court in an amicus curiae ("friend of the court") brief from the American Psychiatric Association, Justice William Clark heatedly disputed the court's policy conclusion.[32] He began by noting that a California statute *prohibits* the release of "all" information about a patient once a person authorized to begin commitment proceedings does so. The majority had avoided that issue by insisting that the pleadings in the case did not state that Dr. Moore was so authorized. Clark insisted he was and further argued that the purpose of the statute applied clearly in the *Tarasoff* case. "The Legislature," he wrote, "obviously is more capable than is this court to investigate, debate, and weigh potential harm through disclosure against the risk of public harm by nondisclosure. We should defer to its judgment.[33]

Clark then turned to common-law analysis itself:

> Assurance of confidentiality is important for three reasons. . . .
>
> First, without substantial assurance of confidentiality, those requiring treatment will be deterred from seeking assistance. (See Sen. Judiciary Com. comment accompanying Sec. 1014 of Evid.Code; Slovenko, *supra*, 6 Wayne L.Rev. 175, 187–188; Goldstein & Katz, *Psychiatrist-Patient Privilege: The GAP Proposal and the Connecticut Statute* (1962) 36 Conn. Bar J. 175, 178.) It remains an unfortunate fact in our society that people seeking psychiatric guidance tend to become stigmatized. Apprehension of such stigma—apparently increased by the propensity of people considering treatment to see themselves in the worst possible light—creates a well-recognized reluctance to seek aid. (Fisher, *The Psychotherapeutic Professions and the Law of Privileged Communications* (1964) 10 Wayne L.Rev. 609, 617; Slovenko, *supra*, 6 Wayne L.Rev. 175, 188; see also Rappeport, *Psychiatrist-Patient Privilege* (1963) 23 Md.L.J. 39, 46–47.) This reluctance is alleviated by the psychiatrist's assurance of confidentiality. . . .

[31]Ibid., pp. 347–348.

[32]William Clark later served President Ronald Reagan, first as National Security Advisor and then as U.S. Secretary of the Interior.

[33]*Op. cit.*, p. 358.

Second, the guarantee of confidentiality is essential in eliciting the full disclosure necessary for effective treatment. (*In re Lifschutz, supra,* 2 Cal.3d 415, 431, 85 Cal.Rptr. 829, 467 P.2d 557; *Taylor v. United States* (1955), 95 U.S. App.D.C. 373, 222 F.2d 398, 401; Goldstein & Katz, *supra,* 36 Conn.Bar.J. 175, 178; Heller, *Some Comments to Lawyers on the Practice of Psychiatry* (1957) 30 Temp.L.Q. 401; Guttmacher & Weihofen, *Privileged Communications between Psychiatrist and Patient* (1952) 28 Ind.L.J. 32, 34.)* The psychiatric patient approaches treatment with conscious and unconscious inhibitions against revealing his innermost thoughts. "Every person, however well-motivated, has to overcome resistances to therapeutic exploration. These resistances seek support from every possible source and the possibility of disclosure would easily be employed in the service of resistance." (Goldstein & Katz, *supra,* 36 Conn. Bar J. 175, 179; see also, 118 Am. J.Psych 734, 735.) Until a patient can trust his psychiatrist not to violate their confidential relationship, "the unconscious psychological control mechanism of repression will prevent the recall of past experiences." (Butler, *Psychotherapy and Griswold: Is Confidentiality a Privilege or a Right?* (1971) 3 Conn.L.Rev. 599, 604). . . .

Third, even if the patient fully discloses his thoughts, assurance that the confidential relationship will not be breached is necessary to maintain his trust in his psychiatrist—the very means by which treatment is effected. "[T]he essence of much psychotherapy is the contribution of trust in the external world and ultimately in the self, modelled upon the trusting relationship established during therapy." (Dawidoff, *The Malpractice of Psychiatrists,* 1966 Duke L.J. 696, 704). Patients will be helped only if they can form a trusting relationship with the psychiatrist. (*Id.* at 704, fn. 34; Burham, *Separation Anxiety* (1965) 13 Arch.Gen. Psychiatry 346, 356; Heller, *supra,* 30 Temp. L.Q. 401, 406.) All authorities appear to agree that if the trust relationship cannot be developed because of collusive communication between the psychiatrist and others, treatment will be frustrated. (See, e.g., Slovenko (1973) *Psychiatry and Law,* p. 61; *Cross, Privileged Communications between Participants in Group Psychotherapy* (1970) Law and Social Order, 191, 199. . . .)

Given the importance of confidentiality to the practice of psychiatry, it becomes clear the duty to warn imposed by the majority will cripple the use and effectiveness of psychiatry. Many people, potentially violent—yet susceptible to treatment—will be deterred from seeking it; those seeking it will be inhibited from making revelations necessary to effective treatment; and, forcing the psychiatrist to violate the patient's trust will destroy the interpersonal relationship by which treatment is effected.[34]

Is Justice Clark correct? Should the court defer here to the legislature's fact-finding abilities? Or is he only using the timeworn argument, condemned by Chief Justice Vanderbilt's powerful dissent in *Fox v. Snow,* that legislatures, not courts, should make policy? Consider two possibilities. First, the court did in fact hear a

---

*One survey indicated that five of every seven people interviewed said they would be less likely to make full disclosure to a psychiatrist in the absence of assurance of confidentiality. (See Comment, *Functional Overlap Between the Lawyer and Other Professionals: Its Implications for the Doctrine of Privileged Communications* (1962) 71 Yale L.J. 1226, 1255). [Asterisk note in original.]

[34]Ibid., pp. 358–360. In 1984, Daniel Givelber, William Bowers, and Carolyn Blitch published the results of their survey of over 2,000 therapists nationwide. They concluded that most therapists found the *Tarasoff* ruling was consistent with their sense of professional ethics and that the ruling did not significantly impair their ability to treat their patients. See "*Tarasoff* Myth and Reality," 1984 *Wisconsin Law Review* 443 (1984). See also Kathleen Quinn's "The Impact of Tarasoff on Clinical Practice," 2 *Behavioral Sciences and the Law* 319 (1984). Quinn, a doctor of medicine, goes so far as to say that the physician may encourage a potentially violent patient voluntarily to commit himself by reminding the patient that in the absence of voluntary commitment, the law may require the psychiatrist to warn potential victims. Compare "More Psychotherapists Held Liable for the Actions of Violent Patients," *Wall Street Journal* 2 March, 1987, p. 23.

wide variety of points of view on the policy questions. The American Psychiatric Association did file an amicus brief. Interest groups lobby courts much as they do legislatures. Is there any reason to believe that a legislature facing this issue would hear substantially more or different or better policy arguments? Does not Justice Clark's dissent tend to undercut his position? He appears to have digested and incorporated into his thinking a wide range of literature bearing on the subject. Second, if Clark's analysis is so compellingly correct, nothing in the common law prevents the California legislature from amending the statute Clark cites to include within its scope the type of situation that occurred in *Tarasoff*.

The *Tarasoff* case, like the *Hynes* case, took the common law of duty in negligence cases a large step forward. The common law does not, however, move smoothly forward in rational increments. True to its nature, the common law did much backing and filling after *Tarasoff*; indeed the false starts, contradictions, and inconsistencies generated in the 1970s only began ironing themselves out in the 1990s.

For example, in *Thompson v. County of Alameda* (614 P.2d 728, 1980), the California Supreme Court reaffirmed *Tarasoff*'s holding that one has a duty to warn only specific victims who were actually identified or were easily identifiable, as was Tatiana herself. However, the facts were different. A juvenile offender in detention told a parole officer that if he were released on furlough he would murder a child chosen at random. He was in fact released, and he did just as he predicted, but the family of the victim child lost because no specific or identifiable victim was named. Similarly in 1984, a federal appellate court affirmed that the therapist of John Hinckley, who attempted to assassinate President Reagan, was not liable for the injuries Brady and others suffered in the attempt because Hinckley had identified no specific or identifiable victim.[35]

The difficulty, as you may already have noted, is that such rulings contradicted California common law as it existed before *Tarasoff*. Recall that California law previously held physicians liable for the damage done by contagious patients who spread disease because they were misdiagnosed. The third-party victims in such cases were not specifically identifiable beforehand. The reality is that in some cases we cannot reasonably expect the doctor to prevent harm to a victim unless she can identify a specific victim, but in other cases we can. As the Wisconsin Supreme Court put it:

> [I]f a patient announces an intention to, for example, leave the psychotherapist's office and commit random acts of violence, the psychotherapist would be unable to warn victims of potential danger. . . . Nevertheless, notwithstanding the absence of a readily identifiable victim, warnings could, in certain instances, effectively be made to, perhaps, the patient's family or police. . . . Society must not become the victim of a dangerous patient's ambiguity.[36]

Over time new and unanticipated problems will inevitably arise, and reasoning by example will apply such precedents in new and not entirely predictable ways. Indeed this is happening with respect to potential responsibility and liability for the spread of HIV and AIDS. Consider the case of a family practitioner who treats a husband and wife and discovers that one of the two is HIV positive. Does she have a duty to warn the other, who is also her patient? Does any physician treating any married patient have an obligation to warn a spouse, even when the spouse is *not* her pa-

---

[35]And see *DeShaney v. Winnebago County Dept. of Social Services*, 109 S.Ct. 998 (1989).
[36]*Schuster v. Altenberg*, 424 N.W.2d 159 (1988), 172–173.

tient? Courts in many states, strongly influenced by *Tarasoff,* have ruled that doctors and other health-care workers do have such duties to third parties. Indeed, *Tarasoff* has created an entire field of law regarding the health-care worker's duty to warn. Thus reasoning by example in common law marches on.[37]

The following case represents a new frontier in third-party liability, lawsuits against gun makers for the carnage caused by their products. Several cities and government agencies have brought such lawsuits, arguing that gun makers have been negligent in supplying weaponry to the public, and claiming that the manufacturers should compensate the government for the cost of treating gun injuries. Their argument parallels the successful claims made by states against tobacco manufacturers, who have agreed to compensate state governments for the cost of treating smoking-related illnesses. Does the judge convince you that this is an area that should be left to the legislature to decide? Or, as in the old tugboat case, is this an appropriate occasion for the courts to make new common law?

Illustrative Case

On March 1, 1997, two would-be bank robbers, stopped in the act, barraged Los Angeles police with heavy fire from an arsenal of "assault weapons." The shootout attracted nationwide attention because the police were outgunned—the robbers had more powerful weapons at their disposal than did the police. One officer who was injured in the shootout brought a lawsuit claiming that the makers of the assault weapons should be held liable for marketing a product seemingly designed for criminal use. A trial judge blocked the lawsuit, concluding that it went beyond the bounds of tort law, and the officer appealed this decision. As you read the appeal court's decision, consider the following facts: (1) while California had enacted a ban on assault weapons in 1989, enforcement of the law at the time of the shootout was tied up by litigation, and the the law was considered ineffective; (2) assault weapon bans have been plagued by the problem of identifying what exactly counts as an assault weapon—manufacturers often rename or slightly modify a banned gun.[38] In light of all you have read about the common law, do you find the appellate court's opinion convincing? Can it be squared with *Tarasoff?*

Whitfield v. Heckler & Koch
California Court of Appeals, Second District
98 *California Reporter* 2d 820 (2000)

Judge CURRY

Appellant Martin Whitfield is a Los Angeles police officer badly injured in a shootout with Emil Matasareanu and Larry Phillips, Jr., in front of the North Hollywood Branch of the Bank of America on February 28, 1997. . . .

[The] appellant alleged that among the various weapons used by Matasareanu and Phillips was a "Heckler & Koch .308 caliber semiautomatic assault rifle, model 91, with drum magazine." The weapons were allegedly used in their attempted robbery of the bank and their attempt to escape, during which nine police officers and two civilians were shot. Appellant was one of the first officers to arrive at the scene. One of the two assailants, believed to be

[37]Many state legislatures, in response to these court decisions, have in turn created statutes specifying the duties and privileges of health care workers who treat HIV-positive patients. For a review of these developments, see Lawrence O. Gostin and James G. Hodge, Jr., "Piercing the Veil of Secrecy in HIV/AIDS and Other Sexually Transmitted Diseases: Theories of Privacy and Disclosure in Partner Notification," 5 *Duke Journal of Gender Law & Policy* 9 (1999).
[38]Carl Ingram, "Assault Rifles Being Altered to Skirt Law," *Los Angeles Times,* 8 November 1999, p. A3.

Phillips, fired at appellant using one of the assault weapons and armor piercing bullets. Appellant ducked behind his patrol car, but was nonetheless struck in the left forearm and left buttock, the bullet which injured his forearm having first traveled through the engine block, transmission, and body of the patrol car. After sustaining these injuries, appellant attempted to reposition himself behind a row of trees, and was shot in the right femur, the lesser trochanter, and the upper torso. As a result of these injuries, appellant has become permanently disabled.

According to the complaint, the weaponry with which Matasareanu and Phillips were armed allowed them to fire at rates in excess of 100 shots per minute, and a total of more than 1,200 rounds during the standoff. . . .

. . . [The appellant alleges that] when they saw the police, Matasareanu and Phillips abandoned their plan to rob the bank "and undertook the completely new and separate task of creating this country's largest single military style shoot-out ever attempted against police officers. The goal of this new plan, which greatly enhanced the risk on the scene and, in fact, created entirely new risks, was to shoot, maim and kill as many police officers and civilians as possible with their massive firepower. . . ." [The appellant attempts] to place the blame for this new plan on respondent's "superior military weaponry"—[the appellant alleges that] "such gun was designed to fire bullets faster than any human being could ever squeeze-and-release the trigger. Such gun was also designed as a military weapon to be used to suppress all small arms fire, penetrate all known body armor, and control the military battle field in hand-to-hand combat settings. . . . [It] was also designed to be extremely accurate at distance, and built with very exacting specifications to be a superior piece of equipment[,] . . . designed to be used in a para-military or military setting, [and] was designed to be modified into a fully automatic weapon, and . . . kill as many people as possible in the shortest period of time. . . ."

Actionable negligence is traditionally regarded as involving the following: (a) a legal duty to use due care; (b) a breach of such legal duty; (c) the breach as the proximate or legal cause of the resulting injury. The question here is whether respondent owed appellant a duty of care. The determination of duty is primarily a question of law. It is the court's "expression of the sum total of those considerations of policy which lead the law to say that the particular plaintiff is entitled to protection." (Prosser, *Law of Torts* (4th ed. 1971) pp. 325–326.) Any number of considerations may justify the imposition of duty in particular circumstances, including the guidance of history, our continually refined concepts of morals and justice, the convenience of the rule, and social judgment as to where the loss should fall. While the question whether one owes a duty to another must be decided on a case-by-case basis, every case is governed by the rule of general application that all persons are required to use ordinary care to prevent others from being injured as the result of their conduct. . . .

To impose ordinary negligence liability on a manufacturer who has done nothing more venal than produce an unflawed, albeit potentially dangerous, product would expand the concept of duty far beyond any current models. Appellant cannot point to a single case where a manufacturer of an unflawed and legal product has been found to have violated a duty of care owed to a person injured by the product.

Generally speaking, the court may not impose a duty on the owner or manufacturer of the instrumentality where the injuries were caused by the criminal actions of a third party. The seminal case in this regard is *Richards v. Stanley,* 43 Cal. 2d 60 (1954), where the defendant left her car on a public street in San Francisco "'unattended and unlocked with the ignition key in said car lock' . . . " A thief took advantage of the situation to steal the car, and, while driving the stolen car, struck the plaintiff. Affirming a judgment for nonsuit, the court emphasized that "when [defendant] left the car it was in a position where it could harm no one, and no harm occurred until it had been taken by a thief. Thus a duty to prevent such harm would involve more than just the duty to control the car, it would involve a duty to prevent action of a third person. Ordinarily, however, in the absence of a special relationship between the parties, there is no duty to control the conduct of a third person so as to prevent him [or her] from causing harm to another."

The Supreme Court found special circumstances present in *Richardson v. Ham* 44 Cal. 2d 772 (1955), where a contractor left a bulldozer unlocked and several intoxicated men started and drove it, and abandoned it when they found they could not stop it. The bulldozer caused massive destruction to property in its path. The court distinguished *Richardson* on the grounds that the bulldozer aroused curiosity, attracted spectators, and was attractive to children, and it was, therefore, reasonably foreseeable that it would be tampered with. In addition, the likelihood that someone tampering with an unattended bulldozer would know how to operate or stop it was small. . . . Appellant attempts to rely on *Richardson,* but can point to no special relationship or special circumstances which would remove this case from the general rule of nonliability for the actions of third parties.

In the final analysis, since courts are in no position to make a value judgment on the usefulness of guns in our society, a decision on whether certain types of weapons should be made available to the general public must rest with the appropriate legislative body. Our Legislature, by its passage of the Roberti-Ross Assault Weapons Control Act of 1989 and the amendments signed into law by Governor Davis has made clear that it is attuned to the issue which is the crux of this litigation: the sale of assault weapons to the general public. In enacting the AWCA, the Legislature found that "the proliferation and use of assault weapons poses a threat to the health, safety, and security of all citizens of this state." The Legislature expressly recognized the problem identified by appellant here—that assault weapons have "such a high rate of fire and capacity for firepower that [their] function as a legitimate sports or recreational firearms [are] substantially outweighed by the danger that [they] can be used to kill and injure human beings." The AWCA restricts the manufacture, sale, and possession of "assault weapons." . . . In view of the ongoing legislative efforts to deal with the evils which led to the type of incident in which appellant was injured, we see no current need for the judiciary to intrude. . . .

Judgment affirmed.

Questions about the Case

1. How does this case compare to *Tarasoff*? How would you compare the duties of a therapist with those of a gun manufacturer? For example, do you see any difference in the foreseeability of harm in the two cases? Do you see any difference in the burden on the defendant to prevent the harm?
2. How does Judge Curry justify his decision? What social background facts and shared values does he muster in the opinion?
3. Is this a case of proper deference to the legislature, or simple spinelessness? Do legislatures have more competence to make policy in this area than courts? Why or why not?

Chapter	**Statutory**
4	**Interpretation**

*Whoever hath an absolute authority to interpret any written or spoken laws,
it is he who is truly the lawgiver, to all intents and purposes, and not the
person who first spoke or wrote them.*

—Benjamin Hoadly

*It is of course dangerous that judges be philosophers—almost as dangerous
as if they were not.*

—Paul Freund

WHAT ARE STATUTES?

Statutes—a dusty and unromantic word. One thinks of endless rows of thick books
in inadequately illuminated library stacks. The librarians have the mildew under
control, but its odor remains faintly on the air.

To understand better the significance of statutory law, we must abandon our reaction to statutes as dull and musty words; we must see them as vital forces in society. Statutes are the skeleton of the body politic. Our elected representatives officially speak to us through the statutes they enact. They form the framework that
gives political power its leverage. People in government, when fortified by statutory
authority, can take our property, our freedom, and our lives. Political campaigns and
elections, indeed much in public life that does excite us, matter because they directly influence the making of statutory policies that can dramatically affect the
quality of our lives.

When judges interpret statutes, they encounter issues that are significantly different from those we discussed in the previous chapter. As we have seen, the common-
law judge has always been a policymaker. Common-law judges often resolve controversies where no legislature has gone before, for example whether therapists owe a
duty to warn to potential victims of their patients, or whether tugboats should be required carry AM radios. In the twentieth century, judges in common-law cases became more explicit and self-conscious about their policymaking role, and their
choices have occasionally created a legislative backlash, as we saw in the case of
tort reform. Judges in common-law cases, then, must wrestle with the proper balance
between legislative and judicial lawmaking, but they do so knowing they are empowered to decide for themselves how to resolve public policy issues.

In statutory disputes the proper balance between legislative and judicial power
is necessarily quite different. Judges who interpret statutes must remember that
even in common-law systems like the United States, legislatures are the primary

lawmakers, so that when legislatures address a social problem, they are supreme.[1] Thus in matters of statutory interpretation the judge's ideas about a public policy problem should not be used to resolve the case.

The history of statutory interpretation in the twentieth century is a series of attempts to respect the supremacy of legislative policymaking by devising some technique for keeping judges within their proper bounds. Statutory law has been haunted by the fear that judges might use their power over statutory interpretation to substitute their own views for those of democratically elected legislators. If judges can interpret statutes any way they wish, it is feared, they can thwart the will of the people and undermine the democratic process.[2] As Appendix B suggests, many believe that the U.S. Supreme Court did just that in the 2000 election cases, although others claim the Court was correcting a runaway state court. Judges in the early twentieth century, one observer has noted, "frequently emasculated legislation designed to protect workers, children, consumers and women."[3] Even where judges in statutory cases don't actively frustrate the will of the majority, they may still "make policy without a license" by acting as (often unelected) superlegislators who feel free to go beyond the law's commands.

In the chapter on constitutional law we will assess more carefully the claim that judicial policymaking violates fundamental principles of democracy. For now, the important point is that concerns about judicial policymaking have led legal theorists—and judges themselves—to try to find ways to limit the role of courts in interpreting statutes. In particular, judges and legal theorists have adopted several approaches to statutory interpretation aimed at neatly separating policymaking and judging.

In this chapter we argue that these approaches are misguided. Each of them involves an attempt to constrain judges by generating a single right answer to statutory disputes, to give the judge a formula by which she can be sure that she's doing exactly what the law commands. But as you should see by now, law does not work that way. Legal disputes usually come to court when the law is uncertain, so that two parties have opposing interpretations of the law. No formula of interpretation can magically dissolve the ambiguities inherent in law. And statutory law, like common-law, has many sources of uncertainty.

First, statutes are written in words, and as we have already seen, words, whether in constitutions, precedents or statutes, are often ambiguous and troublesome. Judges who arm themselves with dictionaries and expect to find a single, unproblematic interpretation of a statute are expecting too much of language—and too little of themselves.

Second, the process by which legislatures make statutes is complex and multi-layered. Attempts to isolate particular moments from the legislative process and glean from them a single correct answer to a statutory dispute usually do injustice to the complexity of legislating. Committee reports, floor speeches, and the rest of the legislative process may help us make sense of the law, but only the duly enacted statute has the force of law. Legislatures can communicate their chosen policies in a

[1]This familiar principle of legislative supremacy has one important exception: Courts in the United States possess the authority to reject statutory supremacy when they conclude that the enforcement of a statute would violate a legal norm expressed in or implied by the constitutions of the states or the nation. Where judges find a violation, their expression of constitutional values becomes supreme, and this political dynamic is part of the familiar set of checks and balances that American government contains.

[2]See Samuel Popkin, *Statutes in Court: The History and Theory of Statutory Interpretation* (Durham, N.C.: Duke University Press, 1999).

[3]Shep Melnick, review of Samuel Popkin, *Statutes in Court: The History and Theory of Statutory Interpretation*, in *Law and Politics Book Review* (2000), www.polsci.wvv.edu/lpbr/subpages/reviews/popkin.html.

legally binding way only by voting favorably on a written proposal. Without the vote by the legislature, no matter how forcefully individual legislators or political parties advocate a policy decision, they create no law. Judges who fruitlessly search dictionaries for the single right answer to a statutory question will be just as frustrated when they turn to the legislative process.

Third, statutes are written in general terms and so do not neatly resolve particular disputes. There are, of course, some statutes that have extremely detailed rules. Tax laws take literally thousands of pages of rules and regulations to specify how government shall raise revenues. But other statutes are incredibly general. Early antitrust statutes said that society has a problem preserving effective business competition, and it shall hereafter be illegal to restrain competition. In 1890 a nearly unanimous Congress passed with very little debate the Sherman Antitrust Act. Its first two sections state: (1) "Every contract, combination in the form of a trust or otherwise, or conspiracy, in restraint of trade or commerce among the several States, or with foreign nations, is hereby declared to be illegal"; and (2) "Every person who shall monopolize, or attempt to monopolize . . . any part of the trade or commerce among the several States, or with foreign nations, shall be deemed guilty of a misdemeanor. . . ." Such general language leaves to judges much freedom to shape and refine law.

Finally, even if they wished to make all statutes as lengthy and detailed as tax codes, legislatures could not possibly anticipate every conflict that might arise under a statute.[4] Legislators are not soothsayers, so they cannot, for example, write laws for technologies that have not yet been invented. The Congress that passed the Sherman Antitrust Law of 1890 could not possibly have conceived of the special antitrust issues posed by computer software. Yet more than a century later, judges must use the Sherman Act to decide whether Microsoft's "bundling" of its Internet browser program to the Windows operating system should be declared illegal. Similarly, the makers of federal copyright law could not possibly have anticipated the unique issues posed by the rise of Napster, the Web site that allows Internet users to swap musical recordings, yet that is the law judges must use to resolve the dispute between Napster and its adversaries. In statutory law, as in common-law, judges must grapple with new kinds of conflicts using old legal rules.

Given all these difficulties, how should judges decide in concrete cases what statutes mean? Because we have focused in both of the previous chapters on the role of precedents in judging, one preliminary answer to this question should be familiar to you: Judges in statutory cases should seek first the guidance of earlier case precedents dealing with the same interpretive problem. Then, as in the common-law, judges can be guided—though of course not bound—by the principle of stare decisis, and by the discipline of reasoning by example.

But what if a particular kind of dispute has never arisen before? We call this *statutory interpretation in the first instance.* When judges decide what uncertain statutes "really" mean the first time, all the problems of statutory intepretation we have just sketched become particularly acute. In *McBoyle,* the airplane theft case in Appendix A, and *Caminetti,* the "weekend affair in Reno" case, judges had to unravel the uncertain commands of Congress with no close precedent to guide them. Similarly, in the dispute over the 2000 election, Florida courts were asked to make sense of confusing and contradictory election laws that had never been previously applied to a presidential contest. Judge Richard Posner likens their

---

[4]In law, as in life, no set of rules can cover every possible situation. This is a point that is explored further in Chapter 6; see pages 128–129.

challenge to that of a field commander in combat who radios his superiors for instructions. He hears the instruction "Go . . ." but immediately loses contact with headquarters. The field commander must decide to go forward or back, but he knows he cannot stay where he is, even if that seems the wisest course to him.[5]

What can judges do in such a messy situation? We argue that they best interpret statutes when they pay attention to the purposes of legislation, an approach that has been labelled "purposivism."[6] A judge must address directly such questions as these: What problem does this statute try to solve? Is the case before me an example of such a problem? If so, how does this statute tell me to solve it? These questions will not yield a single right answer to the legal problem the judge confronts, nor will they wholly eliminate the influence of the judge's worldviews on the answer she reaches. We argue, though, that a purpose-oriented approach strikes the best balance between legislative and judicial power in statutory interpretation. The judge who approaches statutory interpretation as a matter of purpose acknowledges legislative supremacy, but does so in a way that does not oversimplify the complexity of legislation, or the difficulty of the task before him.

Judges who approach statutes wisely know that they cannot treat the words as a series of Webster's definitions strung together. Wise judges intuitively appreciate the saying, "The greatest difficulty with communication is the illusion that it has been achieved." They know that words gain meaning not from dictionaries, but from their context. They know that a sign on an outdoor escalator reading, "Dogs Must Be Carried" does not mean that everyone riding the escalator must carry a dog.[7] They know, as Judge Learned Hand has written, that the words of statutes become meaningful only when they are applied sensibly to the solution of public problems:

> . . . it is one of the surest indexes of a mature and developed jurisprudence not to make a fortress out of the dictionary; but to remember that statutes always have some purpose or object to accomplish, whose sympathetic and imaginative discovery is the surest guide to their meaning.[8]

FOUR MISGUIDED APPROACHES TO STATUTORY INTERPRETATION

We have just outlined how judges should interpret statutes in the first instance, and why we think other approaches to statutory interpretation are misguided. The rest of the chapter fills in the details. As we will demonstrate, in attempting to evade the responsibility inherent in statutory interpretation, judges not only end up on the wrong path, but sometimes get downright silly.[9]

---

[5]See Posner's "Legal Formalism, Legal Realism, and the Interpretation of Statutes and the Constitution," 37 *Case Western Reserve Law Review* 179 (1986–1987), p. 189.

[6]Popkin, *Statutes in Court*, p. 125–149.

[7]Our thanks to Professor Allan Hutchinson for this illustration.

[8]This is from Learned Hand's opinion in *Cabell v. Markham*, 148 F2d 737, 739 (1945) as quoted in Popkin, *Statutes in Court*, p. 133.

[9]The persistence of what verges on downright silliness in statutory interpretation thus illustrates a critical point made near the beginning of Chapter 2: The law's language, practices, and traditions, like those in any field of organized human action, tend to perpetuate themselves even when they no longer square well with contemporary social background facts and values, i.e., they perpetuate bad legal reasoning.

Literalism: Sticking to the Words

Perhaps the most celebrated problem of statutory interpretation in American jurisprudence involves the seemingly straightforward and rather boring statutes governing inheritances. When someone with property dies with a valid will, statutes direct that the property go to the named heirs. When a person dies without a will, statutes designate which relatives—spouses, children, parents, siblings, and so on—take priority, and in what order. Until specific cases arose, these statutes said nothing to prevent people who committed murder in order to get an inheritance, either under a valid will or by statute, from getting the money. In an Ohio case, where the statute said the children would inherit from a parent who died without a spouse and without a will, one Elmer Sharkey took out mortgages on his mother's real estate and then murdered her. The court held that the law entitled him—or rather his creditors, since Elmer had since been hanged—to the money because the statute did not, by its literal words, forbid murderers from inheriting from their victims. The Ohio court reviewed a New York case holding that a grandson named to inherit in his grandfather's will should, despite the law, *not* inherit after he poisoned his grandfather. The Ohio court nevertheless reasoned: "[W]hen the legislature, not transcending the limits of its power, speaks in clear language upon a question of policy, it becomes the judicial tribunals to remain silent." Is this good legal reasoning? The New York court had reasoned that it would not serve any valid statutory purpose to let someone inherit who had murdered to do so.[10]

In 1912 Lord Atkinson, speaking for the British House of Lords in its appellate judicial role, said:

> If the language of a statute be plain, admitting of only one meaning, the Legislature must be taken to have meant and intended what it has plainly expressed, and whatever it has in clear terms enacted must be enforced though it should lead to absurd or mischievous results.[11]

Lord Atkinson, no doubt, respected legislative powers and responsibilities—in this case, those of the House of Commons. The problem he perceived, we can safely guess, is this: If courts can go beyond the words at all, they can go anywhere they want, setting their own limits and destroying legislative supremacy in the process. This is the classic rationale for the literal, sometimes absurd, reading of statutes.

Legislative supremacy deserves our deepest respect. But how would the good Lord react to this hypothetical statute: "A uniformed police officer may require any person driving a motor vehicle in a public place to provide a specimen of breath for a breath test if the officer has reasonable cause to suspect him of having alcohol in his body." Presumably Lord Atkinson would not exempt women from this law just because the last sentence reads "him" rather than "him or her." The earlier use of the word *person*, even to a literalist, can cover both sexes. But how would he handle the following argument by an equally literalistic defendant? "The statute plainly says the officer may require the specimen from a person driving. I may have been slightly inebriated when the officer pulled me over, but when the officer required the

---

[10]*Deem v. Millikin,* 6 O.C.C. Rep. 357 (1892), 360, and 53 Ohio St. 668 (1895); *Riggs v. Palmer,* 115 N.Y. 506 (1889). See the discussion in Hart and Sacks, above (fn. 11, p. 5), beginning at page 75. See also Richard Posner, *The Problems of Jurisprudence* (Cambridge: Harvard University Press, 1990), pp. 105–107. For Ronald Dworkin's famous discussion of this classic problem, see his *Taking Rights Seriously* (Cambridge: Harvard University Press, 1977), pp. 23–31. And see Joel Levin's discussion of the same problem in his *How Judges Reason* (New York: Peter Lang, 1992), Chapter 6.

[11]*Vacher and Sons, Ltd., v. London Society of Compositors,* A.C. 107 (1912), 121.

specimen I was *not* 'driving a motor vehicle.' I wasn't even in my car. I was doing my imitation of a pig in the middle of the pavement when the officer requested the specimen."[12] This result is absurd, but Lord Atkinson seems willing to accept absurd results. Should he be?

American judges have also been seduced by the appeal of adhering to the words. A Virginia statute stated: "No cemetery shall be hereafter established within the corporate limits of any city or town; nor shall any cemetery be established within two hundred and fifty yards of any residence without the consent of the owner. . . ." In 1942, after the legislature passed this statute, the town of Petersburg, Virginia, bought an acre of land within its corporate limits on which to relocate bodies exhumed during a road-widening project. The acre adjoined and would be incorporated into a long-established cemetery. A city resident well within the proscribed distance of the added acre brought suit to prevent the expansion and cited the statute. He lost. Justice Gregory wrote for the appellate court:

> If the language of a statute is plain and unambiguous, and its meaning perfectly clear and definite, effect must be given to it regardless of what courts think of its wisdom or policy. . . .
>
> The word "established" is defined in *Webster's New International Dictionary,* second edition, 1936, thus: "To originate and secure the permanent existence of; to found; to institute; to create and regulate. . . ."
>
> Just why the Legislature, in its wisdom, saw fit to prohibit the establishment of cemeteries in cities and towns, and did not see fit to prohibit enlargements or additions, is no concern of ours. Certain it is that language could not be plainer than that employed to express the legislative will. From it we can see with certainty that . . . a cemetery . . . may be added to or enlarged without running counter to the inhibition found in [the statute]. . . . Our duty is to construe the statute as written.[13]

Judges, like Justice Gregory, who cling to the literal meaning of words fail to appreciate that the dictionary staff did not sit in Virginia's legislature. By sticking to the words, the judges prevent themselves from asking what problem the legislature sought to address. Just why the legislature might purposely allow enlargement but not establishment of cemeteries in cities and towns *is* Justice Gregory's concern. Unless he tries to solve that puzzle, we can have no confidence that he has applied the statute to achieve its purpose.

The Golden Rule

Of course, Lord Atkinson could have solved his problem another way, by sticking to the words except when they produce absurd results. The Golden Rule of statutory interpretation holds that judges should follow

> the grammatical and ordinary sense of the words . . . unless that would lead to some absurdity, or some repugnance or inconsistency with the rest of the instrument, in which case the grammatical and ordinary sense of the words may be modified, so as to avoid the absurdity and inconsistency, but no farther.[14]

---

[12]See Sir Rupert Cross, *Statutory Interpretation* (London: Butterworths, 1976), p. 59. Or imagine a city ordinance requiring all liquor stores "to cease doing business at 10:00 P.M." Does the ordinance permit them to reopen at 10:01 P.M.?

[13]*Temple v. City of Petersburg*, 182 Va. 418 (1994), pp. 423–424. Responding to the vague words of the Mann Act (quoted in Chapter 2), Justice Day wrote in his majority opinion in *Caminetti*, "Where the language is plain and admits of no more than one meaning the duty of interpretation does not arise. . . ." Was the language of the Mann Act plain?

[14]*Grey v. Pearson*, 6 H.L. Cas. 61 (1857), 106, quoted in Cross, p. 15.

The Golden Rule solves the problem of the clever intoxicated driver. It would be absurd and possibly dangerous to require that the officer ride with him and collect the specimen while weaving down the road. But the Golden Rule, unfortunately, does not solve much more because it does not tell us how to separate the absurd from the merely questionable.

Take for example the case of Elian Gonzalez, the six-year-old Cuban boy found clinging to an inner tube in the Atlantic Ocean off the coast of Florida. Elian had been travelling by boat with his mother in an attempt to flee Cuba. When the boat capsized, eleven passengers, including Elian's mother, died. Elian was brought to the United States and put in the temporary custody of his great uncle, Lazaro Gonzalez. When Elian's father requested that his son be returned to Cuba, Lozaro Gonzalez asked the Immigration and Naturalization Service (INS) to grant the child asylum in the United States. The INS refused, concluding that since a six-year-old is incompetent to apply for asylum on his own, only Elian's father could submit an application for him. Lazaro Gonzalez then sued the INS in federal court, claiming that he had acted at the request of Elian, and noting that federal law fails to restrict asylum applications by age, providing only that "any alien . . . may apply for asylum." In a preliminary order barring the removal of Elian from the United States before a final decision in the case could be made, three federal appeals court judges ruled in favor of Lazaro Gonzalez. The judges agreed that the meaning of "any alien" is "pretty clear," and that if Congress had wanted to restrict asylum applications by age, it would not have written the statute to include "any alien":

> To some people, the idea that a six-year-old child may file for asylum in the United States, contrary to the express wishes of his parents, may seem a strange or even foolish policy. But this Court does not make immigration policy, and we cannot review the wisdom of statutes duly enacted by Congress.[15]

Is it absurd to let a six-year-old apply for asylum, or merely unwise? The Golden Rule provides no help, and so the Court simply throws up its hands.[16]

To further test the weakness of the Golden Rule, ask yourself two questions: (1) Is it absurd to allow expansion of existing graveyards while prohibiting the creation of new ones, or only questionable? (2) Is it absurd to use the Mann Act to prevent the transportation of willing girlfriends and mistresses across state lines along with unwilling "white slaves" and prostitutes, or merely questionable? The Golden Rule provides no answer.

Both the literal approach and the superficially more sensible Golden Rule fail. They deceive judges into believing that words in isolation can be and usually are clear, and that the words communicate by themselves. But they don't. The word "establish" in *Temple* (the graveyard case), the phrase "immoral purpose" in *Caminetti* (our first Mann Act case), and the word "vehicle" in *McBoyle* (the airplane theft case) simply are not clear, and no blunt assertion to the contrary will make them so. Even when words in isolation do seem unambiguous, the process of coordinating

[15]*Elian Gonzalez v. Janet Reno,* 2000 U.S. App. Lexis 7025 (11th Circuit, April 19, 2000), at footnote 9.

[16]Two months later, the same judges decided that since "Congress has left a gap in the statutory scheme" by failing to describe *how* an alien should apply for asylum, the INS could reasonably fill that gap by deciding that a six-year-old could not go through the process of applying for asylum without the assistance of his parents. The final decision in *Gonzalez* rested on a basic principle of administrative law, deference to executive agencies. The opinion in this case concluded that the Court should not second-guess the way the INS had interpreted the statute; only if the agency's interpretation was "unreasonable" should the Court step in. (*Gonzalez v. Reno* 212 F.3d 1338, 11th Circuit, June 1, 2000.) The question of how much deference courts owe to administrative agencies in statutory interpretation is also addressed in this chapter's illustrative case, *FDA v. Brown and Williamson.*

them with the facts of a particular case may make them unclear. In the Elian Gonzalez case, the words "any alien . . . may apply" seem straightforward until a judge contemplates the mental world of a six-year-old, who may not be able to understand what it means to apply for asylum, let alone fill out the application forms on his own. The judge who simply examines words like *any alien* by themselves and asserts that they are clear seeks only an easy exit. Interpreting words in isolation, then, is a danger because it leads judges to believe that they have thought a problem through to its end when they have only thought it through to its beginning.

To summarize, words become meaningful only in context. In statutory interpretation, judges must analyze two contexts. The first is the legislative context—what general problem exists and what kind of policy response to it the legislature has created. The second is the case context—what the litigants are disputing and whether their dispute involves the problem the statute addresses. To say that words are clear or unclear depending on the context really means that the words would become clear if we could imagine a different case or context arising under each of the same statutes this book has mentioned so far. If Elian Gonzalez had been 25 years old, or if Mr. McBoyle had stolen a car rather than a plane, judges would have had no difficulty concluding that the statutory words clearly and unambiguously determine the case. Judges would similarly not have hesitated to prohibit Petersburg from opening a brand new cemetery within the city limits.

The idea that words read literally will mislead has been around a very long time. In 1615, Galileo explained in a letter to the Grand Duchess of Tuscany the same idea. After strongly affirming that "the Bible can never speak untruth," Galileo went on to write that the Bible

> is often very abstruse, and may say things which are quite different from what its bare words signify. Hence in expounding the Bible if one were always to confine oneself to the unadorned grammatical meaning, one might fall into error. Not only contradictions and propositions far from true might thus be made to appear in the Bible, but even grave heresies and follies.

Literally read, the Bible would have God forgetting the past and clueless about the future, clearly contradictory to church teachings about the omnipotence of God. It is not too much to expect that judges learn what Galileo taught the Grand Duchess.

Canons of Statutory Construction

Judges have defended themselves against the imprecision of words by arming themselves with interpretive weapons called "canons of construction." As one part of a broader interpretative approach, canons of construction can be useful. The problem comes when judges use canons as if they were mathematical equations that can provide precise answers to problems in statutory interpretation.

A canon of construction or interpretation (they are, for our purposes, the same), is really a rule for interpreting rules. These canons, developed over hundreds of years by judges in statutory cases, provide rules for resolving ambiguities in the language of laws. Take for example the *McBoyle* case, which you will remember involved the theft of an airplane. The relevant statute forbade transportation across state lines of a stolen "automobile, automobile truck, automobile wagon, motorcycle or any other self-propelled vehicle not designed for running on rails." The question raised by the case is whether an airplane is a vehicle. Can the canons help?

One of the canons of construction says:

Where general words follow a statutory specification, they are to be held as applying only to persons and things of the same general kind or class of thing to which the specified things belong.

By invoking this canon, called *ejusdem generis* ("of the same kind"), a judge could conclude that the general words "or any other self-propelled vehicle" refer only to items *like* (in the same genus as) the objects the statute specifically mentions (the species). In this case, all the specific items run on land. Therefore, an airplane is not a vehicle.

Similarly, in *Caminetti* Justice Day invoked the ejusdem generis canon in reaching the conclusion that the Mann Act did cover concubines. He said that the general words "other immoral purposes" refer only to sexual immorality because all the specific examples fit that genus. If you take your mother or a female friend across a state line to rob a bank, you will not violate the Mann Act even though *immoral,* by its plain meaning, clearly includes robbery.

Before we consider how the canons can become a vice rather than a virtue in statutory interpretation, it will help to review a few more examples from among dozens of canons that judges utilize. One frequently cited canon instructs judges to interpret criminal statutes narrowly. This means that when a judge finds that the statute does not clearly resolve his case, he should resolve it in favor of the defendant. Again *McBoyle* can illustrate. Justice Holmes wrote for the Supreme Court in that case:

[I]t is reasonable that a fair warning should be given to the world in language that the common world will understand of what the law intends to do if a certain line is passed. To make the warning fair, so far as possible the line should be clear.

Holmes argues, in other words, that unless judges interpret criminal statutes narrowly, judges will send to jail people who had no clear notice that they had committed a crime.[17]

Holmes's concern for fairness in *McBoyle* reminds us that the canons are not totally ineffective or undesirable weapons. Felix Frankfurter said that "even generalized restatements from time to time may not be wholly wasteful. Out of them may come a sharper rephrasing of the conscious factors of interpretation; new instances may make them more vivid but also disclose more clearly their limitations."[18] Nearly every canon that judges have created contains at least a small charge of sensibility. Canons exist to support each of the principles of proper interpretation that this chapter covers. For example, the canon *noscitur a sociis* ("it is known by its associates") states that words are affected by their context. One British court used this canon to confine a statute regulating houses "for public refreshment, resort and entertainment" only to places where people received food and drink and excluded musical and other theatrical places, refreshing though their shows might be. The statute bore the title Refreshment House Act.[19]

---

[17]*McBoyle v. United States*, p. 27. A narrow interpretation may produce a very different decision from that of a literal interpretation. A literal interpretation of the words "other immoral purposes" in the Mann Act would make the act cover my taking my wife to another state to rob a bank. A narrow interpretation would not.

[18]Felix Frankfurter, "Some Reflections on the Reading of Statutes," 2 *Record of the Association of the Bar of the City of New York* 213 (1947), p. 236.

[19]Cross, p. 118. The list of canons is lengthy. Karl Llewellyn cites and provides judicial citations for 56 canons in "Remarks on the Theory of Appellate Decision and the Rules or Canons about How Statutes Are to Be Construed," 3 *Vanderbilt Law Review* 395 (1950), pp. 401–406.

So what exactly is wrong about using canons? By making disorderly words appear orderly, canons can deceive judges into thinking they have found a sensible and purposeful application of the statute to the case. In fact, the canons often allow judges to evade the difficult task of untangling statutory purpose and of weighing all four elements of legal reasoning. One example of this judicial evasion of purpose occurred after Congress passed a statute in 1893 designed to promote railway safety.[20] In part, Section 2 of the statute reads:

> [I]t shall be unlawful for any . . . common carrier [engaged in interstate commerce] to haul or permit to be hauled or used on its line any car . . . not equipped with couplers coupling automatically by impact, and which can be uncoupled without the necessity of men going between the ends of the cars.

Section 8 of the act placed the right to sue for damages in the hands of "any employee of any such common carrier who may be injured by any locomotive, car or train in use contrary to the provisions of this act. . . ." At common-law, the injured employee often had no right of action against his employer; Section 8 created that right. Additionally, the act imposed criminal penalties on railroads that failed to comply.

A workman was injured while positioned between a locomotive and a car. He had tried to couple them by hand because the locomotive did not possess a coupler that coupled automatically with the car. He sued for damages and lost both in the trial court and in the U.S. Court of Appeals, the latter holding that the statute did not require locomotives to possess the same automatic couplers. Judge Sanborn fired canon after canon in defense of his conclusion that the statutory word *cars* did not include locomotives:

- "The familiar rule that the expression of one thing is the exclusion of the others leads to [this] conclusion.
- "A statute which thus changes the common-law must be strictly construed.
- "This is a penal statute, and it may not be so broadened by judicial construction as to make it cover and permit the punishment of an act which is not denounced by the fair import of its terms.
- "The intention of the legislature and the meaning of a penal statute must be found in the language actually used."[21]

Do any of these canons convince you that this statute does not require locomotives to have automatic couplers? Again, the canons are not themselves absurd; the damage occurs when they seduce judges into applying them simplistically and into thinking the canon gives *the* answer when the canon only justifies *an* answer. Does not Judge Sanborn's reasoning at least create the suspicion in your mind that he wanted, for whatever reasons, to rule for the railroads, and that the easy availability of canons only provided convenient camouflage for his personal preferences?

The vice of the canons resembles the familiar law of mechanics. For each and every canon, there is an equal and opposite canon. Llewellyn organizes his fifty-six canons, noted in footnote 19, into twenty-eight sets of opposing canons: "THRUST BUT PARRY," he calls them. The judge who, for whatever reason, reaches any conclusion can find a canon to defend it.

Consider this example of Llewellyn's point: A federal statute prohibits the interstate shipment of any "obscene . . . book, pamphlet, picture, motion-picture film,

---

[20]27 Stat. c. 196, p. 531.

[21]*Johnson v. Southern Pacific Co.*, 117 Fed. 462 (C.C.A. 8th 1902). Fortunately the United States Supreme Court reversed, 196 U.S. 1 (1904).

paper, letter, writing, print or other matter of indecent character." One Mr. Alpers shipped interstate some phonograph records that, admitted for the sake of argument, were obscene. On the basis of ejusdem generis and "strict construction of criminal statutes," two canons, we might expect Mr. Alpers to win his case. After all, the genus to which all the species belong is "things comprehended through sight." Instead, Justice Minton, for the Supreme Court, alluded to noscitur a sociis, another canon, and upheld the conviction.[22]

In short, the canons themselves are at war. In *Caminetti,* ejusdem generis pushes toward conviction, but "narrow construction" pushes toward acquittal. Clearly canons, whatever their virtues, cannot provide the "right answer" to a question of statutory interpretation that some judges seek.

Legislative Intent

Another common way in which judges attempt to justify their interpretations of statutes is to try to discover what the legislature "intended" its statutory words to mean. We can define an *intention* as a determination to act in some way. Judges who use a "legislative intent" approach, then, attempt to resolve statutory conflicts by studying the intentions of legislators who voted for a statute. They try to figure out how the legislators thought the statute should apply to the case in question. We shall try in a moment to persuade you that "legislative intent" is a mirage, and that the quest for it almost inevitably leads judges astray. For now, think carefully about the following use of legislative intent. How much more comfortable are you with Chief Justice Rugg's reasoning in the next case than you were with Lord Atkinson's literal approach, or Justice Gregory's reasoning in the cemetery case, or Justice Day's argument in *Caminetti*?

Shortly after it became a state, and long before the Nineteenth Amendment to the United States Constitution guaranteed women the right to vote, Massachusetts passed a statute providing that "a person qualified to vote for representative to the General Court [the official name of the Massachusetts legislature] shall be liable to serve as a juror." Ten years after the passage of the Nineteenth Amendment, one Genevieve Welosky, a criminal defendant, found herself facing a Massachusetts jury that excluded all women. Welosky protested the exclusion, appealed, and lost. Under the literal or Golden Rule approaches she would surely have won, for *person* includes women, and women were "qualified to vote." Even before the days of women's liberation, we would hardly label it absurd to seat women on juries.

But Massachusetts Chief Justice Rugg invoked the intent of the legislature:

> It is clear beyond peradventure that the words of [the statute] when originally enacted could not by any possibility have included or been intended by the General Court to include women among those liable to jury duty. . . . Manifestly, therefore, the intent of the Legislature must have been, in using the word "person" in statutes concerning jurors and jury lists, to confine its meaning to men.[23]

The legislature didn't intend women to become jurors when they passed the statute, because at that time women could not vote. Despite the literal meaning of the words, women cannot therefore sit on juries.

---

[22]*United States v. Alpers*, 338 U.S. 680 (1950).
[23]*Commonwealth v. Welosky*, 276 Mass. 398 (1931), pp. 402–406.

The title of this section offered the hope that judges can find statutory truth by discovering legislative intent. The Massachusetts court has identified an uncontested social background fact—that women could not vote when the statute was passed—and concluded logically that the legislature did not intend women to sit on juries. This logic is straightforward enough, but the *Welosky* opinion is a virtual fraud. Rugg says the simple sequence of historical events reveals the legislature's intent; because the statute came before the amendment, the legislature did not intend to include women. But Rugg's first quoted sentence sends us on a wild goose chase. It is plausible that the legislature did not consider the possibility of women— or for that matter, immigrant Martians—becoming jurors. But it is simultaneously plausible that the Massachusetts legislature "intended" to settle the problem of who may sit as a juror once and for all by simply gearing jury liability automatically to all future changes in the voting laws. A legislature that did so would hardly act absurdly. Rugg completely fails to show that it did not so act. In Appendix B, we will see that the U.S. Supreme Court in *Bush v. Gore* reasoned about the intent of the Florida legislature much like the Massachusetts court reasoned about the intent of the Massachusetts legislature in *Welosky*.

Does the hope that legislative intent will reveal the meaning of statutory language hence fail? Yes, but not because of poorly reasoned cases like *Bush* or *Welosky*. The quest for legislative intent is a search for hard evidence. It is detective work in the legal field, not Rugg's idle armchair speculations or the *Bush* majority's desperate grasp for justification, so we should not abandon the field of legislative intent so quickly.

Judges have many sleuthing techniques for discovering "hard evidence" of intent, of which we now review three of the most prominent. What do you think of them?

Other Words in the Statute   The brief excerpt from the cemetery case, discussed earlier in this chapter, may have treated Justice Gregory unfairly, for he did not simply rest his opinion on Webster's dictionary. He continued by pointing out that another section of the cemetery statute of Virginia

> affords a complete answer to the question of legislative intent in the use of the word "established" in Section 56, for the former section [Section 53] makes a distinction between "establish" and "enlarge" in these words: "If it be desired at any time to establish a cemetery, for the use of a city, town, county, or magisterial district, or to enlarge any such already established, and the title to land needed cannot be otherwise acquired, land sufficient for the purpose may be condemned. . . ."
>
> The foregoing language, taken from Section 53, completely demonstrates that the legislature did not intend the words "establish" and "enlarge" to be used interchangeably, but that the use of one excluded any idea that it embraced or meant the other.[24]

Similarly, Justice McKenna, dissenting in *Caminetti*, found support in the official title of the Mann Act:

> For the context I must refer to the statute; of the purpose of the statute Congress itself has given us illumination. It devotes a section to the declaration that the "Act shall be known and referred to as the 'White Slave Traffic Act.'" And its prominence gives it prevalence in the construction of the statute. It cannot be pushed aside or subordinated by indefinite words in other sentences, limited even there by the context.[25]

---

[24]*Temple v. City of Petersburg*, p. 424.
[25]*Caminetti v. United States*, p. 497.

The title of the statute tells Justice McKenna that Congress did not intend to police the activities of willing girlfriends. Willing girlfriends are not white slaves; the conclusion sounds sensible.

The Expressed Intent of Individual Legislators and Committee Reports
Like Justice Gregory, Justice McKenna, in his *Caminetti* dissent, made more than one argument to support his conclusion.[26] In fact, he went directly to the words of the bill's author and quoted extensively from Representative Mann:

> The author of the bill was Mr. Mann, and in reporting it from the House committee on interstate and foreign commerce he declared for the committee that it was not the purpose of the bill to interfere with or usurp in any way the police power of the states, and further, that it was not the intention of the bill to regulate prostitution or the places where prostitution or immorality was practiced, which was said to be matters wholly within the power of the states, and over which the Federal government had no jurisdiction. . . . [Mann stated]:
> "The White Slave Trade—A material portion of the legislation suggested and proposed is necessary to meet conditions which have arisen within the past few years. The legislation is needed to put a stop to the villainous interstate and international traffic in women and girls. The legislation is not needed or intended as an aid to the states in the exercise of their police powers in the suppression or regulation of immorality in general. It does not attempt to regulate the practice of voluntary prostitution, but aims solely to prevent panderers and procurers from compelling thousands of women and girls against their will and desire to enter and continue in a life of prostitution." *Congressional Record,* vol. 50, pp. 3368, 3370.
> In other words, it is vice as a business at which the law is directed, using interstate commerce as a facility to procure or distribute its victims.

Judges rarely argue that the expressed views of any one legislator necessarily convey legislative intent, but they frequently cite committee reports and statements of authors as proof of intent. This is a curious practice, for it seems to allow a minority of legislators to determine what the law holds despite the fact that in a legislature only a voting majority has the power to make law.

Other Actions, Events, and Decisions in the Legislature   To establish legislative intent, judges may also look at how the legislature handled related legislation. In *Welosky,* Chief Justice Rugg noted that the Massachusetts legislature had in 1920 changed several laws relating to women in order to make them conform to the Eighteenth and Nineteenth Amendments, but said nothing about the problem of female jurors. He argued regarding the 1920 legislation:

> It is most unlikely that the Legislature should, for the first time require women to serve as jurors without making provision respecting the exemption of the considerable numbers of women who ought not to be required to serve as jurors, and without directing that changes for the convenience of women be made in court houses, some of which are notoriously over-crowded and unfit for their accommodation as jurors.

Judges may even find in the physical evidence presented to committees the key to intent. In the 1940s the postmaster general refused to grant the preferential lower postage rate to books, like workbooks and notebooks, that contained many blank

---

[26]Appellate judges often give multiple arguments for the conclusions in their opinions, but they rarely articulate whether one argument, by itself, would justify the same result. They don't, in other words, spell out the relative importance of the arguments they use.

pages. Congress then amended the relevant statute to grant the preferential postal rates to books with space for notes. However, the postmaster general continued to refuse the rate to so-called looseleaf notebooks with blank pages on the basis that they were not permanently bound. A shipper of such notebooks eager for the cheaper postage rate sued for an order granting the preferential rate.

The opinion of Judge Groner concluded that Congress did intend to give the preferential rate to looseleaf notebooks because the many physical exhibits placed before the committee that handled the bill included some such notebooks. Groner wrote, "[I]t follows logically that textbooks of the make and quality of those of appellant were considered and purposely included by Congress in the list of publications entitled to the book rate."[27]

The list of possibilities in this category could continue for pages. For example, judges are fond of finding legislative intent by discovering that one house's version of a bill contained a clause that does not appear in the final law, approved by both houses. They conclude from this discovery that the legislature intended that the remaining words *not* mean what the dropped clause meant. Superficially, these discoveries of "hard evidence" of legislative intent appeal to us because they seem to reveal the purpose of the statute. But comparing the examples of sleuthing with our "first principles" of statutory interpretation reveals that legislative intent fails as badly as our other two approaches. Only the statute, the words for which the majority of both houses of the legislature voted, has the force of law.

When Judge Groner concludes "logically" that the legislature intended to include looseleaf notebooks for the preferential rate, he is logically completely incorrect. He does not give one shred of evidence that any legislator, much less the majority, actually thought about the physical exhibits when they voted. Of course, Representative Mann's thoughts give us some clue to his intent, but we do not know that a majority heard or read his thoughts. Even if a majority in the House and Senate did know what Mann intended, we don't know that they agreed with him. After all, the statute uses the word *prostitution* without Mann's qualifications. Maybe the majority voted for the act because they wanted a tougher response than did Mann.

The Perils of Legislative Intent   Why then, precisely, does legislative intent fail as a tool of statutory interpretation? A legislature is an organizational unit of government. By itself a legislature can no more intend something than can a government car or an office building. *People* intend things, and, because the elected representatives in a legislature are people, they may intend something when they vote. If all members of the voting majority intended the same thing, then that might well state the purpose of the statute. However, here three difficulties fatal to the cause of legislative intent arise.

First, intent is subjective. It is usually impossible to tell with 100 percent certainty what anyone, ourselves included, intends. Thus, if a majority of legislators were fortunate enough to intend the same thing, it is highly unlikely that judges could actually discover what that thing was. For centuries, the difficulties of knowing a person's actual intentions have led common-law principles of contract and tort to reject the relevance of evidence about the actual intentions of the parties. Instead the law asks what a reasonable and prudent person would think or do in such a situation.

---

[27]*McCormick-Mathers Publishing Co. v. Hannegan*, 161 F.2d 873 (D.C. Cir. 1947), p. 875. See Arthur Phelps, "Factors Influencing Judges in Interpreting Statutes," 3 *Vanderbilt Law Review* 456 (1950).

Second, we know enough about politics to know that in all likelihood the individuals making up the voting majority do not intend the same thing. Most will not have read the statute they vote on. By casting their vote some will intend to repay a debt, or to be a loyal follower of their party leaders, or to encourage a campaign contribution from a private source in the future. If we want to deduce collective intent on anything, we must take a poll, and the only poll we ever take of legislators is when the presiding officer of the house calls for the vote to enact or defeat a bill. "Yes" voters intend to vote yes, and "No" voters intend to vote no, but that's about all we can accurately say about their intentions.

The third and most serious difficulty is that if by a miracle we overcome the first two difficulties, so that we actually know that the majority intended the same thing about a statute, it is highly unlikely, if not absolutely impossible, that they intended anything about the unique facts of the case before the court. Legislatures simply do not confront the concrete and always unique factual case. In this sense, as former Attorney General Levi once said, "Despite much gospel to the contrary, a legislature is not a fact-finding body. There is no mechanism, as there is with a court, to require the legislature to sift facts and to make a decision about specific situations."[28] In all probability no one in the legislature foresaw the precise problem facing the judge, and it is even less likely that the legislature consciously intended to resolve the case one way or another. Pose to the Congress that created the Mann Act the problems of migrating Mormons or vacationing prostitutes and you would probably get a gruff instruction to "ask a judge about the details." And if you were to somehow bring back to life the makers of the 1890 Sherman Antitrust Act to ask for their opinions about the Microsoft monopoly case, you would undoubtedly get blank stares.

Those are just the most basic problems with using legislative history to discern legislative intent. Consider a few more:

- Legislators and lobbyists often "cook" legislative history, inserting comments and planting evidence in the legislative record solely for the purpose of persuading judges later on in litigation that the legislature had a particular intent. The looseleaf notebooks that Judge Groner put so much weight on in the postal rate case might well have been planted there by a lobbyist. As long ago as 1947, Archibald Cox wrote that "it is becoming increasingly common to manufacture 'legislative history' during the course of legislation."[29]
- The institutional dynamics of contemporary policymaking are so complex and the political cross-pressures so intense that Congress often makes garbled policy and sends conflicting messages. Indeed, judges often ignore the possibility that the lawmaking process might purposely create unclear law because legislatures *want* the courts to fill in the details. This may amount to buck-passing in the hope that the courts will take the pressure for an unpopular result. But legislators may also believe that case-by-case judicial action is the best way to decide precisely what the statute should include and exclude.
- Often there is no real legislative history at all. Most state legislatures still do not produce complete documentation of proceedings that most lawyers can access. Even Congress sometimes acts without hearings or meaningful debate. In practice, a legislative aide often drafts the legislation after getting

---

[28]Edward H. Levi, *An Introduction to Legal Reasoning* (Chicago: University of Chicago Press, 1949), p. 31.

[29]Archibald Cox, "Some Aspects of the Labor Management Relations Act, 1947," 61 *Harvard Law Review* 1 (1947), p. 44. Justice Antonin Scalia, who describes himself as a "textualist" in the battle over statutory interpretation, has made this point one of his main arguments against legislative history. See Scalia, *A Matter of Interpretation* (Princeton, N.J.: Princeton University Press, 1997), pp. 32–36.

advice from a variety of members of Congress and its committees. The drafter will construct, as best he or she sees it, the language that accommodates the competing interests within Congress. Thus, practically, this drafter will be the only person who thinks fully about where the purposes of a particular piece of legislation stop. If that person is an attorney (and this is usually the case), the attorney-client privilege actually forbids communication with the courts about the actual intentions of the people whom he or she represented in the drafting process!

Much can be (and has been) said for abandoning the concept of legislative intent permanently. The ever-skeptical Holmes wrote, "I don't care what their intention was, I only want to know what the words mean." And Frankfurter added, "You may have observed that I have not yet used the word 'intention.' All these years I have avoided speaking of the 'legislative intent' and I shall continue to be on my guard against using it."[30] The candid judge looking for firm evidence of intent simply won't find it very often. A candid Rugg would, for example, have concluded, "I simply can't say whether the Massachusetts legislature thought about women becoming jurors or not." The names Holmes and Frankfurter endure more prominently than Rugg because they were especially able to make such candid judgments.[31] Given the realities of the legislative process, judges should be wary of concluding that the legislature ever intended anything.

The ultimate danger in all the methods of statutory interpretation we've described—the literal and Golden Rule approaches, the use of canons, and the search for legislative intent in legislative history—is that each allows the judge to reach a conclusion without ever struggling with the fundamental question of whether one interpretation or another actually copes with social problems effectively. These methods, in other words, perpetuate decisions that may not promote law's basic goal—social cooperation. The next section describes a better way for judges to interpret statutes.

PURPOSE: THE KEY TO WISE
STATUTORY INTERPRETATION

Statutory interpretation so frequently seems inadequate because judges face an unavoidable necessity. Judges must say what the law "is" in order to resolve the case before them. This is necessary because our society, our culture, believes that judges act unfairly when they do not decide on the basis of what the law says and is. Judges cannot hear a case and then refuse to render a decision because they cannot determine the legal answer.[32] We do not pay judges to say, "Maybe the law is X. Maybe the law is Y. I'll guess Y. You lose!" (Or worse, "I don't care if it's X or Y. You still lose!") In order to render justice in our culture, judges must persuade us to believe with certainty that which is inherently uncertain.

---

[30]Frankfurter, pp. 227–228.

[31]The eminent jurisprudent John Gray wrote, "The fact is that the difficulties of so-called interpretation arise when the Legislature has had no meaning at all; when the question which is raised on the statute never occurred to it. . . ." *The Nature and Sources of the Law* (New York: Macmillan, 1927), p. 173.

[32]This is true of most formal legal systems. For example, the French Civil Code dating from 1804 states, "A judge who refuses to enter judgment on the pretext of silence, obscurity, or inadequacy of the statute is subject to prosecution for the denial of justice."

Making the murky and muddled appear clear and composed (the *art* in judging and in everything else) is particularly difficult in statutory interpretation. In common-law and in constitutional law, the courts know that they have authority to make law. In these realms judges can say, "The law ought to be X, not Y. Therefore the law is X." But legislative supremacy bars judges from interpreting statutes so boldly. They must try to find the "oughts" somewhere in the legislative process, an uncertain and distant proceeding in which judges themselves play little part. It is like sending forth a knight with orders to find the Holy Grail, requiring him to return in a week with anything he finds as long as he can persuade us that what he found is the Grail, and repeating this order week after week.

Judges will continue to make uncertain statutes certain in their application by creating and asserting that certainty can and does emerge from the generality, the vagueness, and the ambiguity in words, and from the disorderly world of politics. They can do so persuasively by identifying the *purpose* of the statute, the problem statutory language tries to solve.

The Centrality of Statutory Purpose

Judges should believe, almost as an article of faith, that words by themselves never possess a plain or clear or literal meaning. Statutes become meaningful only to the extent that their words fit some intelligible purpose. The problem the statute addresses always gives direction to the search for purpose. A dictionary never does.

Judges must satisfy themselves that their application of a statute to the case before them serves the statute's purpose. Sometimes a statute seems automatically to determine a case. We saw that this would occur if McBoyle had driven a stolen car across state lines rather than flying a plane. But judges must understand that no conclusion is totally automatic. We can imagine that an individual could transport an automobile across state lines, knowing the car to be stolen, and yet not violate the act: an FBI agent driving the car back to its owner. The agent does not violate the act, because he is not part of the problem the act tries to solve—he is part of the solution.

Let us explain this in a slightly different way. The questions people ask determine the answers they receive. The right answer to the wrong question should never satisfy a judge. In statutory interpretation, the right questions always begin with questions about statutory purpose: What social problems does this statute try to correct? Does the case before us in court now represent the problem the statute addresses? Think of the difference it can make in *Johnson* (the locomotive coupling case) to ask (1) "Is a locomotive a railroad car?" versus (2) "Is protecting the safety of workers coupling locomotives to cars as well as cars to cars a sensible part of the problem this law tries to cope with?" Notice that whenever a judge inquires into the purpose of the legislation, he must inevitably inquire into the social background facts in order to disover the nature of the social problems involved in the case and how the statute tries to cope with them.

In its rulings on the contested 2000 presidential election, the Florida Supreme Court adopted a purpose-oriented approach in interpreting state election laws. In *Palm Beach Canvassing Board v. Harris,* decided on November 21, the court emphasized legislative purpose:

> Courts must not lose sight of the fundamental purpose of election laws: The laws are intended to facilitate and safeguard the right of each voter to express his or her will in the context of our representative democracy. . . .

In *Gore v. Harris,* decided on December 8, the court reasoned that the purpose of the Florida election "contest" statute was to ensure that "the right to vote will not be frustrated. . . ." As Appendix B shows, the court resolved ambiguities and inconsistencies in Florida statutes by relying on this account of legislative purpose.

To further illustrate purpose, consider an updated Mann Act. Suppose some imaginary international legislature passed a law making it a crime "to transport women or girls from one nation to another for purposes of prostitution, debauchery, or any other immoral purpose." In interpreting the purpose of such a statute, it would be entirely appropriate for courts to consider evidence that the monstrous trade in unwilling women, Representative Mann's original concern, persists to this day. Indeed, attention to the problem of international trafficking of girls and women in the sex trade has grown in recent years. For example, a National Public Radio report recently estimated that between 5,000 and 20,000 girls in Nepal are sold each year to brothels in India. The girls are as young as 10 and 11. National and international organizations are working to stop this trade.[33] In late 1996, the *Bangkok Post* headlined "Asia's Trafficking Shame." The story, in reporting on the recent World Congress Against Exploitation of Children held in Sweden, noted that approximately one million females worldwide are sold into forced prostitution each year, and that approximately 35 percent of these are under age 18. The story noted that the ease of traveling between Thailand, Burma, Laos, Cambodia, Vietnam, and the Yunan province of China helped traffickers evade prosecution.[34] Our hypothetical law, an international Mann Act, would have to be interpreted in light of the problems it was designed to solve.

Determining Purpose: Words Can Help

It is the language of a statute that alone has the force of law. Nothing else that individual legislators and legislative bodies say and do legally binds a judge. Some legislation includes specific definitions of key words. These definitions in statutes may or may not agree with a dictionary definition, but they are law and they bind the judge. Legislation, though lacking an internal dictionary, always contains words whose ordinary definitions unambiguously shape its purpose. By including the word *prostitution,* the Mann Act unambiguously covers more than White slavery because by no ordinary definition are prostitutes necessarily enslaved in that occupation. Judges must never give words a meaning that the words, in their context, cannot bear. Except for its euphemistic title, the "White Slave Act" contains not one word to indicate that the women whose transportation it forbids must be "slaves." It is in this context that the word *prostitution* unambiguously shapes the Mann Act's meaning.

Context is always crucial. Some contexts require courts to decide precisely the opposite of the literal command of words. If, through some printing error, the officially published version of a statute omits a key word, judges properly include the word if the context makes such a purpose clear. Suppose that a statute prohibiting some very undesirable behavior omits in its official version the key prohibitory word *not.* Although the statute would then literally permit or even require the unwarranted behavior, judges may apply the statute as if it contained the missing and critical *not.*

---

[33]Michael Sullivan, "Sex Slaves in Nepal," on *Morning Edition,* National Public Radio, September 19, 2000. See also "Slavery's New Face," *Newsweek,* December 18, 2000, pp. 61–63.
[34]*New York Times,* 12 September 1995, p. A12; *Bangkok Post,* 18 September 1996, p. C3.

Canons of interpretation may help reassure judges that a given word, phrase, or sentence has a certain meaning in a specific context. They may serve as shorthand reminders of ways of thinking about purpose. But a canon should never dictate to a judge that words must have only one meaning regardless of context. The canons of ejusdem generis and narrow construction in criminal law may help a judge exclude airplanes and obscene records from the reach of those two statutes, but they do not compel that conclusion, as the next section illustrates. The Florida Supreme Court used several canons to interpret state election laws in *Palm Beach County Canvassing Board v. Harris.* The Florida court was faced with the daunting task of turning a series of inconsistent election provisions into a coherent statutory scheme aimed at ensuring that "the vote reflect[s] the will of the voters" (see Appendix B).

Noscitur a sociis can also be a helpful reminder for a way of thinking about purpose. The context of neighboring words may crystallize the meaning of an ambiguous phrase. What, for example, is "indecent conduct"? In the abstract, we might agree that it depends on individual perceptions and moralities and that we can't really tell what it is. But consider two statutes, one that prohibits "indecent conduct at a divine service of worship" and another that prohibits "indecent conduct at a public beach or bathing place." The contexts of worship and beach could both classify total nudity as indecent conduct, but only one context would classify playing a game of volleyball in string bikinis as indecent.

Let us put this even more strongly. In life, as in law, things don't exist "in the abstract." In the abstract, there is no such thing as, say, indecent conduct. We might, trying to pick an extreme and hence conclusive example, say that cannibalism is automatically indecent conduct. Jeffrey Dahmer's crimes certainly were, but when the survivors of a plane crash high in the Andes consume the flesh of the dead in the hope of staying alive, does not the specific context, the spectre of imminent death by starvation, change our feelings drastically about the "indecency" of cannibalism?

Determining Purpose: The Audience

Legislatures direct different statutes to different kinds of audiences. Some statutes, especially criminal statutes, communicate to the community at large. Criminal statutes thus have the purpose of communicating general standards of conduct to large populations containing people of widely varying degrees of literacy and local customs and habits. Judges properly interpret such words according to the common meanings they may expect these words to convey to this diverse population. Other perhaps highly technical laws may communicate only to special classes of people, such as commercial television broadcasters or insurance underwriters. Here the words may assume technical meanings that only the special audience understands. Similarly, judges should hold that a statute purposely changes a long-held principle of common-law or the legality of a behavior widely believed proper in the past only when they think a statute makes that purpose unambiguously clear.

Determining Purpose: The Assumption of Legislative Rationality and the Uses of Legislative History

In determining whether an issue in a lawsuit is part of the problem that a statute purposely tries to address, judges should treat the people who make laws and the process of lawmaking as rational and sensible, "reasonable persons pursuing reasonable purposes reasonably," as Hart and Sacks put it.[35] This assumption helps judges determine purpose because it forces them to determine what portion of the law, prior to the enactment of the statute, worked so poorly that a rational legislature wanted to change it.[36] Again, think about how the result in the locomotive coupling case would differ if the court had approached the problem this way. Finally, what purposes would a rational legislator have for inserting the "good moral character" test in our naturalization laws? Is such a purpose well served by making moral judgments about incest or mercy killing in the abstract?

The judge who thinks about lawmaking as a logical process also recognizes that no statute exists in isolation, for rational lawmakers understand that no one act can completely define where its policy stops and another competing policy ought, instead, to govern. Members of Congress realize (and the courts grasp that they know) that state law, not federal law, assumes the major responsibility for defining and policing criminal behavior. Knowing that state laws purposely define and prohibit sexual immorality limited the purpose the Court attributed to the Mann Act in *Mortensen.*

Sometimes, as we have seen, no helpful legislative history exists at all. But at other times courts can generate sensible conclusions about the purpose of statutes from the statements of legislative committees, sponsors of the bill, and so forth. This history may allow a judge to understand what aspects or consequences of prior law failed to cope with a social problem so that the legislature needed to create a new law. Legislative history may also clarify where one policy should give way to another. Legislative history relating to specific applications of the statute, as in the looseleaf notebook case, helps the judge only to the extent that it provides good evidence of the legislation's general purpose.

Illustrations of Statutory Purpose

Two Easy Cases   You should now have little difficulty resolving some of this chapter's cases. Despite the ambiguities in the statutory language, you should not hesitate (1) to allow the officer to collect the breath specimen from a driver standing on the shoulder of the road, not while the driver weaves down the highway; and (2) to prohibit the liquor store from reopening at 10:01 (see footnote 12). The words don't require these conclusions, and judges probably lack any legislative history for these state and local laws, but judges can still reach sensible results. The words can bear these interpretations, and our knowledge of social problems and purposes compels these conclusions. Notice, by the way, how the solution to both of these cases hinges on the judge's realistic assessment of the social background facts and widespread public values that bear on these cases, not merely on the rules and case facts alone.

Of course, other cases could arise under these same statutes in which the words themselves would not bear the interpretation claimed for them. Our officer cannot collect breath specimens in parking lots and driveways outside cocktail parties at midnight, even if he safely assumes that many will soon drive home and even if we believe it a highly wise social policy to prevent intoxicated drivers from driving in the first place. This action might be an effective preventive, but it is not found in the meaning and purpose of this law because the words make "driving" a prerequisite for demanding the specimen.

---

[35]Hart and Sacks, p. 1415.
[36]Lord Coke originated this helpful approach, sometimes labeled the mischief rule, in 1584.

The Case of the Lady Jurors, or Why Legislative Intent Does Not Determine Statutory Purpose   Recall briefly Chief Justice Rugg's justification for excluding women from jury liability despite the fact that they could vote and despite the fact that the statute required jury duty of "persons" (not "men") qualified to vote. The legislature did not intend *person* to include females, because females could not then vote, he said.

Like the case of the automatic couplers, *Welosky* offers a classic example of a judge reaching the right answer to the wrong question. Of course the legislature did not intend to include women, but that doesn't answer the right question. The proper question is, "What purpose does legislation serve that gears jury liability to voter eligibility?"

Efficiency is one possible answer, because this policy spares the legislature from repeatedly rehashing the question of who should sit on juries. Quality is another, for this policy provides a test of qualifications that will insure at least the same minimum degree of responsibility, competence, education, and permanence of residence for both jurors and voters. Both voting and jury duty are general civic functions of citizens. Gearing the right to practice medicine, for instance, to voting eligibility would not make much sense; but gearing these two similar civic functions sounds reasonable. But where does turning the problem around leave us? Does it serve a purpose to pass a statute saying, in effect, the following? "If you are qualified to vote, you are qualified to serve as a juror; however, any changes in voter eligibility hereafter enacted won't count because we haven't thought of them yet." If the legislation had this purpose, why didn't it simply list the desirable qualifications for jurors? Read the statute as Rugg did and the gearing loses purpose. Rugg did not treat the policy process as rational and sensible. He did not admit that juror qualifications could have been purposely designed to change with the times.

The difference between a search for legislative intent and a search for purpose, then, is the difference in the evidence judges seek. Judges who believe they must show intent will examine reports, speeches, and prior drafts of bills. This evidence probably won't give clear meaning to the statute, because it will contain internal inconsistencies or raise issues only in general terms. Moreover, judges who think they must find intent can fool themselves into believing that they have found it in the evidence. On the other hand, judges who feel they must articulate a sensible statement of purpose will necessarily search much further, into dictionaries, canons, verbal contexts, and competing social policies as well as history itself. They will coordinate the materials in order to reach a confident articulation of purpose. They will perform the judicial function as Benjamin Cardozo described it (see the epigraph that opens this book). They will work harder than will judges who stop when they have found a nugget of legislative history, which is why so many judges, possessing the all-too-human tendency to laziness, are satisfied with the nugget.

Statutory Purpose in the Cases of Criminal Commerce: *Caminetti,* *McBoyle,* **and** *Alpers*   In each of these three cases, Congress, under the authority of the Commerce Clause of the U.S. Constitution, forbade citizens from moving what Congress deemed evil from one state to another. Let us assume that every state had laws to deal with each of the evil things—statutes punishing theft, prostitution, and pornography. What purpose, then, does additional *federal* legislation on these matters serve? For each of the federal statutes we possess records of committee reports, floor speeches, and other legislative history. In no case, however, does the solid data of legislative history reveal whether the purpose of the statute does or does not include the cases of our defendants. After a delightfully detailed review of the House and Senate reports on the Mann Act and of the discussions reported in the *Congressional Record*—showing, if not total confusion about the act, at least much disagreement about its specific meaning—Levi concludes, "The Mann Act was passed after there had been many extensive governmental investigations. Yet there was no common understanding of the facts, and whatever understanding seems to have been achieved concerning the white-slave trade seems incorrectly based. The words used were broad and ambiguous."[37]

These cases resemble each other not only in their constitutional origins but also because the canons of construction could resolve each of them. The canon dictating narrow construction of criminal statutes could allow a judge to reverse the three convictions, since the law does not unambiguously apply to any of these special factual situations. A judge who adopted Holmes's belief that criminal laws must communicate to a general lay audience with a clarity the average man can understand would reach the same result. Following ejusdem generis, however, Mr. Caminetti might go to jail, but McBoyle, the airplane thief, and Alpers, the seller of obscene records, would still go free.

Despite these similarities, these cases do not come out this way. The smut peddler and the boyfriend went to jail. McBoyle went free. The three judicial opinions together articulate no coherent linkages between purposes and outcomes. To link purposes and outcomes, we must begin with the right question: Why would Congress, "reasonable persons pursuing reasonable purposes reasonably," pass laws making actions crimes when all the states already have, through their criminal laws, expressed a policy? Does not the purpose lie in the fact that movement from state to state makes it difficult for the states to detect or enforce the violation? A car owner who has his car stolen may have trouble tracking it in another state. The prosecutor in the state where citizens receive wanted or unwanted pornography cannot reach the man who peddles by mail from another state. Men who hustle girls far from home may make both detection and social pressure to resist prostitution impossible. Movement has consequences. It makes objects and behaviors physically harder to locate. It makes apprehension and prosecution more difficult, because police and prosecutors in one jurisdiction don't have authority in another. The presence of physical movement thus helps to reveal purpose.

In *McBoyle*, then, the proper questions ought to look something like this: (1) Do airplanes, because they are movable, complicate the task of catching people who steal them? (2) Does it, secondarily, serve any purpose to assume that McBoyle thought flying a stolen airplane to another state was legal because of the ambiguities in the word *vehicle*? Is it, in other words, unfair to McBoyle to convict him under this act because the act does not unambiguously include airplanes? You should reach your own conclusion, but we would answer the first question with a yes, the second with a no, and respectfully dissent from Justice Holmes.

You should ask one other question about *McBoyle*. Suppose McBoyle's lawyer had argued that when the Motor Vehicle Theft Act was passed, air travel was in such infancy that Congress probably did not intend to include airplanes. Notice that this argument should matter to you only if you think it important to ask what Congress intended. If you instead consider legislation as policy designed to adjust to future technological and other changes that lawmakers cannot in the present foresee, and if you ask instead what kind of crimes call for the kind of law enforcement help that this act provides, you would find McBoyle's lawyer's argument trivial.

[37]Levi, p. 40, and see pp. 33–40.

Is *Alpers* any different? It might be, particularly if you see the case as presenting a constitutional problem of free expression. The purpose of this statute might be said to be to prevent exposing children or unwilling people, people who open mail or see magazines left around, to visual pornography. Is this purpose served by prohibiting the shipment of obscene records?

Alpers is an especially difficult case. Unlike Mr. McBoyle, Mr. Alpers could reasonably have interpreted the act as not banning records for two reasons. First, the competing principle of free expression does set limits on government interference with the communication of ideas. No such principle limits governmental interference with the movement of property known to be stolen. Second, the purpose of the Motor Vehicle Theft Act specifically seems to apply to airplanes. They are very transportable. The act's purpose may therefore especially apply to airplanes. However, one reading of the purpose of the statute in *Alpers*—visual pornography left around may offend, while a phonograph record lying around does not—reduces its applicability to *Alpers*. But, although it reduces it, it doesn't eliminate it. The recipient might play the dirty record for an unwilling person and cause that person great offense. However, does not the *McBoyle* example provide a strong argument for excusing Alpers? Isn't transporting stolen property at least as morally ambiguous as pornography?

Finally, consider the man who brings in a willing girlfriend from out of state for a night or for the big-game weekend. Conceivably, the Mann Act could purposely try to police all forms of sexual immorality involving, somehow, interstate transportation. But what are the probabilities that this legislation has such purpose in light of (1) the title of the act; (2) the canons of narrow construction of and clear communication in criminal statutes; (3) the problem arousing public concern at the time; (4) the fact that states are just as able, if they so choose, to discover and crack down on noncommercial illegal sex as the FBI; (5) Representative Mann's report and the widespread belief that the general police powers reside in state and not federal hands?

Notice how it is only by weaving together many different techniques of interpretation that we begin to develop confidence about the purpose of the Mann Act.

A Final Complication

This summary of sensible judicial approaches to statutes may have misled you in one critical respect. You may now feel that in every case the "right-thinking" judge will find the one "right" solution simply by uncovering a single purpose of the statute. This chapter's illustrations all make sense when we analyze them in terms of purpose. *We may, however, still honestly disagree about purpose.* The task of judging is choosing among plausible alternative possibilities, not solving an algebra problem. A purpose-oriented approach does not eliminate judicial discretion in statutory interpretation. Judges who thoughtfully and diligently consider legislative purpose may nonetheless disagree about the resolution of a specific case.

To illustrate, suppose Holmes had said in *McBoyle:*

> The purpose of this act is to permit federal assistance to states in finding easily moved and hidden vehicles. But airplanes, while easily moved, are really like trains, which the act expressly excludes, because, like trains, they are tied to places where they cannot be hidden—airports. What goes up must come down, and only in certain places. One black Ford may look like a thousand other black Fords almost anywhere, but an airplane is much more like a train in this respect. Therefore, since we believe states, not the federal government, possess primary police powers, this act does not cover airplanes.

Finally, suppose in the cemetery case Justice Gregory argued,

> Establishment and expansion of cemeteries differ because the people near an expanded cemetery are already used to its presence, but to create a new cemetery in a place where residents had not planned on seeing funeral processions and graves and other unwanted reminders of life's transience is another matter.

Whether we agree or disagree with these analyses, at least these analyses rest on purpose. We should prefer them to the automatic citation of a canon, a quotation from a dictionary, or to any technique of interpretation that allows judges to evade the difficult task of determining statutory purpose.

STARE DECISIS IN STATUTORY INTERPRETATION

We have thus far studied an atypical occurrence in statutory interpretation, interpretation in the first instance. This may have puzzled you, for in the previous chapters we have seen that reasoning by example—using precedents as guides for resolving legal conflicts—is central to legal reasoning. So far, however, in this chapter we have not mentioned reasoning by example at all. In the interpretation of statutes in the first instance, courts by definition have no precedents with which to work. In this chapter, we have examined some methods for interpreting statutes in the first instance, but these methods do not resolve the more typical problem: Once a court has given direction and meaning to a statute by interpreting it in the first instance, when should courts in the future follow that interpretation? When, conversely, should courts prefer a different interpretation and ignore or overrule an earlier court's first effort to make sense of the statute's meaning?

Let us make this point more sharply. Assume that the *McBoyle* decision wrongly interpreted the National Motor Vehicle Theft Act because its purpose does cover the theft of airplanes. Or assume that *Caminetti* wrongly applied the Mann Act to include the transportation of girlfriends. Should a court facing a new airplane or girlfriend case feel bound to accept that interpretation? Once a precedent or series of precedents gives a clear answer on a point of law, should courts leave it to legislatures to change that questionable interpretation by statutory amendment? In what circumstances should judges adhere to stare decisis in statutory interpretation?

It might seem sensible to you to answer these questions by referring to the justifications for stare decisis that appeared near the end of Chapter 2. When adherence to a prior interpretation or series of cases interpreting a statute promotes stability in law, and this stability in turn allows citizens to plan their affairs by relying on specific legal rules—in short, when stability promotes the paramount social goal of cooperation—courts should not abandon stare decisis. Similarly, if a citizen now deserves to receive the same treatment a citizen in a precedent did, or if we feel stare decisis would preserve efficient judicial administration or a positive public image of justice, then courts should honor it. When stare decisis does not promote these goals, courts should freely ignore it. Thus, assuming a court felt that both *McBoyle* and *Caminetti* were wrongly decided, normal stare decisis theory would permit overruling *Caminetti* but not *McBoyle*. It injures no citizen to declare that something once held criminal is no longer so, but it does seem unfair to convict someone after declaring that his actions were not crimes.

Unfortunately, some judges and legal scholars believe that judges should invariably follow the first judicial attempt to find statutory meaning even when they have doubts about the wisdom of the first attempt and, worse, when the characteristics of the problem do not call for stare decisis. We shall first review an example of this "one-shot theory" of statutory interpretation in action.[38] Then we shall evaluate its shortcomings. We shall see that, in part, it fails because it depicts judges once again misunderstanding how legislatures operate and how courts should reason from legislative action and inaction. We shall also see in this example considerable judicial ignorance about stare decisis itself.

Major League Baseball, Haviland's Dog and Pony Show, and Government Regulation of Business

The power of the federal government to regulate business derives from the constitutional clause empowering Congress to make laws that regulate commerce "among the several states." Armed with this authority, Congress has passed many statutes regulating wages, hours of work, safety and health standards, and other aspects of business. Such laws apply not only to businesses and businesspersons that physically cross state lines or transact business among states. They also apply to businesses operating within one state entirely, on the theory that these businesses nevertheless may compete with and affect businesses operating from other states.[39] Modern economic and political theory also suggest that the collective health of small businesses and of labor can and does affect the national welfare.

Among the many such statutes regulating business, we shall consider only two. The more substantial of the two, the federal antitrust laws, responded to the huge cartels and monopolies that emerged in the nineteenth century by prohibiting certain activities that restrain competition in business. They authorize criminal and civil proceedings by government and by citizens privately when they feel they are damaged by anticompetitive business practices. The antitrust laws were in the news in the 1990s after the Justice Department filed suit against MIT and the eight elite Ivy League universities because the admissions officials had met annually to decide how much financial aid to offer individual students with applications at more than one of these elite schools. The Justice Department argued that the schools were conspiring to fix the "price" of top-quality students. The same kind of collusion in business to avoid costly price competition presumptively would violate the antitrust prohibitions. MIT alone defended the lawsuit, insisting the law did not apply to that situation.[40] This story confirms the basic assumption on which antitrust law rests: Despite popular rhetoric, economic competition is *not* the "natural" state of affairs; cooperation is. Cooperation reduces risks and uncertainties to parties but imposes external costs on those excluded, here the students and other less elite universities.

The Animal Welfare Act of 1970, our second statutory example, specifies a variety of requirements for handling animals in a humane manner.[41] The statute requires "exhibitors" of animals "purchased in commerce or the intended distribution of which affects commerce or will affect commerce" to obtain an exhibitor's license.

---

[38]William Eskridge calls the theory "the super-strong presumption against overruling statutory precedents." "Overruling Statutory Precedents," 76 *Georgetown Law Journal* 1361 (1988) at 1363. Eskridge's very thorough analysis agrees in nearly all respects with the position we take in this chapter. Calling the notion "a very odd doctrine," he analyzes cases from 1961 to 1987 and finds that "in only twenty-six instances (or one per term) has the Court explicitly repudiated both the reasoning and the result of a statutory precedent." p. 1368. He concurs with Justice Scalia's statement that "vindication by Congressional inaction is a canard." p. 1405n.

[39]*United States v. Darby*, 312 U.S. 100 (1941), and *Wickard v. Filburn*, 317 U.S. 111 (1942).

[40]See "What's An A Student Worth?", *Newsweek*, July 6, 1992, p. 52.

[41]15 U.S.C. 1 et seq. and 7 U.S.C. 2131 et seq.

The statute explicitly includes carnivals, circuses, and zoos. It empowers the Agriculture Department to administer its regulatory provisions.

Within the context of these two statutes, we shall now observe a truly wondrous phenomenon in contemporary law. Within the past forty years courts have held: (1) that the multimillion-dollar industry of professional baseball, with all its national commercial television coverage and travel from state to state and to foreign countries, *is not* a business in interstate commerce such that the antitrust laws govern the owners of baseball clubs; and (2) that "Haviland's Dog and Pony Show," consisting of a maximum of two ponies and five dogs traveling the rural byways of the American Midwest and earning a handful of dollars weekly, *is* a business in interstate commerce that must therefore meet the requirements of the Animal Welfare Act.[42]

We need say little more about the *Haviland* case. Haviland refused to obtain an exhibitor's license. The court held that he was wrong to refuse. Given the current legal definition of commerce, the interpretation is entirely defensible constitutionally. This interpretation and result also make sense in terms of the presumed purpose of the statute. Owners of dog-and-pony shows, we can assume, are no less likely to abuse their animals than is the staff of the San Diego Zoo; rather more likely we should think.

But why don't antitrust statutes regulate major league baseball? Rigid adherence to stare decisis in statutory interpretation provides the answer, as the following chronology of decisions illustrates.

1922 The "Federal Baseball Club of Baltimore," a member of a short-lived third major league, sued the National and American Leagues claiming that the two leagues had, in violation of the antitrust laws, bought out some Federal League clubs and induced other owners not to join the league at all. The Baltimore franchise found itself frozen out and sued to recover the financial losses caused by the anticompetitive practices of the other leagues. The case reached the United States Supreme Court, where Justice Holmes's opinion held that the essence of baseball, playing games, did not involve interstate commerce. The travel from city to city by the teams, Holmes thought, was so incidental that it did not bring baseball within the scope of the act. Thus, without reaching the question whether the defendants did behave anticompetitively within the meaning of the statute, Holmes ruled that the act did not apply to professional baseball any more than it would apply to a Chautauqua lecturer traveling the circuit.[43]

Comment: We should not hastily condemn Holmes's reasoning. His opinion predated by 20 years a major enlargement in the scope of "commerce" that came in *Wickard v. Filburn,* so we cannot blame him for an antiquated definition. Also, to his credit, Holmes did not try to discover whether Congress intended to include baseball within the scope of the antitrust laws. There is nothing in the opinion that stamps its results with indelibility, nothing that says if the commercial character of baseball changes, baseball club owners would nevertheless remain free to behave monopolistically. For its time, *Federal Baseball* rested on defensible if not indisputable reasoning.

[42]*Flood v. Kuhn,* 407 U.S. 258 (1972); *Haviland v. Butz,* 543 F.2d 169 (D.C. Circuit 1976).
[43]*Federal Baseball Club of Baltimore v. National League of Professional Baseball Clubs,* 259 U.S. 200 (1922).

1923 A year later Justice Holmes addressed the applicability of the antitrust
laws in the field of public entertainment. In this case, the plaintiff, a Mr.
Hart, acted as a booking agent and manager for a variety of actors. He
specialized in negotiating contracts between vaudeville performers, on
one hand, and large theater chains sponsoring vaudeville shows on the
other. Hart sued the Keith Circuit, the Orpheum Circuit, and other theatrical chains, claiming that, in violation of the antitrust laws, they col-
luded to prevent any of his actors from obtaining contracts in their the-
aters unless Hart granted them what we would today call kickbacks.
Holmes noted that some of these contracts called for the transportation of
performers, scenery, music, and costumes. Distinguishing *Federal
Baseball,* he held that "in the transportation of vaudeville acts the apparatus sometimes is more important than the performers and . . . the defendant's conduct is within the [antitrust] statute to that extent at least."[44]

Comment: Note fact freedom at work here. Holmes does not, despite
vaudeville's obvious resemblance to baseball, find that the two are factually similar enough to govern vaudeville by baseball's precedent. There
was, he said, a difference. Some of the disputed contracts did involve
transportation itself. Holmes could have chosen to follow the previous
year's precedent. The travel is still incidental to local performance of either baseball or vaudeville. Compare this with what happened in 1953.

1948 Blacklisted by the major league owners because he had once chosen to
play in Mexico rather than for the major leagues, an outfielder named
Danny Gardella sued. The Second Circuit Court of Appeals ruled that, in
part due to increased radio and television revenues, baseball was interstate commerce and subject to the Sherman Act. The court also called the
major league's treatment of the players a "shockingly repugnant" form of
slavery, outlawed by the Thirteenth Amendment after the Civil War.[45]

Question: Do you believe by now, since the business aspects of baseball had changed, since the constitutional basis for *Federal Baseball* had
evaporated, and since an appellate court had ruled that baseball was now
covered by the antitrust laws, that the baseball owners had *any* reason to
rely on the *Federal Baseball* precedent?

1953 Baseball again, but not an alleged attempt to prevent the formation of a
third league. Now it was the players' turn to allege violation of the antitrust laws. The violation took the form of the well-publicized reserve
clause,[46] or so players claimed. The players contended that the clause
prevented open competition for better salaries. In *Toolson v. New York
Yankees* the Supreme Court ruled in an unsigned (*per curiam*) opinion that
baseball still did not fall under the coverage of the antitrust laws. It so
held despite the efforts of Justices Burton and Reed, who dissented, to
marshall extensive evidence of baseball's dramatic growth since 1922.
The majority opinion stated:

> Congress has had the [*Federal Baseball*] ruling under consideration but
> has not seen fit to bring such business under these laws by legislation
> having prospective effect. The business has thus been left for thirty years

[44]*Hart v. B. F. Keith Vaudeville Exchange,* 262 U.S. 271 (1923), p. 273.
[45]See Andrew Zimbalist, *Baseball and Billions* (New York: Basic Books, 1992), p. 13. See also Stephen Jay
Gould's "Dreams That Money Can Buy," *New York Review of Books,* November 5, 1992, pp. 41–45.
[46]*Toolson v. New York Yankees,* 346 U.S. 356 (1953), pp. 362–363.

to develop, on the understanding that it was not subject to existing antitrust legislation. The present cases ask us to overrule the prior decision and, with retrospective effect, hold the legislation applicable. . . . Without reexamination of the underlying issues, the judgments below are affirmed on the authority of *Federal Baseball* . . . so far as that decision determines that Congress had no intention of including the business of baseball within the scope of the federal antitrust laws.

Questions: Did Justice Holmes conclude in 1922 that "Congress had no intention of including the business of baseball within the scope of the federal antitrust laws?" Do you believe that because Congress has not legislated on the subject of baseball and the antitrust laws, therefore professional baseball does not fall within the act? Remember that not only had baseball become more businesslike since 1922, but the definition of commerce had also changed so that travel or movement from state to state did not have to be an essential part of a business's activities in order to put it under the act. Why is it necessary to follow the 1922 precedent? Why could not the *Toolson* opinion simply say that both the law and the sport have changed and the owners have no justified expectation to rely on an outdated judicial ruling? Do you think, in other words, that because in 1922 the Court told the established leagues they could try to prevent the formation of a third league, they therefore rightly planned in 1953 to deal with their players by contracts that prevented free competition in that business?

1955 In *United States v. Shubert,* Chief Justice Warren, speaking for the Supreme Court, upheld the government's claim that theater owners who monopolized the booking of theater attractions violated the antitrust laws.[47] The Court acknowledged *Hart*, though only in passing. It refused to follow *Toolson,* calling it "a narrow application of the rule of *stare decisis.*"

Question: One purpose of stare decisis is to promote equality. On what basis should the law treat actors and baseball players unequally, as this case concludes the law must?

Chief Justice Warren, in a companion case to *Shubert,* held that professional boxing did fall within the scope of antitrust laws.[48] He distinguished *Toolson* for the same reasons he gave in Shubert.

Questions: How equally do you think baseball players felt the courts applied the law in 1955? If you had managed the Boxing Club, would you have relied on the *Toolson* decision? Would you think of boxing as any more a business than baseball? Would the new boxing decision possibly surprise you?

1957 In *Radovich v. National Football League,* the lower appellate court, mystified by the distinction between baseball and boxing that the Supreme Court had created, decided that football did not fall under the antitrust laws because football, like baseball but unlike boxing, was a team sport. The Supreme Court reversed.[49]

Comment: "Foolish consistency is the hobgoblin of little minds."

---

[47]*United States v. Shubert*, 348 U.S. 222 (1955).
[48]*United States v. International Boxing Club of New York, Inc.*, 348 U.S. 236 (1955).
[49]*Radovich v. National Football League*, 352 U.S. 445 (1957).

1971   The Supreme Court held that the antitrust laws did govern professional basketball.[50]

   Question: By now do you think the Court could safely overrule *Federal Baseball*?

1972   Fifty years after *Federal Baseball,* Curt Flood's challenge to the reserve clause reached the Supreme Court. After a panegyrical review of baseball's history, replete with references to Thayer's "Casey at the Bat" and a long and curious list of baseball's greats (the list includes such immortals as Three-Finger Brown and Hans Lobert but omits Stan Musial, Joe DiMaggio, Ted Williams, and Hank Aaron), Justice Blackmun refused to abandon *Toolson* or stare decisis. Flood lost. Blackmun wrote:

> [W]e adhere once again to *Federal Baseball* and *Toolson* and to their application to professional baseball. We adhere also to *International Boxing* and *Radovich* and to their respective applications to professional boxing and professional football. If there is any inconsistency or illogic in all this, it is an inconsistency and illogic of long-standing that is to be remedied by the Congress and not by this Court. If we were to act otherwise, we would be withdrawing from the conclusion as to congressional intent made in *Toolson* and from the concerns as to retrospectivity therein expressed. Under these circumstances, there is merit in consistency even though some might claim that beneath that consistency is a layer of inconsistency.[51]

   Justice Douglas dissented. He wrote, "The unbroken silence of Congress should not prevent us from correcting our own mistakes."[52]

That's enough of the chronology of judicial decisions. In the wake of judicial and congressional failure to deal with the reserve clause, the baseball players struck in the early 1970s. The strike successfully freed the players from the clause, and recent increases in players' salaries can be credited to this change.

What went wrong here? In the immediate case of sports and the antitrust laws, *Toolson's* utterly inaccurate insistence that *Federal Baseball* means that Congress did not intend to include baseball wreaked the most havoc. *Toolson,* to paraphrase, says, "The highest lawmaking body in the country, Congress, has determined that the antitrust laws should not apply to professional baseball. Therefore the owners of baseball teams have made many business arrangements in reliance on this state of the law. It would be wrong to upset these expectations legitimized by the intent of Congress." This position is pure nonsense. Congress did not intend to exclude baseball. Holmes in *Federal Baseball* never said Congress so intended. As our questions at the end of the *Toolson* excerpt imply, the baseball owners had no reason to rely on *Federal Baseball,* at least not in 1953, given intervening precedents. Stability and reliance do not in this instance require the Court to invoke stare decisis and follow *Federal Baseball. Toolson* reached that different result by merely saying, without supporting evidence, that Congress so commanded.

[50]*Heywood v. National Basketball Association,* 401 U.S. 1204 (1971).
[51]*Flood v. Kuhn,* p. 284.
[52]The mess created by these decisions will not go away. In 1996 the Court returned to them in *Brown v. Pro Football, Inc., dba Washington Redskins,* 116 S.Ct. 2116 (1996). See particularly Justice Stevens's dissent, where he cites *Federal Baseball, Toolson, Radovich,* and *Flood.* The lawsuit alleged that the National Football League's unilateral arrangement to pay "taxi squad" members a flat rate of $1,000 per week violated the Sherman Antitrust Act.

Unfortunately, the Supreme Court's reasoning in these cases is worse than that. At least, you might say, baseball owners probably did honestly believe that they had a good chance of escaping the antitrust laws and acted on that basis. There is some merit in the reliance argument. But if stare decisis seeks to assist people to make plans in reliance on stable law, then surely owners of football, basketball, and boxing franchises and athletes had every bit as much reason for relying on *Federal Baseball* or *Toolson* as did the baseball owners. After all, in terms of the antitrust law, there is no difference among these sports that ought to induce baseball owners to rely on the original precedent while preventing those in the other sports from doing so.

In the name of stare decisis, then, we have a series of decisions that hardly seems stable, that violates reliance expectations to the extent that there are any, and that does not treat equals equally. To complete the list of justifications for adhering to precedent, do these decisions strike you as efficient judicial administration? What image of justice do these cases flash in your mind? Crazy, perhaps?

Fortunately, we have deliberately chosen an extreme example. Faced with statutory precedents, courts do not invariably invoke stare decisis in order to wreak havoc on the very justifications for stare decisis. Nevertheless, this critical question remains: *If* a judge feels that an existing judicial interpretation of a statute is erroneous, and *if* the judge also feels that he may overrule it without doing violence to the five justifications of stare decisis, do *any* aspects of the court's relationship to the legislature nevertheless compel adherence to the questionable interpretation? We believe the proper answer to this question is no. However, on two analytical levels, judges and legal scholars have at times reached a different conclusion. Let us review their reasons for the one-shot theory on both levels.

The Case against Increased Adherence to Precedent in Statutory Interpretation

The first, and more superficial, analytical level holds that the legislature may take certain actions that compel the courts to adhere to precedent. In *Toolson*, for example, the Supreme Court seemed to say that since Congress had not passed a statute to cover baseball by the antitrust laws, Congress had somehow converted *Federal Baseball* into statutory law. Would any of the following events in Congress, or in any legislature, strengthen such a conclusion?

- Many bills were introduced to cover baseball, but none of them passed.
- Many bills were introduced to exempt baseball, but none of them passed.
- Congress reenacted the relevant antitrust provisions, with some modifications, none of which attempted to cover or exempt baseball specifically.
- Congress passed a statute explicitly placing, say, professional boxing prior to 1955, under the antitrust laws that makes no mention of baseball's status.
- Congress passed a joint resolution that officially states that baseball is hereinafter to be considered "The National Pastime of the United States."

Judges often buttress their adherence to precedents on such grounds, but these grounds are insufficient. Congress possesses no power to make law other than by passing statutes. Statutes are, among other items, subject to presidential veto power. Not even joint resolutions, which escape presidential veto, therefore create law. To say that any of the legislative acts we just listed create law is to give Congress a lawmaking power not found in the Constitution.

Furthermore, consider these reasons that a legislature might not, in fact, directly respond to a judicial interpretation by law.[53]

- Legislators never learn of the judicial interpretation in the first place.
- Legislators don't care about the issue the interpretation raises.
- Legislators care but feel they must spend their limited time and political resources on other more important matters.
- Legislators like the proposed new statute or amendment but feel it politically unwise to vote for it.
- Legislators decide to vote against the bill because they do not like another unrelated provision of the bill.
- Legislators feel the bill does not go far enough and vote against it in hopes of promulgating more comprehensive law later.
- Legislators don't like the bill's sponsor personally and therefore vote negatively.
- Legislators believe, in the words of Hart and Sacks, "that the matter should be left to be handled by the normal process of judicial development of decisional law, including the overruling of outstanding decisions to the extent that the sound growth of the law requires. . . ."[54]

Do not all these possibilities, especially the last, convince you that courts should not speculate about the meaning of a statutory interpretation by guessing at why the legislature didn't pass a law affecting the interpretation?

Professor Beth Henschen writes:

Congress rarely responds to the statutory decisions of the Court in at least . . . labor and antitrust policy. . . . Over a 28-year period, Congress considered legislation constituting reactions to only 27 of 222 cases in which the Court interpreted labor and antitrust statutes. . . . Moreover, only 9 of those decisions . . . were modified by the enactment of a bill that was signed into law.[55]

In a more recent and more comprehensive survey, William Eskridge calculates that from 1967 to 1990, the Supreme Court issued approximately 1,900 opinions interpreting statutes. In the same period, Congress overrode or substantially modified 121 decisions, some of which (including *Caminetti*) predated the period. Eskridge does find that the contemporary Congress considers bills to revise court interpretations much more frequently than in the past. He estimates that half of the Supreme Court's decisions get some kind of review. The majority of these efforts die in committee. Eskridge's data reveal some important political observations. Thirty-eight percent of the overrides overrode distinctly conservative Court decisions, while 20 percent overrode liberal decisions. More interesting for our purposes, Eskridge coded the reasons Congress gave for overriding into such categories as bad interpretation, confusion in law, bad or outdated policy, and need to clarify law. If the courts were doing a consistently bad job of interpretation, we would expect "bad interpre-

[53]Hart and Sacks, pp. 1395–1396.
[54]Ibid, p. 1396.
[55]Beth Henschen, "Statutory Interpretations of the Supreme Court: Congressional Response," 11 *American Politics Quarterly* 441 (1983). R. Shep Melnick closely examines the court/Congress interaction in statutory interpretation in *Between the Lines: Interpreting Welfare Rights* (Washington, D.C.: The Brookings Institution, 1994).

tation" to crop up frequently. If, on the other hand, the Congress was doing a consistently bad job of writing statutes, we would expect other reasons, like "bad policy" or "confusion," to crop up more frequently. Of the total of 311 congressional actions so coded (including overrides of lower court decisions and of multiple aspects of the same statute), only 40 actions (13 percent) cited bad or unfair interpretation as the reason. On the other hand, Eskridge lists bad or unfair policy as the reason for overriding in 240 of the 311 cases (77 percent). From this we might conclude that the courts faithfully implement a foolish policy six times more often than they interpret a statute poorly.[56]

The second analytical level is more complex. Sophisticated proponents of the one-shot theory of statutory interpretation admit that legislative silence is meaningless.[57] They worry instead about the proper apportionment of legislative and judicial responsibilities. Their argument goes this way: Legislatures deliberately use ambiguous language in statutes, not simply to bring many somewhat different specific events under one policy roof but also to allow room for the compromises necessary to generate a majority vote. Once written, the words of a statute will not change; but because they are general, vague, and ambiguous, courts will certainly have the opportunity to interpret those same words in many different ways.

If, the argument continues, words have different meanings at different times and places, the legislature's power to make law becomes pointless, or at least quite subordinated to judicial power of interpretation. Courts must find one meaning. They do so by determining legislative intent. The judiciary insults the legislature if it says that at one time the legislature intended the words to carry one meaning and at another time another meaning. To say this is to say of the legislature that it had no intent and that it did not understand its actions. That assertion would embarrass the legislature, to say the least.

The argument thus holds that part of the judicial responsibility to the legislature is to reinforce the concept that the legislature did in fact have a specific intention, because that is what the public expects of legislatures. In the first half of this chapter, we have revealed why this argument fails.

Fortunately, the argument does not stop there. Levi asserts:

> Legislatures and courts are cooperative law-making bodies. It is important to know where the responsibility lies. If legislation which is disfavored can be interpreted away from time to time, then it is not to be expected, particularly if controversy is high, that the legislature will ever act. It will always be possible to say that new legislation is not needed because the court in the future will make a more appropriate interpretation. If the court is to have freedom to reinterpret legislation, the result will be to relieve the legislature from pressure. The legislation needs judicial consistency. Moreover, the court's own behavior in the face of pressure is likely to be indecisive. In all likelihood it will do enough to prevent legislative revision and not much more. Therefore it seems better to say that once a decisive interpretation of legislative intent has been made, and in that sense a direction has been fixed within the gap of ambiguity, the court should take that direction as given. In this sense a court's interpretation of legislation is not dictum. The words it uses do more than decide the case. They give broad direction to the statute.[58]

---

[56]William Eskridge, Jr., "Overriding Supreme Court Statutory Interpretation Decisions," 101 *Yale Law Journal* 331 (1991). See more generally Eskridge's *Dynamic Statutory Interpretation* (Cambridge: Harvard University Press, 1994).

[57] See especially Levi, pp. 31–33.

[58]Ibid., p. 32.

Levi's argument cuts too deeply. Indeed, there are instances in which legislators breathe sighs of relief that courts have taken delicate political problems from them. (Curiously enough, courts most often do so by applying constitutional standards to legislation, and in this area Levi does not demand similarly strict stare decisis.) But Levi's position is simply inaccurate in its assumption that most questions of interpretation raise highly charged public issues that legislatures ought to deal with, but won't if the Court does it for them. For the most part, judicial errors in statutory interpretation involve borderline application of statutes. The interpretations may do considerable injustice to the parties who find themselves in borderline situations without, in any significant way, damaging the central purposes of the statutory policy as a whole. In the large majority of cases, then, it is wholly unrealistic to assume that either overruling or adherence will affect how legislators perform. Try to imagine, for example, how Congress would have reacted had the Supreme Court held in 1946 that the traveling bigamous Mormons did not violate the Mann Act. Probably with a yawn.[59]

A SUMMARY STATEMENT OF THE APPROPRIATE JUDICIAL APPROACH TO STATUTORY INTERPRETATION

To conclude, notice how many of the problems that courts have created for themselves regarding the place of stare decisis in statutory interpretations would evaporate if only judges convinced themselves to seek the purpose of a statute and not to speculate about legislative intent from inconclusive legislative evidence. The inadequate conclusions that judges reach when they reason on the first and more superficial analytical level would disappear altogether. At the more sophisticated level, the concept that the courts embarrass legislatures by implying the rather obvious truth that the legislators probably had no intent regarding the precise issue before the court would also disappear. Is this truth so awful? Of course not. That statutes speak in general terms is a simple necessity in political life. Such generality explains and justifies the existence of courts.

Judges should follow precedents when the justifications of stare decisis so dictate. Their primary obligation to the legislature is to apply the statutes it creates so as to achieve, as best judges can determine it, the intelligible solution of problems the statute exists to solve. Judges should try to determine purpose accurately, but they will err from time to time. It is no embarrassment to the legislature for judges to admit that they erred in determining statutory purpose and applying it to cases properly before them. They should therefore give stare decisis no special weight in statutory interpretation. They should do so with the confidence that to the extent that they can predict legislative behavior at all, they can predict that the legislature is no less likely to correct them if they err today than if they erred yesterday. Of course, legis-

---

[59]However, nearly three-quarters of a century after the *Caminetti* decision, Congress quietly rewrote the Mann Act with the Child Sexual Abuse and Pornography Act of 1986. The amendments eliminated the reference to White slavery, substituted *individual* for *female* and *woman or girl*, and instead of debauchery or immoral purpose, wrote "any sexual activity for which any person can be charged with a criminal offense. . . ." This presumptive tightening of the law still leaves some hypothetically questionable applications. Consensual oral sex between married people remains a criminal offense in some states. If a spouse flies a spouse who is temporarily working out of state home to a state with such a law for a romantic visit, would this violate the purpose of the Mann Act? What if this separated couple periodically reunites to reduce the temptations to have adulterous liaisons while lonely and apart?

lation needs judicial consistency. Affixing proper legislative responsibility will occur only when courts consistently discern sensible statutory purposes.[60]

Illustrative Case

As we noted in the first chapter, this book does not cover in depth an important and flourishing field of law, administrative law. Administrative law is, in fact, such a complex and important realm that one of the authors, Lief Carter, has devoted an entire book to it.[61] That said, we have included in this chapter an administrative law case that is also a fascinating example of dueling statutory interpretations. In 1996, the Food and Drug Administration (FDA) announced it would impose new rules on sales of tobacco to minors. The tobacco companies challenged these new rules, arguing that the FDA had no statutory authority to regulate tobacco. In 2000, the case came before the Supreme Court. The case raised two major questions: (1) Does the Food, Drug, and Cosmetic Act (FDCA) give the FDA the power to regulate tobacco? (2) Should the Court defer to the FDA's own interpretation of its powers under the statute? As you will see, the majority and dissenting justices answered these questions in strikingly different ways.

FDA v. Brown and Williamson Tobacco Corporation
529 U.S. 120 (2000)

Justice O'CONNOR announced the judgment of the Court and delivered an opinion, in which the Chief Justice, Justice SCALIA, Justice KENNEDY, and Justice THOMAS joined.

This case involves one of the most troubling public health problems facing our Nation today: the thousands of premature deaths that occur each year because of tobacco use. In 1996, the Food and Drug Administration (FDA), after having expressly disavowed any such authority since its inception, asserted jurisdiction to regulate tobacco products. The FDA concluded that nicotine is a "drug" within the meaning of the Food, Drug, and Cosmetic Act (FDCA), and that cigarettes and smokeless tobacco are "combination products" that deliver nicotine to the body. Pursuant to this authority, it promulgated regulations intended to reduce tobacco consumption among children and adolescents. The agency believed that, because most tobacco consumers begin their use before reaching the age of 18, curbing tobacco use by minors could substantially reduce the prevalence of addiction in future generations and thus the incidence of tobacco-related death and disease . . .

Regardless of how serious the problem an administrative agency seeks to address, however, it may not exercise its authority "in a manner that is inconsistent with the administrative structure that Congress enacted into law." And although agencies are generally entitled to deference in the interpretation of statutes that they administer, a reviewing "court, as well as the agency, must give effect to the unambiguously expressed intent of Congress." *Chevron U.S.A. Inc. v. Natural Resources Defense Council, Inc.,* 467 U.S. 837, 842–843 (1984). In this case, we believe that Congress has clearly precluded the FDA from asserting jurisdiction to regulate

---

[60]The one-shot theory is, sadly, alive and well. In *Neal v. United States,* 116 S.Ct. 763 (1996), the Court in 1996 insisted on following its own interpretation of a 1986 drug law. The Court had concluded in 1991 that LSD dealers should be sentenced based on the weight of the LSD they sold plus the weight of the blotter paper that contained it. The United States Sentencing Commission subsequently concluded that the blotter paper weight should not count toward the amount of LSD sold. Justice Kennedy's opinion for the Court made the standard "one-shot" argument for following precedent blindly and ignoring the Sentencing Commission rules. The Court also ignored the fact that the Court, not Congress, created the "blotter paper rule" in the first place.

[61]Lief Carter and Christine Harrington, *Administrative Law and Politics,* 3rd edition (New York: Longman, 2000).

tobacco products. Such authority is inconsistent with the intent that Congress has expressed in the FDCA's overall regulatory scheme and in the tobacco-specific legislation that it has enacted subsequent to the FDCA. In light of this clear intent, the FDA's assertion of jurisdiction is impermissible.

The FDCA grants the FDA . . . the authority to regulate, among other items, "drugs" and "devices." The Act defines "drug" to include "articles (other than food) intended to affect the structure or any function of the body." It defines "device," in part, as "an instrument, apparatus, implement, machine, contrivance, . . . or other similar or related article, including any component, part, or accessory, which is . . . intended to affect the structure or any function of the body." The Act also grants the FDA the authority to regulate so-called "combination products," which "constitute a combination of a drug, device, or biologic product . . ."

In determining whether Congress has specifically addressed the question at issue, a reviewing court should not confine itself to examining a particular statutory provision in isolation. The meaning—or ambiguity—of certain words or phrases may only become evident when placed in context . . . It is a "fundamental canon of statutory construction that the words of a statute must be read in their context and with a view to their place in the overall statutory scheme." A court must therefore interpret the statute "as a symmetrical and coherent regulatory scheme," and "fit, if possible, all parts into an harmonious whole . . ."

Viewing the FDCA as a whole, it is evident that one of the Act's core objectives is to ensure that any product regulated by the FDA is "safe" and "effective" for its intended use . . . This essential purpose pervades the FDCA. For instance [one section of the FDCA] defines the FDA's "mission" to include "protect[ing] the public health by ensuring that . . . drugs are safe and effective" and that "there is reasonable assurance of the safety and effectiveness of devices intended for human use . . ."

Considering the FDCA as a whole, it is clear that Congress intended to exclude tobacco products from the FDA's jurisdiction. A fundamental precept of the FDCA is that any product regulated by the FDA—but not banned—must be safe for its intended use. Various provisions of the Act make clear that this refers to the safety of using the product to obtain its intended effects, not the public health ramifications of alternative administrative actions by the FDA. That is, the FDA must determine that there is a reasonable assurance that the product's therapeutic benefits outweigh the risk of harm to the consumer. According to this standard, the FDA has concluded that, although tobacco products might be effective in delivering certain pharmacological effects, they are "unsafe" and "dangerous" when used for these purposes. Consequently, if tobacco products were within the FDA's jurisdiction, the Act would require the FDA to remove them from the market entirely. But a ban would contradict Congress' clear intent as expressed in its more recent, tobacco-specific legislation. The inescapable conclusion is that there is no room for tobacco products within the FDCA's regulatory scheme. If they cannot be used safely for any therapeutic purpose, and yet they cannot be banned, they simply do not fit.

Justice BREYER filed a dissenting opinion, in which Justice STEVENS, Justice SOUTER, and Justice GINSBURG joined.

The majority . . . reaches the "inescapable conclusion" that the language and structure of the FDCA as a whole "simply do not fit" the kind of public health problem that tobacco creates. That is because, in the majority's view, the FDCA requires the FDA to ban outright "dangerous" drugs or devices (such as cigarettes); yet, the FDA concedes that an immediate and total cigarette-sale ban is inappropriate.

This argument is curious because it leads with similarly "inescapable" force to precisely the opposite conclusion, namely, that the FDA *does* have jurisdiction but that it must ban cigarettes. More importantly, the argument fails to take into account the fact that a statute interpreted as requiring the FDA to pick a more dangerous over a less dangerous remedy would be a perverse statute, *causing*, rather than preventing, unnecessary harm whenever a total ban is likely the more dangerous response. And one can at least imagine such circumstances.

Suppose, for example, that a commonly used, mildly addictive sleeping pill (or, say, a kind of popular contact lens), plainly within the FDA's jurisdiction, turned out to pose serious health risks for certain consumers. Suppose further that many of those addicted consumers would ignore an immediate total ban, turning to a potentially more dangerous black-market substitute, while a less draconian remedy (say, adequate notice) would wean them gradually away to a safer product. Would the FDCA still *force* the FDA to impose the more dangerous remedy? For the following reasons, I think not.

First, the statute's language does not restrict the FDA's remedial powers in this way. The FDCA permits the FDA to regulate a "combination product"—*i.e.*, a "device" (such as a cigarette) that contains a "drug" (such as nicotine)—under its "device" provisions. And the FDCA's "device" provisions explicitly grant the FDA wide remedial discretion. For example, where the FDA cannot "otherwise" obtain "reasonable assurance" of a device's "safety and effectiveness," the agency may restrict by regulation a product's "sale, distribution, or use" upon "*such . . . conditions as the Secretary may prescribe.*" (Emphasis added.) And the statutory section that most clearly addresses the FDA's power to ban (entitled "Banned devices") says that, where a device presents "an unreasonable and substantial risk of illness or injury," the Secretary "*may*"—not *must*—"initiate a proceeding . . . to make such device a banned device . . ."

The second reason the FDCA does not require the FDA to select the more dangerous remedy is that, despite the majority's assertions to the contrary, the statute does not distinguish among the kinds of health effects that the agency may take into account when assessing safety. The Court insists that the statute only permits the agency to take into account the health risks and benefits of the *"product itself"* as used by individual consumers, and, thus, that the FDA is prohibited from considering that a ban on smoking would lead many smokers to suffer severe withdrawal symptoms or to buy possibly stronger, more dangerous, black market cigarettes—considerations that the majority calls "the aggregate health effects of alternative administrative actions." But the FDCA expressly *permits* the FDA to take account of comparative safety in precisely this manner. [Here Breyer quotes from the FDCA to show that it empowers the FDA not to recall a product if the risk of a recall presents a greater health risk than no recall.]

. . . In my view, where linguistically permissible, we should interpret the FDCA in light of Congress' overall desire to protect health. That purpose requires a flexible interpretation that both permits the FDA to take into account the realities of human behavior and allows it, in appropriate cases, to choose from its arsenal of statutory remedies. A statute so interpreted easily "fit[s]" this, and other, drug- and device-related health problems.

Questions about the Case

1. What approach to statutory interpretation do Justice O'Connor and Justice Breyer take in this case? Are they literalists? Devotees of legislative intent? Purposivists?
2. What purpose does Justice O'Connor ascribe to the Food and Drug Control Act? What purpose does Justice Breyer see in the statute?
3. What techniques of statutory interpretation do Justice O'Connor and Justice Breyer use to support their conclusions about legislative purpose?
4. In your opinion, have these justices used good legal reasoning? Which opinion do you find more persuasive? Why?[62]

---

[62]For another example in which the Supreme Court decided a major public policy, by the same 5–4 division, about the meaning of a statute, see *Solid Waste Agency of Northern Cook County v. U.S. Army Corps of Engineers,* U.S. Lexis 640 (2001). This same divided Court, with Justices Stevens, Breyer, Souter, and Ginsburg dissenting, decided *Bush v. Gore.*

Chapter	# Interpreting
5	# the United States
	# Constitution

We are under a Constitution—but the Constitution is what the Judges say it is.

—CHARLES EVANS HUGHES

I look forward to seeing my plays staged so that I can find out what they mean.

—TOM STOPPARD, PLAYWRIGHT

At the beginning of the book, we discussed *legal reasoning* as a shorthand term for evaluating the fairness by which courts and judges exercise political power. Let us review why we use this shorthand. First, because we believe in something called the *rule of law,* we care that people act consistently with the law. Second, because we have inherited a common-law tradition, we give courts power to interpret what the law means in legal cases. (This is not true, for example, in a *civil law* nation like France, where judges do not give extensive justifications for their decisions.) Third, rules of law are often unclear when applied to specific cases, so cases constantly get appealed on points of law, and judges must choose what the law means. Fourth, liberal democracy requires judges to *justify* these choices because they exert judicial power. We expect judges to do so through the medium of legal reasoning, which requires them to render decisions that fit together or harmonize rules of law, facts of cases, social background facts, and widespread social values.

In constitutional law, the third and final type of law this text examines, we encounter what we conventionally think of as the most truly political part of law. Common and statutory law have never been the political science staple that constitutional law has traditionally been. All 50 states have constitutions, but it is only the Constitution of the United States that we conventionally teach. Why should this be so?

The Constitution does two important things. First, it allocates specific powers. It allocates powers both among the branches of the national government and between national and state governments. (Only the national government may coin money; the states have primary but not exclusive power over alcohol regulation.) Second, the Constitution declares rights that no branch of government at any level can exert power over—freedom of speech or the free exercise of religion for example. But

104

state constitutions also simultaneously convey powers and provide rights to resist power. The question remains, why is the U.S. Constitution uniquely important?[1]

"THE SUPREME LAW OF THE LAND"

The short answer is that the Constitution of the United States is "the supreme law of the land," as stated in Article VI. If the Constitution is supreme, it presumably overrides all state constitutions and all statutes and common-law rulings. In other words, when one rule of law is inconsistent with a constitutional rule, the other rule has got to go. Furthermore, the Constitution in Article III gives the U.S. Supreme Court, and all federal courts, jurisdiction to hear cases "arising under this Constitution." In the famous case of *Marbury v. Madison* in 1803, Chief Justice John Marshall, a lifetime appointee from the repudiated Federalist government of John Adams, put the jurisdiction clause and the supremacy clause together and declared that the federal courts could declare the acts of democratically elected Congress—in 1803 a very Republican Congress—null and void. We call this process "judicial review."

Judicial review of constitutionality puts the courts in a uniquely strong position. Legislatures can, as previous chapters demonstrated, overturn both common-law and statutory decisions. In constitutional interpretation, no such democratic backstopping exists. Short of holding a constitutional convention (a difficult and potentially risky procedure), those who dislike a constitutional ruling must either persuade the Court to change its mind or amend the Constitution. But a constitutional amendment requires approval of two-thirds of both houses of Congress *and* three-fourths of the states. Therefore, relatively small minorities can block a proposed amendment's passage. Only two of the eleven amendments ratified in the twentieth century (the Sixteenth Amendment, authorizing a federal income tax, and the Nineteenth, granting women's suffrage) can be said to have corrected controversial Supreme Court readings of the Constitution. To a very great extent, then, the Constitution really is, as Justice Charles Evans Hughes put it in this chapter's epigraph, "what the Judges say it is."

Interpretations of the Constitution are at the center of many of our most urgent political controversies. Based on their reading of the Constitution, courts declare some affirmative action programs illegal. Courts strike down laws prohibiting abortions, even so-called partial-birth abortions. Courts tell the federal government what it can and can't do to regulate the Internet. Courts reverse the convictions of killers because of what some critics call "technicalities." Additionally, in the 2000 election, the Supreme Court ended Al Gore's campaign for the presidency.

Why, in a democracy, should decisions like these be made by judges who do not subject themselves to the rigors of the electoral process? As we shall see, that question has created an entire academic industry of legal theorists and social scientists who have attempted to square judicial review with democratic theory. Even more than statutory law, the subject of the previous chapter, scholarship on constitutional

---

[1]State supreme courts can make major policy innovations by interpreting clauses of state constitutions. For example, on December 20, 1999, the Vermont Supreme Court ruled that the Vermont Constitution required the state to offer same-sex couples the same legal protections offered heterosexual married couples. It did so by interpreting the "Common Benefits Clause" of Vermont's Constitution. See *Baker v. Vermont* 98 Vt. 32, 744 A.2d 864 (Vermont Supreme Court, 2000). The "Common Benefits Clause" reads, in part:

> [G]overnment is, or ought to be, instituted for the common benefit, protection, and security of the people, nation, or community, and not for the particular emolument or advantage of any single person, family, or set of persons, who are a part only of that community.

law is haunted by the fear that judges, insulated from the people, will use their position to remake society according to their own visions. It's not clear, however, what the alternative to constitutional interpretation by judges would be. All government officers have a duty to take care that they are acting constitutionally in carrying out their duties. But when disputes over what the Constitution commands arise, some group or individual must settle them. And, as more and more of the nations of the world are deciding, courts are appropriate institutions for that task.[2]

The need for an authoritative interpretation of constitutional language is especially acute in the United States because of the "openness" of our Constitution. The Constitution speaks in some instances with considerable clarity, but in many others with generality, ambiguity, and vagueness. As you would expect, the clear parts of the Constitution rarely create much dispute. For example, the Constitution says that the president must be 35 years old, and while we can imagine hypothetical cases— an 18-year-old guru claims to be reincarnated and "really" 105—in fact no one has ever litigated that clause. But the Constitution's most frequently litigated clauses do little more than command the courts to *care* about basic political and governmental values without specifying with any precision the values or the problems to which the provisions apply:

- "Care," says the First Amendment to the courts, "that government not take sides on religious matters. Care that it not constrain religious freedom, or speech, or the press, unduly. But it's up to you to define religion, speech, and press and to decide when government action and those values simply cannot stand together."
- "Care," say the Fourth, Fifth, Sixth, and Eighth Amendments, "that government not become too zealous in fighting crime. Respect people's homes and property. Give them a fair chance to prove their innocence in court and do not punish the guilty too harshly. In short, be fair. But it's up to you to decide what's fair."
- "People must be able to trade effectively," say the commerce clause and the contract clause. "Work it out so they can."

The Constitution omits references to some rights that the structure of our government seems to require. For example, the Constitution contains no guarantee of a right to vote. Obviously the Constitution's words could not anticipate some violations of liberty and privacy, such as wiretapping, thermal imaging, and surveillance by airplanes.[3] On the other hand, the Constitution omits reference to some rights that we assume the framers knew about and took for granted—rights that are so much a part of our "liberty" as to "go without saying." The right to marry may well fall in this category. Thus to interpret the Constitution only according to what its words actually say seems to defeat its purpose. And once we accept that there are some liberties that the Constitution protects without specifically mentioning, someone has to decide where to draw the line.[4]

---

[2]On the growing importance of judicial review around the world, see C. Neil Tate and Torban Vallinder (eds.), *The Global Expansion of Judicial Power* (New York: New York University Press, 1995) and Alex Stone Sweet, *Governing with Judges: Constitutional Politics in Europe* (New York: Oxford University Press, 2000).

[3]Jeffrey Rosen, *The Unwanted Gaze: The Destruction of Privacy in America* (New York: Random House, 2000).

[4]See Judge Richard Posner's case against strict constructionism, aptly titled, "What Am I? A Potted Plant?" *New Republic*, September 28, 1987, pp. 23–25.

The Supreme Court has declared the right to choose whether to carry a fetus to term to be an unspecified liberty. The right of parents to raise children as they wish was vindicated in the 2000 case *Troxel v. Granville*.[5] On the other hand, in 1986 the Supreme Court concluded, in *Bowers v. Hardwick*, that the constitutional right of privacy did not bar Georgia from enforcing its sodomy law. Hardwick, a gay male, had been the victim of overt police harassment.[6] In a rare public statement, retired Justice Lewis Powell admitted regret for his vote supporting the decision, and since *Hardwick* several state courts have ruled that their state constitutions make sodomy laws illegal. The limits of a right of privacy, or of the right to raise children without interference from the state, or of the right to have a living will, are unclear. So, even if we could assume that every governmental representative—whether a legislator before voting for a statute or a policeman before deciding to arrest—stopped and made a conscientious determination of the constitutionality of a decision, under our Constitution, we would still need a constitution-interpreting organization like the courts. The Constitution is so vague, general, and ambiguous that people with the best of intentions do not necessarily reach the same interpretation.

Federalism also seems to require a Supreme Court to interpret the Constitution. We have one national constitution but many state constitutions. If we take its legal status seriously, then the Constitution should mean the same everywhere, just as the Mann Act should not have one meaning in Utah and another in the District of Columbia. If we lived under a unitary government, then maybe (but only maybe) we could count on a conscientious Congress to determine uniform constitutional applications. Under our Constitution, however, Congress is neither structured nor empowered to review the constitutionality of the actions of state and local governments.

For all these reasons—the finality of the Supreme Court, the importance of constitutional issues, the inconclusiveness of the Constitution's text, and the need for constitutional uniformity—we might expect the Supreme Court to take particular care to honor the conventional formulas for good legal reasoning in order to persuade us that justice is done. The bulk of this chapter explains why just the opposite happens, and why the practice of justification in constitutional law differs from the practices of legal reasoning described in previous chapters.

Readers will have to put up with a higher level of abstraction in this chapter than the two that precede it. In part, one must move toward the general and the abstract in order to say anything at all about such an immense subject—one on which books about the Rehnquist Court, the Robert Bork and Clarence Thomas nominations, or constitutional interpretation itself—flow steadily forth.[7] But there is a much more profound reason for the abstraction to follow, and the reason itself will seem difficult and abstract at first: Because the Constitution is supreme and because we believe we should follow it, we have throughout the many turbulent changes in our

---

[5]*Troxel v. Granville*, 530 U.S. 65 (2000).

[6]See Peter Irons, *The Courage of Their Convictions* (New York: Penguin Books, 1990), Chapter 16, and "Powell Regrets Backing Sodomy Law," *Washington Post*, 26 October 1990, p. A3.

[7]Here is a small sampling of recent books on the subject. Bruce Ackerman, *We the People, Vol. 1: Foundations* and *Vol. 2: Transformations* (Cambridge: Belknap Press of Harvard University Press, 1991 and 1997); Robert J. Lipkin, *Constitutional Revolutions* (Durham: Duke University Press, 2000); Akhil Reed Amar, *The Bill of Rights* (New Haven: Yale University Press, 1998); Robert C. Post, *Constitutional Domains* (Cambridge: Harvard University Press, 1995); Bernard Schwartz, *Decision: How the Supreme Court Decides Cases* (New York: Oxford University Press, 1996); John Maltese, *The Selling of Supreme Court Nominees* (Baltimore: The Johns Hopkins University Press, 1995); Stephen Griffin, *American Constitutionalism: From Theory to Politics* (Princeton, N.J.: Princeton University Press, 1996).

history worked very hard to make the Constitution fit and harmonize with what we do and what we believe. Bruce Ackerman's *We the People: Foundations* emphasizes that the United States has had—under one written document—two profound constitutional revolutions since the original revolutionary period: the Civil War and the New Deal.

Constitutional law, in other words, gets abstract because most of the Constitution's meaning is purely symbolic. We need the security of believing we are one political community with a continuous history, so we say we are living under one Constitution when in fact we work hard to change our interpretations of it to legitimate contemporary realities. Recall, however, that this is just the way the common law works.

CONVENTIONAL LEGAL REASONING
IN CONSTITUTIONAL INTERPRETATION

The Court's unique political position, we shall now see, makes it unwise to use the conventional techniques of legal reasoning that might be appropriate in common and statutory law. You might well think that factors described in the last section—the inconclusiveness of the Constitutional text, the centrality of constitutional issues in American politics, the need for uniform constitutional meaning both within the national government and among all the states—call for especially stable and clear patterns of legal reasoning and justification. However, this is precisely what 200 years of constitutional interpretation has *never* achieved, and for good reason. Precisely because "the Constitution is what the Judges say it is" (Justice Hughes's epigraph again), the Constitution is always open to new contructions. As in statutory interpretation, the formulas (literalism and intent, for example) that some judges use in a vain attempt to avoid making public policy are doomed to fail. But in constitutional law, the more open-ended, purpose-oriented techniques we recommended last chapter fall short as well. Let us see why.

Words as Channels of Meaning

Four words drawn from the Constitution loomed over the battle over the impeachment of Bill Clinton: *high crimes and misdemeanors,* the Constitution says, are impeachable offenses. But what exactly are "high crimes and misdemeanors"? Naturally, Republicans and Democrats in Congress had different views. Democrats argued that whatever Bill Clinton's sins, they did not relate closely enough to his performance in office, and so clearly were not "high crimes and misdemeanors." Republicans believed, on the other hand, that Clinton had broken the law, betrayed the trust of the American people, and demeaned the office of the presidency—a combination that amounted to "high crimes and misdemeanors." As usual in constitutional conflicts, the language divided rather than united.[8]

---

[8]For a provocative analysis of the impeachment battle, see Richard A. Posner, *An Affair of State: The Investigation, Impeachment and Trial of President Clinton* (Cambridge: Harvard University Press, 1999); for an equally provocative rebuttal, see Ronald Dworkin, "Philosophy and Monica Lewinsky," *New York Review of Books,* March 9, 2000.

By now this should be an old story to you: The mechanical jurisprudence that Judge Cardozo condemned in the *Hynes* common-law case has no place in constitutional law either. Indeed in constitutional law, the Supreme Court sometimes ignores *even unambiguous language*.

For example, Article I, Section 10 of the Constitution prohibits the states from engaging in certain activities altogether. It prohibits them from making treaties, coining money, or keeping a state militia during times of peace without Congressional permission. The section also includes these words: "No state shall . . . pass any . . . law impairing the obligation of contracts."

Debts provide the best example of the kind of contract the state may not impair under the contract clause. In the typical case of such a contract—"executory" contracts in legal language—Pauline borrows money, say from a bank, and promises to pay the money back some time in the future. Until she pays the money back (and at the stated time), she has a contractual obligation to do so. The contract clause prevents the state from impairing Pauline's "obligation" to repay. In short, the state can't pass a law saying people don't have to pay back what they owe, even if a popularly elected legislature voted to do so. Thus the word *impairing* would seem to prevent the state from allowing Pauline to forget about paying the interest or to pay back years later than she promised.

During the Great Depression, a number of states passed laws allowing owners of homes and land to postpone paying their mortgage payments as the mortgage contracts required. These statutes forbade banks and other mortgage holders from foreclosing. The Depression, of course, destroyed the financial ability of hundreds of thousands of "Paulines" to repay mortgages on time, but these mortgage moratorium laws spared the Paulines from this peril by impairing the bank's ability to recover the debt. Yet the Supreme Court ruled, in *Home Building and Loan Association v. Blaisdell,* that these laws did not violate the contract clause.[9]

The political context of Minnesota's moratorium statute was volatile. In Brest and Levinson's words, "angry farmers denounced and in some instances forcibly stopped foreclosure of their farms. In Iowa, a local judge who refused to suspend foreclosure proceedings was dragged from a courtroom and had a rope put around his neck before the crowd let him go."[10] Yet surely the Supreme Court should not decide cases simply to minimize violence. That only invites constitutional blackmail.

We *can* defend such a result. Just as in nature, survival of economic and political values depends on adaptation, on change, and on the ability to reevaluate policies in light of new information. The Supreme Court rejected the contract clause's words and upheld the Depression's mortgage moratorium laws because these laws were based on economic knowledge not fully available to the framers. In the forced-panic sale of land following massive numbers of foreclosures of mortgages, what would happen to the price of land? Supply and demand analysis predicted that the price would drastically decline—quite possibly to the point where creditors as well as debtors would lose—because the land could be sold for only a fraction of what the banks had originally loaned on it. The Court upheld the law as a defensible method for attempting to prevent further collapse of the economy.

A decision in the monumental school desegregation cases provides another example of prudent judicial flight from constitutional words. In its celebrated decision,

---

[9]*Home Building and Loan Association v. Blaisdell,* 290 U.S. 398 (1934). See also *East New York Savings Bank v. Hahn,* 326 U.S. 230 (1945) and *El Paso v. Simmons,* 379 U.S. 497 (1965).

[10]Paul Brest and Sanford Levinson, *Processes of Constitutional Decisionmaking* (Boston: Little, Brown & Co., 3rd ed., 1992), p. 352.

Brown v. Board of Education, the Court held that the equal protection clause of the Fourteenth Amendment prohibited laws and policies designed to maintain segregation in public schools of the then forty-eight states.[11] A case decided the same day as *Brown, Bolling v. Sharpe,* concerned the problem of segregation of schools in the nation's capital. The Fourteenth Amendment's sentence containing the equal protection clause begins with the words *no state shall.* It does not govern the District of Columbia. The original Bill of Rights does govern the national government and hence the District, but it contains no equal protection clause. Nonetheless, the Court in *Bolling* forbade segregation in the District's public schools by invoking the due process clause of the Fifth Amendment.[12] The Court did this even though the due process clause does not address the problem of equality. Its words—"No person shall . . . be deprived of life, liberty, or property, without due process of law . . ."— seem to address the problem of the fairness of procedures, the "due process," in the courts. The Fourteenth Amendment contains both due process and equal protection clauses, which further suggests that they convey different messages.

Yet the Court was right to go beyond the words of the Fifth and Fourteenth amendments. If the Constitution denies government the power to segregate schools by race, it would be absurd to permit segregation only in the national capital. It is proper to say in this instance that the due process clause of the Fifth Amendment does address this problem of equality despite its words. Sometimes even when the words of a constitutional provision are clear, the Supreme Court must pay attention instead to "the felt necessities of the time," as Justice Holmes famously put it.

Original Intent and Purpose

In 1985 Attorney General Edwin Meese called for a style of constitutional interpretation derived from the original understandings of the framers of the Constitution.[13] Meese's call, seconded by others, was nevertheless unrealistic. Searching for the actual intent of the framers of the original Constitution (or of its later amendments) proves just as frustrating as the search for legislative intent. The processes of constitution- and statute-making are equally political. People make arguments they don't fully believe in order to win support. Others do not express what they do believe in order to avoid offending. The painful process of negotiation and accommodation that produced the Constitution in 1787 left many questions unresolved. Most confounding of all, the authors could have had no intent in relation to the new facts that have surfaced since their work concluded.[14]

Thus, the Court ignored the original purpose of the Sixth Amendment's command when it expanded the right to counsel. This amendment states in part that "In all criminal prosecutions, the accused shall enjoy the right . . . to have the assistance of counsel for his defense." The framers who drafted it sought to alter the common-law rule that prohibited accused felons from having any lawyer at all. They wanted to stop the government from preventing the accused from bringing his lawyer to court with him. It makes no reference to the problem that a man's poverty may stop him from hiring a lawyer. Yet in 1938 the Court held that these words required

[11]*Brown v. Board of Education,* 347 U.S. 483 (1954).
[12]*Bolling v. Sharpe,* 347 U.S. 497 (1954). See also *Hirabayashi v. United States,* 320 U.S. 81 (1943).
[13]Edwin Meese III, "Toward a Jurisprudence of Original Intention," 45 *Public Administration Review* 701 (1985).
[14]For further elaboration see Lief Carter, *Contemporary Constitutional Lawmaking: The Supreme Court and the Art of Politics* (Elmsford, N.Y.: Pergamon Press, 1985), pp. 52–55. For a very thorough review of the intellectual history of the founding period, see Jack N. Rakove, *Original Meanings* (New York: Alfred A. Knopf, 1996).

the federal government to provide lawyers for the poor, and the court has since expanded the right to protect those accused of felonies and misdemeanors in state and local courts.[15]

And consider again the mortgage moratorium laws of the Depression. If we examine the purpose of the contract clause from the framers' viewpoint, we discover that they feared excessive democracy—feared that popularly elected legislators would enact the "selfish" interests of the masses. The masses contain more debtors than creditors, and it was in economically difficult times that the framers most feared that debtors would put irresistible pressure on legislators to ease their debts. Hence the Court in *Home Building and Loan* rejected more than constitutional words, and more than the specific intent of some individual framers; it arguably rejected the purpose of the provision. But it did so wisely because it understood, as presumably the framers did not, how postponing mortgage foreclosures could benefit creditors and debtors alike.

Finally, H. Jefferson Powell has shown two reasons why the leading figures of the founding period repeatedly and expressly rejected the idea that their own actual hopes and expectations of the Constitution would dictate legal conclusions in the future. First, at common-law, the reading of texts like wills and contracts rejected actual intent in favor of giving words their "reasonable," "grammatical," or "popular" meaning. Second, the framers, as members of the Protestant tradition, believed that texts ought to speak for themselves, unmediated by church or scholarly authority. They believed each person should be free to interpret biblical texts for himself, and that complex scholarly interpretations—interpretations imposed by "experts"—had no presumptive authority.

Powell describes how George Washington required in his will the nonlegal arbitration of any ambiguity in administering its provisions precisely in order that the decision maker might consider Washington's actual intent in the matter. None of the debaters in Philadelphia acknowledged that their words might shape the future, and James Madison believed that usage ("usus") and the lessons learned from political practice should override any "abstract opinion of the text." Thus, as president he signed the Second Bank Bill. He thought the First U.S. Bank had been unconstitutional, but he approved the successor because the people had approved it and it had worked.[16]

In this historical evidence we find the beginnings of America's major contribution to Western philosophy—pragmatism. Despite the way it is sometimes used in everyday discourse, *pragmatism* does not refer to an unprincipled, selfish attempt to "do whatever it takes to win." Pragmatism holds that our attitudes and choices should follow primarily from the lessons experience teaches us about what works, not from abstract rules or theories. The "radicalism of the American revolution," as Gordon Wood calls it, succeeded in implanting a democracy that made a pragmatic move away from the values and beliefs of the framers inevitable. Wood quotes a political leader of the generation that followed the framers:

"We cannot rely on the views of the founding fathers anymore," Martin Van Buren told the New York convention in 1820. "We have to rely on our own experience, not

---

[15]*Johnson v. Zerbst*, 304 U.S. 458 (1938); *Gideon v. Wainwright*, 372 U.S. 335 (1963); *Argersinger v. Hamlin*, 407 U.S. 25 (1972). For a persuasive defense of this trend, see Anthony Lewis's classic, *Gideon's Trumpet* (New York: Random House, 1964).

[16]H. Jefferson Powell, "The Original Understanding of Original Intent," 98 *Harvard Law Review* 885 (1985). Compare Richard Kay, "Adherence to the Original Intentions in Constitutional Adjudication: Three Objections and Responses," 82 *Northwestern University Law Review* 226 (1987).

on what they said or thought." "They had many fears," said Van Buren, "fears of democracy, that American experience had not borne out."[17]

In constitutional law, as in statutory law, "intent" is a deeply problematic concept. We have argued in favor of a purpose-oriented approach to statutory interpretation, acknowledging that it often leaves some discretion to judges to pick among competing purposes. But in constitutional law, even where "intent" or "purpose" are relatively clear, judges must sometimes ignore them.

Stare (In)Decisis

In 1940 the Supreme Court held that a public school could require all children—including Jehovah's Witnesses, whose religious convictions forbade it—to salute the flag each day. In 1943 the Court overruled itself and held the opposite.[18] In 1946 the Court refused to require state legislatures to make electoral districts roughly equal, but in 1962 the Court began to do just that.[19]

While the Justices sometimes make stare decisis a primary rationale for their decisions,[20] they have also from time to time recognized reasons to ignore precedents in constitutional law. After all, no legislature sits mainly to update constitutional policy in light of new conditions. It is not simply that the Court should correct its own mistakes—that, as we have argued in the previous chapter, is always wise policy. It is rather that wise policy at one time is not necessarily wise policy at another. If we take seriously the idea that the Constitution is law—ought to have teeth—then the courts must do the updating. As Justice William O. Douglas once said:

> The place of *stare decisis* in constitutional law is . . . tenuous. A judge looking at a constitutional decision may have compulsions to revere past history and accept what was once written. But he remembers above all else that it is the Constitution which he swore to support and defend, not the gloss which his predecessors may have put on it. So he comes to formulate his own views, rejecting some earlier ones as false and embracing others. He cannot do otherwise unless he lets men long dead and unaware of the problems of the age in which he lives do his thinking for him.[21]

Of course people rely on constitutional decisions. Teachers in 1943 believed they could require all students—regardless of their individual beliefs—to salute the flag. State judges in 1963 did not believe they had to appoint counsel in all felonies. Candidates for political office and their parties in the early 1960s may have created their election strategies assuming malapportionment in voting districts. The point is that constitutional values may be important enough to override reliance on past policy.

JUDICIAL REVIEW AND DEMOCRATIC THEORY

If neither the conventions of legal justification nor the backstop of legislative correction of judicial decisions limits the Supreme Court's power and discretion, then what does? This question has preoccupied constitutional scholarship for nearly a century.

---

[17]*The Radicalism of the American Revolution* (New York: Alfred A. Knopf, 1992), pp. 368–369.

[18]*Minersville School District v. Gobitis*, 310 U.S. 586 (1940), and *West Virginia State Board of Education v. Barnette*, 319 U.S. 624 (1943).

[19]*Colegrove v. Green*, 328 U.S. 549 (1946), and *Baker v. Carr*, 369 U.S. 186 (1962).

[20]One such instance was *Planned Parenthood v. Casey*, as discussed in Chapter 2 at p. 29.

[21]William O. Douglas, "Stare Decisis," 4 *Record of the Association of the Bar of the City of New York* 152 (1949), pp. 153–154.

The great constitutional theorist Alexander Bickel coined the phrase "the Countermajoritarian Difficulty" to summarize the problem: How could a democracy empower unelected judges to make decisions about many of the nation's most important controversies, sometimes against the wishes of the majority of the people?[22]

This issue surfaced in the 2000 presidential debates. When George Bush was asked what kind of judges he would pick for the Supreme Court, he contended that, unlike his opponent, he would appoint competent judges who would not seek to use their position to "write social policy":

> I believe that the judges ought not to take the place of the legislative branch of government, that they're appointed for life and that they ought to look at the Constitution as sacred. They . . . shouldn't misuse their bench. I don't believe in liberal activist judges . . .[23]

We have argued that in constitutional law, as in statutory and common-law, judges cannot help but write social policy. Another problem with Bush's position, though, is that it's not clear that judges can avoid being "activists," whether of the conservative, liberal, or moderate varieties. This is because activism has several dimensions, and a decision that is inactivist on one dimension may be activist on others.[24] Professor Bradley C. Canon suggests six such dimensions:

1. Majoritarianism—Does the decision nullify an act of an elected legislature?
2. Interpretive stability—Does the decision overrule prior court precedent?
3. Interpretive fidelity—Does the decision contradict the manifest intent of the framers?
4. Substance—Does the decision make new basic policy for the society (as for example *Brown v. Board of Education* began a new policy of school desegregation)?
5. Specificity—Does the decision require people to follow specific, court-created rules?
6. Availability of political alternatives—Are other political institutions equally able and willing to formulate effective policy in the area the decision touches?

In this light consider *Casey*, the Supreme Court's 1992 decision reaffirming the right to an abortion, a case we discussed in the second chapter of this book. By striking down part of a Pennsylvania law restricting abortions, the Supreme Court overturned the policy choice of an elected legislature (though not necessarily the policy choice of the majority of Americans) and so according to dimensions 1 and 6 was being activist. But notice that if the Supreme Court had decided in favor of Pennsylvania, it also would have been activist, this time according to 2 and perhaps 4 (since the Court would be approving a new policy regarding abortion). Moreover, the decision the Court did make in *Casey* seems to be "nonactivist" according to dimension 5 (since the Court did not announce a detailed set of rules for abortion regulation), and to 3 (since it's doubtful any of the framers had any intent about the constitutionality of abortion, much less a "manifest" one).

As this example suggests, activism is a much more complex concept than politicians like George W. Bush typically acknowledge. And yet Bush's comments do

---

[22]Alexander Bickel, *The Least Dangerous Branch: The Supreme Court at the Bar of Politics*, 2nd ed. (New Haven: Yale University Press, 1986), 16.

[23]"The 2000 Campaign: Transcript of Debate between Vice President Gore and Governor Bush," *New York Times*, 4 October 2000, p. A30.

[24]"A Framework for the Analysis of Judicial Activism," in Halpern and Lamb (eds.), *Supreme Court Activism and Restraint* (Lexington, Mass.: Lexington Books, 1982), Chapter 15.

point to an oft-voiced concern about the Supreme Court's role in American democracy. That concern is underlined when we realize that the Court has (rightly, we have argued) at times ignored the clear words of the Constitution, the clear intent of the framers, and the clear purposes of constitutional provisions. How can we keep (again, mostly) unelected judges from misusing their power to interpret the Constitution?

Theories of Judicial Self-Restraint

Academic legal sleuths have been on the case for more than a century now. They seek a theory of constitutional justification that would constrain the justices and thus resolve the countermajoritarian difficulty. Their concern is not merely "academic," for the Supreme Court has time and time again misused its power. In the late nineteenth and early twentieth centuries, for example, the Supreme Court tried to proclaim itself the final arbiter of social and economic policy and of political morality. It actively thwarted economic and social reforms at all levels of government for the sake of then-popular beliefs in social Darwinism, which seemed to many judges to equate unregulated private business activity with the improvement of the human race. So in *U.S. v. E.C. Knight* (1895), the Court aggressively reduced national power over commerce by defining the commerce power (contrary to precedents going back to John Marshall) to cover only the physical movement of goods among the states.[25] In 1905, in *Lochner v. New York*, the Court struck down statutory amelioration of harsh working conditions in bakeries by creating, under the Fourteenth Amendment's due process clause, a constitutional right to individuals' freedom to make any contracts they chose subject only to the "reasonable" exercise of the state's police power. The Court decided what was reasonable.[26] In 1918, Congress forbade the shipment in interstate commerce of goods made with child labor. Although the statute seemed to honor restrictions on the commerce power set in *E.C. Knight*, the Court struck down this statute because there was nothing inherently harmful about the goods shipped.[27]

The Court's official version of social Darwinism mistook the absence of regulation for free competition. Social Darwinism promised the improvement of the species through free competition, but such government regulations as the antitrust laws (which *E.C. Knight* curtailed) actually encouraged the sort of competition that social Darwinism required; that is, the Court claimed the power to review and reverse social policy on the basis of a theory that contradicted itself. Thus, Justice David Brewer in 1893 told the New York Bar Association that strengthening the judiciary was necessary to protect the country "against the tumultuous ocean of democracy!" He believed that

> the permanence of government of and by the people . . . rests upon the independence and vigor of the judiciary, . . . to restrain the greedy hand of the many from filching from the few that which they have honestly acquired. . . .[28]

This claim to unlimited judicial power prompted a search for theories that would solve the mystery of judicial power, a search that has continued to this day.

---

[25] 156 U.S. 1.
[26] 198 U.S. 45.
[27] *Hammer v. Dagenhart*, 247 U.S. 251.
[28] *Proceedings of the New York State Bar Association* (1893), p. 37.

The first of these theories, authored by James B. Thayer of the Harvard Law School, tried to reaffirm the representative nature of American constitutional government. All acts of elected bodies carry a heavy presumption of constitutionality. The courts may properly overturn legislation only on a showing that the legislature has made a very clear mistake.[29]

Thayer's thesis proved unsatisfactory for two reasons. First, like the "golden rule" of statutory interpretation, it contained no standards for determining what counted as a clear mistake. From the perspective of David Brewer (and Justice Field, who thought the income tax marked the beginning of a war waged by the poor against the rich), economic regulation *was* a clear mistake. Thayer's position left to courts the responsibility for doing the extralegal analysis necessary to decide what counts as a clear mistake: "The ultimate arbiter of what is rational and permissible is indeed always the courts, so far as litigated cases bring the question before them."

Second, if Thayer's theory did nudge the court into a posture of judicial self-restraint, the Court would then lack power to protect violations of civil liberties. Yet before the final collapse of the Court's economic activism in 1937, it had begun to move into the civil liberties area. In 1931, in *Near v. Minnesota,* the Court struck down a Minnesota law permitting prior censorship of the press.[30] In a 1932 case, *Powell v. Alabama,* it reversed the death sentences of six Black defendants sentenced to death after a one-day trial in Scottsboro, Alabama, in which the six were denied adequate representation of counsel.[31]

The synthesis of the two extremes—the theory that justified judicial abstinence from evaluating the rationality of economic policy without curtailing its power to protect civil liberties—appeared quietly (and in the most obscure legalese possible) in the fourth footnote to a 1938 case, in which the Court upheld congressional authority to regulate the ingredients in milk products processed for interstate commerce. This now-famous "Carolene footnote four" reads:

> There may be narrower scope for operation of the presumption of constitutionality when legislation appears on its face to be within a specific prohibition of the Constitution, such as those of the first ten amendments, which are deemed equally specific when held to be embraced within the Fourteenth. . . .
>
> It is unnecessary to consider now whether legislation which restricts those political processes which can ordinarily be expected to bring about a repeal of undesirable legislation, is to be subjected to more exacting judicial scrutiny under the general prohibitions of the Fourteenth Amendment than are most other types of legislation. . . .
>
> Nor need we inquire whether similar considerations enter into the review of statutes directed at particular religious . . . or national . . . or racial minorities . . . whether prejudice against discrete and insular minorities may be a special condition, which tends seriously to curtail the operation of those political processes ordinarily to be relied upon to protect minorities, and which may call for a correspondingly more searching judicial inquiry. . . .[32]

The first paragraph justified cases like *Near* because the First Amendment guarantees a free press—and *Powell* because the Fifth and Sixth Amendments guarantee a fair trial. In such cases the Court deemed that the Fourteenth

[29]"The Origin and Scope of the American Doctrine of Constitutional Law," 7 *Harvard Law Review* 129 (1893).

[30]*Near v. Minnesota*, 283 U.S. 697.

[31]*Powell v. Alabama*, 287 U.S. 45.

[32]*United States v. Carolene Products Co.*, 304 U.S. 114, pp. 152–153.

Amendment's due process clause applied these federal restrictions to state and local governmental actions.

The note's second paragraph explained why the Court need not intervene in economic policy: Fights over allocation of economic resources—like the debate over the working conditions in bakeries in *Lochner*—are usually waged by well-organized groups on various sides of the issue. The political compromises among those interests may not equate with a professional economist's definition of rationality, but they are legally acceptable because all sides participate in the process. But if the electoral machinery itself breaks down so as to bias the messages policymakers receive, the Court may intervene, for example, as in the reapportionment cases.[33]

The footnote's third paragraph suggests that even when the machinery of electoral politics works properly, prejudice against racial, religious, or other minorities (including people accused of serious crimes like murder, rape, and robbery) may prevent them from being heard. The Court's leadership regarding racial segregation took place at a time when Blacks in the deep South were systematically denied the chance to organize and vote. These racist policies arguably violated all three parts of the *Carolene* theory.

In 1980, John Hart Ely and Jesse Choper developed the details of these theories.[34] To the three *Carolene Products* points, Choper added a fourth: The Court should avoid upsetting political decisions about the balance of power between national and local government. The fact that state and local parties and elections select the members of Congress and that reelection depends on satisfying local demands, ensures a rough balance of state and local power without help from the Supreme Court.[35]

Many more scholarly theories of the Court's role have emerged since 1937. Herbert Wechsler, for example, has advocated that the Court decide cases only on the basis of "neutral principles," on the basis of rules that future courts can apply in cases with very different partisan or political alignments. A principle protecting those who demonstrate for racial justice must be articulated in such a way as to protect demonstrating members of the American Nazi Party.[36]

Wechsler, Choper, and Ely are among a vast array of constitutional theorists who seek to find a place for judicial review in democratic theory. But despite the scholarly elegance of each of the theories, they do not answer *our* fundamental question. We seek legal and political dynamics that actually do limit the constitutional power of the Supreme Court—not merely a resolution of an academic debate about what might, in theory, limit the Court. We seek an understanding of the Court's actual practices that can assure us that its justifications are good—and the fact of the matter is that, in practice, the Court does not consistently follow these theories any better than it follows more conventional methods of legal reasoning.

Consider the Court's decision in *Griswold v. Connecticut,* in which the Court struck down state laws prohibiting the distribution of contraceptives. The "right of privacy" created by the Court to justify the result is hardly a "specific prohibition" in the Bill of Rights, and the people it protects—women and men both—are as far

---

[33]*Baker v. Carr,* 369 U.S. 186 (1962), and see *Reynolds v. Sims,* 377 U.S. 533 (1964).

[34]John Hart Ely, *Democracy and Distrust: A Theory of Judicial Review* (Cambridge: Harvard University Press, 1980); and Jesse Choper, *Judicial Review and the National Political Process: A Functional Reconsideration of the Role of the Supreme Court* (Chicago: University of Chicago Press, 1980).

[35]The Rehnquist Court has decisively rejected Choper's theory, becoming particularly "activist" (in almost all dimensions) in the area of federal-state relations. The Court has struck down a host of federal laws that it believes interfere with the constitutional powers of states.

[36]Herbert Wechsler, "Toward Neutral Principles of Constitutional Law," 73 *Harvard Law Review* 1 (1959).

from an insular and discrete minority as we could imagine.[37] The Court's extension of the principle of privacy in the abortion case—including the right of a single female—might seem to practice Wechsler's neutral principles concept but for the fact that the Court also ruled that the Constitution permits government to deny funds for abortion to the indigent who are otherwise qualified to receive them.[38] Indeed Justice Stone, the coauthor of *Carolene Products'* footnote four, voted (perhaps for Bickelian reasons) *against* allowing the Court to intervene in legislative reapportionment, in direct contradiction to his note's second paragraph.[39]

We have already seen that a precedent does not dictate how a judge applies it. (If it did, the case would usually not reach the appellate courts in the first place.) Just as "fact freedom" allows different judges to apply the same precedents in opposite ways, so each constitutional theory does not dictate or constrain. The history of judicial review, starting with *Marbury v. Madison*,[40] more resembles a tool bench where the judge decides how the case ought to come out and then chooses whatever tool seems handiest to get the job done. All abstract theories about the Supreme Court's role fail to answer our question. But perhaps the political role of the Supreme Court makes theoretical consistency both impossible and unnecessary. We explore that possibility next.

Political Constraints on the Court

One school of thought, which political scientists have called "political jurisprudence," supplies constraints on the Supreme Court not through political theory or legal doctrine but from the practical operation of politics itself. This resolution of the constitutional paradox was expressed most pithily by Mr. Dooley's conclusion that "th' Supreme Court follows th' iliction returns." Martin Shapiro, a leading figure in political jurisprudence, put it this way:

> No regime is likely to allow significant political power to be wielded by an isolated judicial corps free of political restraints. To the extent that courts make law, judges will be incorporated into the governing coalition, the ruling elite, responsible representatives of the people, or however else the political regime may be expressed.[41]

Subject to a few historical exceptions, particularly the Court's advocacy of social Darwinism and laissez-faire economics, the theory holds that the Court rarely strays far enough from dominant popular opinion to worry about checking it through legal doctrine or theories of judicial review.[42] This approach combines historical observations of instances in which presidential selections of justices have steered the Court onto more popular courses with analyses of the structural and procedural characteristics of the Court's work that make it politically responsive. Here are the major threads this perspective weaves together.

Many constitutional decisions do not invalidate the work of popularly elected legislators in the first place. They set aside—as in the decisions regarding search

[37]*Griswold v. Connecticut*, 381 U.S. 479 (1965).
[38]*Roe v. Wade*, 410 U.S. 113 (1973), but see *Harris v. McRae*, 448 U.S. 297 (1980).
[39]*Colegrove v. Green*, 328 U.S. 549 (1946).
[40]*Marbury v. Madison*, 5 U.S. 87 (1803).
[41]Martin Shapiro, *Courts: A Comparative Political Analysis* (Chicago: University of Chicago Press, 1981), p. 34.
[42]See Robert Dahl, "Decision-Making in a Democracy: The Supreme Court as National Policy Maker," 6 *Journal of Public Law* 294 (1958).

and seizure of criminal evidence and of interrogation of suspects—decisions of non-elected administrative personnel who are, like judges, only indirectly affected by electoral politics. In less than one-half of 1 percent of all statutes passed by Congress since World War II, the Court has found a point to invalidate. In nearly all of these instances, the Court has invalidated not an entire statutory scheme or policy but only an offending clause or provision.[43] The most activist of courts touches only a tiny fraction of the democratic work of Congress.

Elected officials do not vote according to the "majority will," because on most policy issues before a legislature the public has no opinion whatsoever. The benefit of elections in the daily operation of politics comes from the fact that elected politicians listen to interest groups and individual citizens because they need as many votes from as many different sources as possible. Elections tend to overcome the natural inertia of all organized human effort. The legal process has a different but equally effective method for forcing judges to listen: Anyone can file a lawsuit about anything, and judges must listen to it at least long enough to determine that the lawsuit alleges no legal injury.

The president fills a vacancy on the Supreme Court on the average of slightly less often than once every two years. Bill Clinton had fewer opportunities to appoint justices than this average, but his two appointees, Ruth Bader Ginsburg and Stephen Breyer, have tempered the conservative tendencies of the Rehnquist Court. Similarly, the Nixon, Ford, and Reagan appointees on the previous Burger Court stalled the expansion of the Warren Court's protection of the rights of the accused, just as President Nixon's "law and order" campaign had pledged.[44] The political jurisprudence solution becomes more persuasive when we consider that, despite predictions to the contrary, Justices Souter and Kennedy voted to follow the *Roe v. Wade* abortion precedent at a time (1992) when popular opinion seemed to favor just that result.

As we saw regarding the case of the sunken barges in Chapter 3, courts process information very much as other decision makers do. Various sides present positions. Lawyers file briefs containing abundant factual as well as legal assertions. They criticize the positions their opponents take. The capacity of judges to understand information depends on two things. First, does the issue really depend on the intelligent digestion and interpretation of a complex body of facts at all? Many of the most dramatic civil rights questions are so fundamentally normative and depend so extensively on moral rather than factual reasoning that the technical competence of judges really does not seem relevant. The decision to forbid mandatory flag salutes does not depend on scientific analysis of data revealing the beneficial and harmful consequences of such practices. Second, when the issue does depend on an understanding of facts, then we should really expect judges to have the capacity to understand the facts before they proceed. Judges must understand the language through which the problem expresses itself. Most judges are well equipped to understand the dimensions of a right-to-counsel issue. Most judges are not equipped to understand the econometric analysis on which the Federal Reserve Board determines its national monetary policy. The problem must not be of the sort in which part of the information is necessarily hidden from judges, as it is in many foreign-policy matters because the information is secret or because the only people who possess it do not

---

[43]Through the year 1978, the Supreme Court had invalidated portions of about 100 acts of Congress, 900 state statutes, and 124 local ordinances. Our thanks to Professor Sam Krislov for pointing out these tabulations.

[44]For an argument favoring independent Senate screening of the President's judicial appointments, see Laurence Tribe, *God Save This Honorable Court* (New York: Random House, 1985).

live or work within reach of the court's jurisdiction. Finally, if a given decision generates feedback information that will produce improved policy, the courts should have access to that information in the course of further litigation.[45]

Constitutional decisions possess all the characteristics of the common-law tradition. No one decision permanently sets the course of law. The process is a thoroughly incremental one in which, case by case, new facts and new arguments pro and con repeatedly come before the courts. The law can change and adjust to new facts and conditions. A judicial commitment to protecting liberties does not require the courts to articulate a complete theory of equal protection or due process.[46]

In the twentieth century the Court avoided creating legal doctrine that appeared to "take sides" along popular partisan lines. Decisions defending the freedom of civil rights activists to organize and demonstrate also protect neo-Nazis and Klansmen. The Burger Court, loaded with Nixon appointees, denied President Nixon's claim of executive privilege in the Watergate crisis. The Court first steered a middle course regarding affirmative action when it ruled that race alone could not determine admissions policies, and since then has gradually chipped away at the constitutionality of affirmative action, rather than banning it entirely.[47]

The main thrust of the Madisonian constitutional scheme was to prevent too much power from accumulating in one place. The dispersion of power takes place more through the sharing than the separating of power. Different institutions must compromise because none can act effectively without cooperating with the others. Perhaps therefore the indeterminacy of constitutional theory is a blessing in disguise, a measure of the success of Madison's vision.[48]

These indisputable characteristics of American politics may help us to answer the challenge posed by Bickel's countermajoritarian difficulty. American government is not constructed to be purely majoritarian, but instead to be a system of separated institutions sharing power. The courts are the least majoritarian of these institutions, but they do not usually fall very far out of line with the dominant political opinions of the time. As Alexander Hamilton said in defending the federal judicial structure in *Federalist Papers* #78, the judiciary is the "least dangerous branch" because it has neither the power of "purse nor sword." It has neither the staff nor the budget to implement its own decisions, so it must rely on others, especially the other branches of government, to put its rulings into effect.[49] No wonder then, that the Court rarely takes on the branch most connected to the people, Congress, in a major dispute.

[45]Lief H. Carter, "When Courts Should Make Policy: An Institutional Approach," in John A. Gardiner (ed.), *Public Law and Public Policy* (New York: Praeger, 1977), pp. 141–157; Donald L. Horowitz, *The Courts and Social Policy* (Washington, D.C.: The Brookings Institution, 1977); Gerald Rosenberg, *The Hollow Hope* (Chicago: University of Chicago Press, 1991); David Schultz (ed.), *Leveraging the Law* (New York: Peter Lang, 1997).

[46]Felix Cohen, "Transcendental Nonsense and the Functional Approach," 35 *Columbia Law Review* 809 (1935). See also Martin Shapiro, "Stability and Change in Judicial Decision Making: Incrementalism or Stare Decisis?" 2 *Law in Transition Quarterly* 134 (1964). And see Janet S. Lindgren, "Beyond Cases: Reconsidering Judicial Review," 1983 *Wisconsin Law Review* 583 (1983).

[47]*Regents of the University of California v. Bakke*, 438 U.S. 265 (1978), was the Supreme Court's first substantive decision on the constitutionality of affirmative action. In *Richmond v. Croson* 488 U.S. 469 (1989) and *Adarand Constructors v. Pena* 515 U.S. 200 (1995), the Rehnquist Court restricted affirmative action programs, but has never declared all racial preferences illegal.

[48]See Walter Murphy, James Fleming, and Sotirios Barber, *American Constitutional Interpretation*, 2nd ed., (Mineola, N.Y.: Foundation Press, 1995), Chapters 1–4, esp. pp. 71–79.

[49]*The Federalist Papers* (New York: Mentor, 1961), 464–472. For a study of the limits of the judiciary in implementing its rulings, see Gerald Rosenberg, *The Hollow Hope: Can Courts Bring about Social Change?* (Chicago: University of Chicago Press, 1991).

Taken together, these facts about the role of courts within American government answer the democracy question that Bickel and others have posed. But do all these facts provide an acceptable substitute for persuasive legal justification? Do they obviate the need for good legal reasoning in constitutional law?

Two lines of reasoning indicate that they do not. First, although these factors do suggest no cause for immediate alarm about the Supreme Court's political role, they completely sidestep the original question. Legal reasoning ought to provide standards of satisfactory justification for specific case decisions. The political factors do not guide judges in the crafting of actual opinions. The political environment may reassure the average voter, but it will hardly satisfy a losing litigant in a concrete case to learn that the president might appoint a more sympathetic justice a year or two later.

Second, the reassuring argument may prove too much. The Constitution in part seeks to protect individuals from what Alexis de Tocqueville called "the tyranny of the majority."[50] The unpopular speaker and the deviant religious belief may thrive only if the courts are not politically too responsive. If we must sustain the belief that the Constitution is a central source of political structure and communal values—if we need to believe in *it*—then conventional political jurisprudence provides no satisfying solution to our problem.

THE TURN TO INDIVIDUAL DIGNITY

One important movement in legal theory—"Critical Legal Studies"—recognizes the two reservations just described. Beginning in the mid-1970s, Duncan Kennedy, Roberto Unger, Mark Tushnet, Robert Gordon, Paul Brest, John Henry Schlagel, and other law professors who came of professional age during the antiwar movement of the 1960s began in their publications to assert that the political culture constrains court and legislature alike from protecting individual dignity adequately. But they also recognized that the solution lay in changing not legal doctrine but the political culture itself. The negative side of the movement has articulated a powerful case for abandoning the search for any doctrinal solution to constitutional interpretation.[51]

The positive contribution of critical legal studies is less clear or convincing, in part because the very success of the movement's critique of doctrine makes a case that no doctrinal solution is possible. Nevertheless, critical legal studies seem to move toward endorsing the idea that constitutional goodness depends on the Court's enhancing our capacity to converse about the moral or normative quality of our communal life. To accomplish this, the Court must do more than protect First Amendment freedoms or individual privacy. It must protect individual integrity and dignity so that people feel empowered to participate in political life. To accomplish that task, the Court must in turn model good conversation. It must speak candidly about the world that law, politics, science, economics, and religion all inhabit.

The critical legal studies movement has retained the radical orientation of its antiwar origins, but its substantive conclusions do not differ substantially from those reached by the more mainstream liberal philosophy of Ronald Dworkin, Walter

[50]Alexis de Tocqueville, *Democracy in America*, George Lawrence, tr., J. P. Mayer, ed. (New York: Harper and Row, 1969), 250.
[51]Lief Carter has discussed critical legal studies in more depth in his *Contemporary Constitutional Lawmaking*, especially pp. 98–101 and 127–133.

Murphy, and Sotirios Barber.[52] Although mainstream liberalism persists in searching for a coherent constitutional philosophy, its approach emphasizes not legal solutions but the process by which we arrive at them. The Constitution reminds us that we aspire to achieve political goodness. We, being imperfect, will never fully achieve it, but it is essential that we not abandon our effort to combine the lessons of the past with our experience in the present to define what is politically good.

The final chapter presents our own theory of justification in all areas of law and will elaborate on this approach. For now, the lesson is that a preoccupation with doctrine may do more harm than good. The judge or scholar who insists on a doctrinally elegant legal resolution of a case may shut herself off from the cares and aspirations of the litigants themselves. The people whose lives the courts shape will not likely have doctrinal elegance at the top of their list of priorities. Perhaps this is what Justice Harry Blackmun meant in a 1983 interview:

> "Maybe I'm oversensitive," Justice Blackmun says, "But these are very personal cases. We're dealing with *people*—the life, liberty, and property of *people*. And because I grew up in poor surroundings, I know there's another world out there we sometimes forget about."[53]

Illustrative Case

To understand the legal issues in the following case, you need to know that the "equal protection clause" of the Fourteenth Amendment potentially invalidates any state law that classifies or differentiates people by sex. This body of law is complex and unsettled, but let us make several assumptions. First, assume that all legislation must pass some minimal test of rationality to be upheld. If, to use John Ely's example, someone were to invent a new, highly effective, "deadstop" brake for trucks, it might be rational for the legislature by law to require only trucks weighing more than five tons to install them, but it would not be rational for the legislature by law to require only blue trucks to install them.[54] That kind of irrationality would strongly imply that a corrupt under-the-table deal had taken place. Second, assume that all laws that treat people unequally on the basis of their race must meet a much higher test of necessity known as "strict scrutiny." Third, assume that for laws that discriminate on the basis of gender—laws that treat men more or less favorably than women, and vice versa—the law must meet a "higher" test of rationality than the minimum rationality test but not as severe as the "strict scrutiny" test for racial classifications. In *Craig v. Boren,* 429 U.S. 190 (1976), the Supreme Court held that "classifications by gender must serve important governmental objectives and must be substantially related to achievement of these objectives." In *Craig* the Court struck down a law that forbade the sale of 3.2 beer to men (but not women) ages 18 to 20. The Court in *Craig* placed on the state the burden of proving that *allowing* the females

[52]Dworkin, *Taking Rights Seriously* (Cambridge: Harvard University Press, 1978), and *A Matter of Principle* (Cambridge: Harvard University Press, 1985); Murphy, "The Art of Constitutional Interpretation: A Preliminary Showing," in M. Judd Harmon (ed.), *Essays on the Constitution of the United States* (Port Washington, N.Y.: Kennikat Press, 1980); Barber, *On What the Constitution Means* (Baltimore: Johns Hopkins University Press, 1984).

[53]John Jenkins, "A Candid Talk with Justice Blackmun," *New York Times Magazine,* February 20, 1983, p. 20, at pp. 23–24.

[54]See Ely's "Legislative and Administrative Motivation in Constitutional Law," 79 *Yale Law Journal* 1205 (1970) and the particularly lucid discussion of rationality analysis generally in Brest and Levinson, *Processes of Constitutional Decisionmaking,* 3rd ed., supra, pp. 559–579.

to buy the beer somehow made life safer than would denying the right to buy beer to both sexes. The state failed to produce such evidence, so the Court invalidated the sex-based classification.

Consider by contrast the Supreme Court's conclusions about what the background facts do and do not prove in the following case. Virginia Military Institute (VMI) is a state-funded college that aims to produce "citizen soldiers," graduates equally able to succeed in the military and in civilian life. It does this through an "adversative," or "doubting," model of education, which exposes the student to extreme physical and mental stress, hyperregulation of even "private" behavior, and indoctrination into a traditional code of values. In 1992, a federal appeals court ruled that VMI's policy of barring women from its program violated the Fourteenth Amendment. Virginia responded by proposing to create a new Women's Institute for Leadership at Mary Baldwin College that Virginia argued would serve as a female equivalent to VMI. Instead of the adversative method, the Institute would use a cooperative, self-esteem enhancing mode of instruction deemed more appropriate for women. Two lower federal courts approved this plan, but it was struck down by the Supreme Court, which ruled that the Mary Baldwin program was in no way equivalent to VMI. As you read the majority opinion, consider whether Virginia has met the burden imposed by *Craig v. Boren* for justifying classifications based on gender. And as you read Justice Scalia's dissent, ask yourself if the arguments advanced in this book undercut or support his view.

United States v. Virginia
523 U. S. 420 (1996)

Justice GINSBURG delivered the opinion of the Court in which Justice STEVENS, Justice O'CONNOR, Justice KENNEDY, Justice SOUTER and Justice BREYER joined.

. . . Virginia . . . asserts two justifications in defense of VMI's exclusion of women. First, the Commonwealth contends, "single sex education provides important educational benefits," and the option of single sex education contributes to "diversity in educational approaches." Second, the Commonwealth argues, "the unique VMI method of character development and leadership training," the school's adversative approach, would have to be modified were VMI to admit women. We consider these two justifications in turn.

Single sex education affords pedagogical benefits to at least some students, Virginia emphasizes, and that reality is uncontested in this litigation. Similarly, it is not disputed that diversity among public educational institutions can serve the public good. But Virginia has not shown that VMI was established, or has been maintained, with a view to diversifying, by its categorical exclusion of women, educational opportunities within the State. In cases of this genre, our precedent instructs that "benign" justifications proffered in defense of categorical exclusions will not be accepted automatically; a tenable justification must describe actual state purposes, not rationalizations for actions in fact differently grounded . . .

Neither recent nor distant history bears out Virginia's alleged pursuit of diversity through single sex educational options. In 1839, when the State established VMI, a range of educational opportunities for men and women was scarcely contemplated. Higher education at the time was considered dangerous for women; reflecting widely held views about women's proper place . . .

Debate concerning women's admission as undergraduates at the main university continued well past the [twentieth] century's midpoint. Familiar arguments were rehearsed. If women were admitted, it was feared, they "would encroach on the rights of men; there would be new problems of government, perhaps scandals; the old honor system would have to be changed; standards would be lowered to those of other coeducational schools; and the glorious reputation of the university, as a school for men, would be trailed in the dust."

Ultimately, in 1970, "the most prestigious institution of higher education in Virginia," the University of Virginia, introduced coeducation and, in 1972, began to admit women on an equal basis with men. . . . Virginia describes the current absence of public single sex higher education for women as "an historical anomaly." But the historical record indicates action more deliberate than anomalous: First, protection of women against higher education; next, schools for women far from equal in resources and stature to schools for men; finally, conversion of the separate schools to coeducation . . .

In sum, we find no persuasive evidence in this record that VMI's male only admission policy "is in furtherance of a state policy of 'diversity.'" No such policy, the Fourth Circuit observed, can be discerned from the movement of all other public colleges and universities in Virginia away from single sex education . . . A purpose genuinely to advance an array of educational options, as the Court of Appeals recognized, is not served by VMI's historic and constant plan—a plan to "affor[d] a unique educational benefit only to males." However "liberally" this plan serves the State's sons, it makes no provision whatever for her daughters. That is not equal protection.

Virginia next argues that VMI's adversative method of training provides educational benefits that cannot be made available, unmodified, to women. Alterations to accommodate women would necessarily be "radical," so "drastic," Virginia asserts, as to transform, indeed "destroy," VMI's program. Neither sex would be favored by the transformation, Virginia maintains: Men would be deprived of the unique opportunity currently available to them; women would not gain that opportunity because their participation would "eliminat[e] the very aspects of [the] program that distinguish [VMI] from . . . other institutions of higher education in Virginia."

The District Court forecast from expert witness testimony, and the Court of Appeals accepted, that coeducation would materially affect "at least these three aspects of VMI's program—physical training, the absence of privacy, and the adversative approach." And it is uncontested that women's admission would require accommodations, primarily in arranging housing assignments and physical training programs for female cadets. It is also undisputed, however, that "the VMI methodology could be used to educate women." The District Court even allowed that some women may prefer it to the methodology a women's college might pursue. "[S]ome women, at least, would want to attend [VMI] if they had the opportunity," the District Court recognized, and "some women," the expert testimony established, "are capable of all of the individual activities required of VMI cadets." The parties, furthermore, agree that "some women can meet the physical standards [VMI] now impose[s] on men." In sum, as the Court of Appeals stated, "neither the goal of producing citizen soldiers," VMI's raison d'être, "nor VMI's implementing methodology is inherently unsuitable to women."

In support of its initial judgment for Virginia, a judgment rejecting all equal protection objections presented by the United States, the District Court made "findings" on "gender based developmental differences." These "findings" restate the opinions of Virginia's expert witnesses, opinions about typically male or typically female "tendencies." For example, "[m]ales tend to need an atmosphere of adversativeness," while "[f]emales tend to thrive in a cooperative atmosphere" . . . VMI's expert on educational institutions testified, "undoubtedly there are some [women] who do"; but educational experiences must be designed "around the rule," this expert maintained, and not "around the exception . . ."

It may be assumed, for purposes of this decision, that most women would not choose VMI's adversative method. As Fourth Circuit Judge Motz observed, however . . . it is also probable that "many men would not want to be educated in such an environment." (On that point, even our dissenting colleague might agree.) Education, to be sure, is not a "one size fits all" business. The issue, however, is not whether "women—or men—should be forced to attend VMI"; rather, the question is whether the State can constitutionally deny to women who have the will and capacity, the training and attendant opportunities that VMI uniquely affords.

The notion that admission of women would downgrade VMI's stature, destroy the adversative system and, with it, even the school, is a judgment hardly proved, a prediction hardly different from other "self fulfilling prophec[ies]," . . . once routinely used to deny rights or opportunities . . .

. . . A prime part of the history of our Constitution, historian Richard Morris recounted, is the story of the extension of constitutional rights and protections to people once ignored or excluded. VMI's story continued as our comprehension of "We the People" expanded. There is no reason to believe that the admission of women capable of all the activities required of VMI cadets would destroy the Institute rather than enhance its capacity to serve the "more perfect Union."

For the reasons stated, the initial judgment of the Court of Appeals, is affirmed, the final judgment of the Court of Appeals, is reversed, and the case is remanded for further proceedings consistent with this opinion.

[Chief Justice REHNQUIST wrote a separate opinion concurring in the result.]

Justice SCALIA (dissenting).

. . . Much of the Court's opinion is devoted to deprecating the closed-mindedness of our forebears with regard to women's education, and even with regard to the treatment of women in areas that have nothing to do with education. Closedminded they were—as every age is, including our own, with regard to matters it cannot guess, because it simply does not consider them debatable. The virtue of a democratic system with a First Amendment is that it readily enables the people, over time, to be persuaded that what they took for granted is not so, and to change their laws accordingly. That system is destroyed if the smug assurances of each age are removed from the democratic process and written into the Constitution. So to counterbalance the Court's criticism of our ancestors, let me say a word in their praise: They left us free to change. The same cannot be said of this most illiberal Court, which has embarked on a course of inscribing one after another of the current preferences of the society (and in some cases only the countermajoritarian preferences of the society's law-trained elite) into our Basic Law. Today it enshrines the notion that no substantial educational value is to be served by an all-men's military academy—so that the decision by the people of Virginia to maintain such an institution denies equal protection to women who cannot attend that institution but can attend others. Since it is entirely clear that the Constitution of the United States—the old one—takes no sides in this educational debate, I dissent.

It is beyond question that Virginia has an important state interest in providing effective college education for its citizens. That single-sex instruction is an approach substantially related to that interest should be evident enough from the long and continuing history in this country of men's and women's colleges. But beyond that, as the Court of Appeals here stated: "That single-gender education at the college level is beneficial to both sexes is a fact established in this case." The evidence establishing that fact was overwhelming—indeed, "virtually uncontradicted" in the words of the court that received the evidence. As an initial matter, Virginia demonstrated at trial that "[a] substantial body of contemporary scholarship and research supports the proposition that, although males and females have significant areas of developmental overlap, they also have differing developmental needs that are deep-seated." While no one questioned that for many students a coeducational environment was nonetheless not inappropriate, that could not obscure the demonstrated benefits of single-sex colleges. For example, the District Court stated as follows:

> "One empirical study in evidence, not questioned by any expert, demonstrates that single-sex colleges provide better educational experiences than coeducational institutions. Students of both sexes become more academically involved, interact with faculty frequently, show larger increases in intellectual self-esteem and are more satisfied with practically all aspects of college experience (the sole exception is social life) compared with their counterparts in coeducational institutions. Attendance at an all-male college substantially increases the likelihood that a student will carry out career plans in law, business and college teaching, and also has a substantial positive effect on starting salaries in business. Women's colleges increase the chances that those who attend will obtain positions of leadership, complete the baccalaureate degree, and aspire to higher degrees."

"In the light of this very substantial authority favoring single-sex education," the District Court concluded that "the VMI Board's decision to maintain an all-male institution is fully justified even without taking into consideration the other unique features of VMI's teaching and training." This finding alone, which even this Court cannot dispute, should be sufficient to demonstrate the constitutionality of VMI's all-male composition.

But besides its single-sex constitution, VMI is different from other colleges in another way. It employs a "distinctive educational method," sometimes referred to as the "adversative, or doubting, model of education." "Physical rigor, mental stress, absolute equality of treatment, absence of privacy, minute regulation of behavior, and indoctrination in desirable values are the salient attributes of the VMI educational experience." No one contends that this method is appropriate for all individuals; education is not a "one size fits all" business. Just as a State may wish to support junior colleges, vocational institutes, or a law school that emphasizes case practice instead of classroom study, so too a State's decision to maintain within its system one school that provides the adversative method is "substantially related" to its goal of good education. Moreover, it was uncontested that "if the state were to establish a women's VMI-type [i.e., adversative] program, the program would attract an insufficient number of participants to make the program work;" and it was found by the District Court that if Virginia were to include women in VMI, the school "would eventually find it necessary to drop the adversative system altogether." Thus, Virginia's options were an adversative method that excludes women or no adversative method at all.

Justice Brandeis said it is "one of the happy incidents of the federal system that a single courageous State may, if its citizens choose, serve as a laboratory; and try novel social and economic experiments without risk to the rest of the country." *New State Ice Co. v. Liebmann.* But it is one of the unhappy incidents of the federal system that a self righteous Supreme Court, acting on its Members' personal view of what would make a "more perfect Union," (a criterion only slightly more restrictive than a "more perfect world"), can impose its own favored social and economic dispositions nationwide . . . The sphere of self government reserved to the people of the Republic is progressively narrowed . . .

In an odd sort of way, it is precisely VMI's attachment to such old-fashioned concepts as manly "honor" that has made it, and the system it represents, the target of those who today succeed in abolishing public single-sex education. The record contains a booklet that all first-year VMI students (the so-called "rats") were required to keep in their possession at all times. Near the end there appears the following period piece, entitled "The Code of a Gentleman":

> "Without a strict observance of the fundamental Code of Honor, no man, no matter how 'polished,' can be considered a gentleman. The honor of a gentleman demands the inviolability of his word, and the incorruptibility of his principles. He is the descendant of the knight, the crusader; he is the defender of the defense-less and the champion of justice or he is not a Gentleman.
>
> "A Gentleman . . .
>
> "Does not discuss his family affairs in public or with acquaintances.
>
> "Does not speak more than casually about his girl friend.
>
> "Does not go to a lady's house if he is affected by alcohol. He is temperate in the use of alcohol.
>
> "Does not lose his temper; nor exhibit anger, fear, hate, embarrassment, ardor or hilarity in public.
>
> "Does not hail a lady from a club window.
>
> "A gentleman never discusses the merits or demerits of a lady.
>
> "Does not mention names exactly as he avoids the mention of what things cost.

"Does not borrow money from a friend, except in dire need. Money borrowed is a debt of honor, and must be repaid as promptly as possible. Debts incurred by a deceased parent, brother, sister or grown child are assumed by honorable men as a debt of honor.

"Does not display his wealth, money or possessions.

"Does not put his manners on and off, whether in the club or in a ballroom. He treats people with courtesy, no matter what their social position may be.

"Does not slap strangers on the back nor so much as lay a finger on a lady.

"Does not 'lick the boots of those above' nor 'kick the face of those below' him on the social ladder.

"Does not take advantage of another's helplessness or ignorance and assumes that no gentleman will take advantage of him.

"A Gentleman respects the reserves of others, but demands that others respect those which are his.

"A Gentleman can become what he wills to be. . . ."

I do not know whether the men of VMI lived by this code; perhaps not. But it is powerfully impressive that a public institution of higher education still in existence sought to have them do so. I do not think any of us, women included, will be better off for its destruction.

[Justice THOMAS took no part in the case.]

Questions about the Case

1. Did Virginia demonstrate, as *Craig v. Boren* requires, a "substantial relationship" between its exclusion of women from VMI and its two goals of excellent education and diversity of educational choices? If not, what could it have done to prove this? (Doesn't Ginsburg's opinion suggest she would have ruled against VMI's male-only policy no matter what evidence Virginia had admitted? How does her interpretation of the *Craig* test lead her in this direction? What social background facts about men and women do you think led her to give the evidence introduced at the trial court level so little weight?)
2. Do you agree with Scalia that it was undemocratic for the Court to rule against VMI? In what sense was VMI's policy democratically decided? Why do you think Scalia ends his opinion with the "gentleman's code"?
3. Do you think the authors of the Fourteenth Amendment intended the equal protection clause to cover sale of 3.2 beer to male versus female customers? To cover admission to military academies? To cover sex issues at all, given that women did not have the vote when the amendment was passed? How much attention do the opinions in this case pay to these questions?

Chapter 6	**Law and Politics**

> *The ultimate goal is to break down the sense that legal argument is autonomous from moral, economic and political discourse.*
>
> —DUNCAN KENNEDY

> *When judges make law and scholars propose rules of law, they necessarily rely on their vision of society as it is and as it ought to be. If law is to be made well, those visions must be accurate and attractive.*
>
> —MARK TUSHNET

*T*his book stated in the beginning that to study legal reasoning is to study politics. The discussion since has touched on many obviously political issues—the common-law power of judges to make law, and the reasons why elected representatives so often make unclear statutes, to name just two. We have, however, focused principally on law and legal reasoning, on judicial "outputs" rather than political "inputs." The time has come to define politics and the connections between politics and law more precisely.

Let us begin by anticipating a potential source of confusion. We live in an age in which politics is a dirty word. Media coverage of the presidential contest between Al Gore and George W. Bush focused on the shortcomings of both candidates, and on the alienation and apathy that American election campaigns seem to foster. If we take our cue from the news media and define *politics* as the sum of all our grievances with public life—declining rates of political participation, the double-talk and self-serving double standards of elected representatives, the power of special interests over public policy—our proposal to connect legal reasoning and politics will surely confuse you. But this conception of politics is far too narrow. *Politics describes the many things we do in our public and collective lives to build and maintain communities.* According to this definition, politics is all around us, in schools, religious institutions, nonprofit agencies, even sports leagues. Once we define *politics* this broadly, we begin to see that people do politics both well and badly, just as people can do "love" and "religion" and many other things both well and badly.

LEGAL REASONING AS LIBERAL JUSTIFICATION

A Recap

Communities are groups of people who seek to work and play cooperatively and productively together. Communities come in all sizes, from families and clusters of "good neighbors" to states and nations—communities of strangers. Sometimes, and particularly in small groups with long histories, cooperation comes easily. People know the customs that bind each other. They trust each other not to cheat, and so

127

they trust the economic and social trades they make with each other. But as communities get larger, some people must rule others. Someone must use power to coerce those who have not cooperated either to become cooperative or to get out of the group. Here formal political institutions emerge—leaders with weapons, codes of rules and courts to enforce them, and so on.

Liberal political systems try to minimize the harm that rulers do to the ruled by imposing on the powerful the obligation to justify their use of power based on collective community good. No matter how shallow and uninformative the presidential debates between Al Gore and George W. Bush may have seemed, these debates nevertheless illustrate the importance of justification in our political culture. In the final presidential debate in Missouri, swing voters got to ask the two candidates virtually any question they wanted, and were able to judge the candidates on the adequacy of their answers.

Here enters legal reasoning. Our political system generates an immense quantity of legal texts—statutes, regulations, constitutional provisions, and the prior judicial opinions that we call *precedents*. These texts represent attempts to give communities rules by which people can live together. Yet inevitably from time to time these attempts fail, and social cooperation falters. A father wants to bring his son back to his family in Cuba, but some others in the family want the child to stay in the United States. A police officer holds a gun manufacturer responsible for selling assault weapons to the men who injured him, but the manufacturer believes it did nothing wrong. Election officials can't agree on how to count the votes in a presidential election. Or, as we shall soon see, a gay man who served for years in the Boy Scouts wants to remain in the organization, but Scout leaders feel that his open homosexuality is inconsistent with the group's traditional values. When conflicts like this arise, a judge is sometimes called in to arbitrate the dispute. And because we insist on justification in our legal culture, we do not simply permit judges to exercise their power by declaring their decisions. They must justify their solutions.

The judge's resolution of the conflict uses the legal texts as a starting point but not, as we have shown, the ending point. This is partly because words are ambiguous, and in a diverse society, people can understand them differently. But it's also because in law, as in life, no set of rules can cover every possible situation. To understand this point better, consider an analogy literary theorist Stanley Fish makes to the game of basketball:

> Suppose you were a basketball coach and taught someone how to shoot baskets and how to dribble the ball, but had imparted these skills without reference to the playing of an actual basketball game. Now you decide to insert your student into a game, and you equip him with some rules. You say to him, for instance, "Take only good shots." "What," he asks reasonably enough, "is a good shot?" "Well," you reply, "a good shot is an 'open shot,' a shot taken when you are close to the basket (so that the chances of success are good) and when your view is not obstructed by the harassing efforts of opposing players." Everything goes well until the last few seconds of the game; your team is behind by a single point; the novice player gets the ball in heavy traffic and holds it as the final buzzer rings. You run up to him and say, "Why didn't you shoot?" and he answers, "It wasn't a good shot." Clearly, the rule must be amended, and accordingly you tell him that if time is running out, and your team is behind, and you have the ball, you should take the shot even if it isn't a good one, because it will then *be* a good one in the sense of being the best shot in the circumstances. (Notice how both the meaning of the rule and the entities it covers are changing shape as this "education" proceeds.) Now suppose there is another game, and the same situation develops. This time the player takes the shot, which under the

circumstances is a very difficult one; he misses, and once again the final buzzer rings. You run up to him and say "Didn't you see that John (a teammate) had gone 'back door' and was perfectly positioned under the basket for an easy shot?" and he answers "But you said. . . ." Now obviously it would be possible once again to amend the rule, and just as obviously there would be no real end to the sequence and number of emendations that would be necessary. Of course, there will eventually come a time when the novice player (like the novice judge) will no longer have to ask questions; but it will not be because the rules have finally been made sufficiently explicit to cover all cases, but because explicitness will have been rendered unnecessary by a kind of knowledge that informs rules rather than follows from them.[1]

Legislatures, constitution makers, and judges who set precedents are each in the position of Fish's basketball coach, unable to anticipate every possible dispute that may arise under the rules they propound. That's why, as we have argued, they need judges to look beyond the words of legal texts if the law is to be effectively implemented. And that's also why judges must justify their decisions rather than simply announcing them.

Legal reasoning is the name we use to describe judges' justifications. This book argues that when a judicial opinion makes the four elements of legal reasoning fit plausibly together, the judicial writer has met his or her obligation to use judicial power the way our political culture expects. By implication we have argued as well that when judges harmonize the four elements—the facts of cases, the official legal texts, social background facts about the world in which we live, and norms widely shared in our polity—they *necessarily* create an image of a viable community. It is the job of this final chapter to explain why you should believe this.

Impartiality and Trust

Governing a large community, a group of total strangers who happen to live—often by the millions—in one city, state, or nation, is a difficult business. It is more difficult than, say, running General Motors or the Seattle Symphony for several reasons.

- The government's rules speak to the public, to the community, to everyone, in a way that General Motors' rules (or for that matter, the pope's rules) do not.
- The community is the greatest source of disruption and uncertainty in our lives because it exposes us to the work of strangers that we individually cannot control: crimes, nuclear wars, and changes in moral standards. The community is the place where people's psychological need for confidence in structure is greatest, for it is the one place that binds everyone, and beyond it we will find no social structure at all. The rules that the *government* makes and enforces must maintain confidence in structure—confidence that even strangers can share values.
- People need to maintain this confidence even when they cannot express precisely the "right" limit or value by which to judge a concrete situation.

The judicial process and legal reasoning therefore play a major part in preserving the confidence that the community can reconcile rules, facts of disputes, social conditions, and ethics. Our confidence does not rest entirely or immediately on the quality of legal reasoning, but the language of legal justification is one important means by which those who govern can reassure us that our communal life is "accurate and attractive." Unlike other social processes in and out of government, courts

[1]Stanley Fish, *"Fish v. Fiss,"* 36 *Stanford Law Review* 1325 (1984), pp. 1329–1330.

must make *some* decision—reach some closure on the problems litigants bring to them. Regardless of the wisdom of the solution, we need to believe that our community contains forums in which decision and action replace indecision and drift. In this book we have criticized many conventional practices, habits, and assumptions in legal reasoning precisely because good legal reasoning is so vital to the flourishing of communities. Reason in law must "break down the sense that legal argument is autonomous from moral, economic, and political discourse," or it will ultimately destroy our confidence in community.

Thus, the ethical view of the legal process holds that, despite its potentially infinite complexity and uncertainty, law must contain a method of applying the abstractions of law to human affairs. This does not require finding the perfect solution. It is much more important that the process attempt to reach acceptable reconciliations of facts, social conditions, laws, and ethical values. For this process to succeed, it is essential that we trust judges to speak for the community and not simply for the profession or for their personal gain. We must therefore shift our attention to the concepts of trust, impartiality, and judgment.

Impartial Judgment

Imagine yourself in each of these three situations:

1. *A midsummer afternoon in Wrigley Field.* The Cubs versus the Cardinals. You are calling balls and strikes behind home plate.
2. *A late Saturday night in Atlantic City in September.* You are judging the finals of the Miss America Pageant.
3. *Eight-thirty in the evening, in the home of your young family.* The children are squabbling. They appeal to you for judgment.
   Laurie: "Daddy, Robbie bit me!"
   Robbie: "I did not!"
   Laurie: "You did too! Look! Tooth marks!"
   Robbie: "But Dad! Laurie took my dime!"
   Laurie: "I took your dime cuz you stepped on my doll and broke it."
   Robbie: "But it was an accident, dum-dum."
   Laurie: "I am not a dum-dum, you fathead!"

Each of these situations calls for judgment. Each judge makes decisions that affect the claims of others, and he decides before an audience that has some expectations about how the judge should decide. Without necessarily determining what the judge should conclude, the audience knows what the judge should look at and will test the judgment against these expectations. Even a child seeking justice from a parent does so.

To judge is to decide the claims of others with reference to the expectations of an audience that define the process of decision. We shall see shortly where this definition leads in law. For the moment, consider what these three nonlegal judging situations do and do not have in common.

First and most important, notice that the three are not equally reasoned. Reasoning—defined as a choice that depends on calculations about future consequences—influences the umpire calling balls and strikes only indirectly. Occasionally, he may reflect on the fact that if he calls a pitch wrong, angry fans may pitch obscenities at him. Basically, however, he simply tries to fit physical—visual—evidence to a category, ball or strike, predetermined by some formula. He judges because the audience (baseball fans) has (have) specific expectations of how umpires should behave. In most households the parent, at the other extreme, cannot escape from making some calculation about the effects of his decision on the children, or at least on his own sanity.

The second difference is that rules do not equally affect all three situations. The umpire works with an elaborate set of written rules about baseball—most of which he commits to memory. He decides most questions literally in a second or less by applying the rules to the facts. In baseball, time is of the essence, which is why its rules are so elaborate. Additionally, baseball allows for precise rules because, as in most sports, we can pinpoint what matters to us in time and space.

On the other hand, we cannot define male or female beauty so precisely in time and space. Beauty contest judges exercise more discretion because their rules do not so precisely tell them what to seek.[2] Finally, the squabbling children may invoke no family rule at all. The family may have no regulation forbidding or punishing Robbie's toothy assault on his sister and his lie, and no conventions governing Laurie's theft or their gratuitous exchange of insults. Expectations, not precepts, create the need for judgment.

Third, these three kinds of judges have different opportunities to make rules for the future. The parent can explicitly respond to the squabble by announcing what is right and wrong and declaring his official policy for the future. Such a setting of limits may be precisely what the children hope the judge will do. But beauty contest judges may do so only informally and the umpires hardly at all, given audience expectations of their roles.

This definition and discussion of the nature of reason makes clear that not all reasoning is legal reasoning. Legal reasoning involves judgment—deciding the claims of others in front of some audience, before a "public." We have also seen, from the example of the home plate umpire in baseball, that not all judgment involves reason. Law therefore employs reasoned judgment, and we shall develop that concept momentarily. First, however, we must pin down that quality inherent in all judging, whether reasoned or not: impartiality.

Impartiality is not a mysterious concept. The *American Heritage Dictionary* defines *partial* as "pertaining to only part; not total; incomplete." To decide impartially is to leave the final decision open until all the relevant information is received. It means that the information—the placement of the pitch, the beauty contestant's stage performance, and the children's actual behavior—rather than a personal affection or preference for one "party" determines the result.[3]

While impartiality is not itself a difficult concept—we have all judged and been judged in our lives—it is often difficult for audiences to satisfy themselves that judges actually decide impartially. Initially a judge may succeed if her mistakes

---

[2]There is another interesting difference: With rare exceptions, when he calls the game on account of rain or ejects an ornery manager or player, the umpire has minimal control over who wins. But the beauty contest judges *declare* the winner. This differential effect on the outcome explains why we have only one home plate umpire but several judges in contests of beauty and on our appellate courts. (Notice that when the umpire does make discretionary calls, he is also more likely to consult other umpires than when he calls balls and strikes.)

[3]Empirical research on how jurors in trials think builds on a very similar definition of impartiality. These studies document the frequency with which jurors close their minds and refuse to admit new facts, sometimes long before a trial ends. These jurors don't come to court biased for one side. They simply jump to a conclusion and thereafter don't listen to the other parts of the argument. They are partial in just that sense. Effective trial lawyers know how to keep minds open: They tell stories. Jurors then have a framework for knowing what facts are missing, just as all of us do when we read or hear a story and stay alert waiting for the final clues to fall into place. See "Study Finds Jurors Often Hear Evidence with Closed Minds," *New York Times*, 29 November 1994, p. B5.

cancel out, if her decisions randomly favor both sides equally. But the loser, being the loser, will probably not take a balanced count of errors. The judge's only long-range security, therefore, is to care about and try as best she can to *fulfill the expectations of judgment that the audience imposes.*

To judge is to be judged. The argument assumes, of course, that audiences can, in fact, distinguish their expectations of the process of decision from their hopes that one side—their side!—will win. Your authors are convinced that people can do so, though we rely more on our experiences as sports fans, employees, teachers, and family members than we do on psychological experimentation. Teams can lose championships, employees can receive poor assignments, students can receive disappointing grades, and children can be ordered to wash the dishes, all without doubting that the judges have decided impartially.

Professor Robert Cover has written:

> The critical dimension of the rule of law is not the degree of specificity with which an actor is constrained, but the very fact that the actor must look outside his own will for criteria of judgment. There is a difference—intelligible to most pre-adolescents—between the directions "Do what you want" and "Do what you think is right or just."[4]

To "look outside his own will for criteria of judgment": If we have any single key to legal judgment, it is here.

To judge is to decide the claims of others before an audience. The judgmental decision need not be reasoned, as the umpire's calling of pitches reveals. But judgmental decisions must be impartial, which means in the end they must, to appear impartial, conform to audience expectations of the process of decision.

In law, as in all contexts in which judging takes place, the audience can never know for sure why the judge decided as he did. It cannot see inside a judge's head. That is why the legal audience is so concerned with the way an appellate judge justifies her decision, because it is the only visible evidence of the judge's impartiality. What criteria will a legal audience use to assess the impartiality of an appellate judge? To answer that question, we must determine the legal audience's expectations of the appellate process. But that has already been done in this book: We believe that the audience of law expects the process to reassure it that society can reconcile and harmonize facts, rules, social conditions, and moral values. This is the test of judicial impartiality and hence of reason in law. When judges explain their results in judicial opinions, they must attempt to convince readers that the result does *not* depend on inaccurate characterization of the facts in the case, does *not* depend on false assumptions about social conditions, does *not* depend upon a tortured reading of a rule, and does *not* depend on an ethical judgment that the community of readers would reject. The result need not please everyone, but that is not the point. Judges cannot and need not discover one right solution that everyone somehow believes best. They convince us of their impartiality as long as they convince us that they have attempted to describe these four elements accurately. We expect law judges, unlike umpires, to engage in *reasoned* judgment when they do so.

---

[4]Robert Cover, book review of R. Berger, *Government by Judiciary, New Republic,* January 14, 1978, p. 27. Two essays in which judges vigorously defended the impartiality of the appellate courts are Harry T. Edwards's "Public Misperceptions Concerning the Politics of Judging," 56 *Colorado Law Review* 619 (1985), and Patricia Wald's "Thoughts on Decisionmaking," 87 *West Virginia Law Review* 1 (1984). And see the Australian film *Breaker Morant,* a powerful essay on the politicization of the judicial process.

Let us here anticipate and resolve two practical problems that often bother alert readers at this stage of the argument. The first problem arises because readers of judicial opinions, reading often many years after the litigation happened, never learn even a small fraction of what the judges and attorneys actually know about a case. How, you may ask, can we ever know if judges who make a coherent and well-harmonized argument are in fact radically falsifying the key facts of the case, or deliberately ignoring a powerful set of legal texts that could justify a very different result?

Well, judges who disagree with a decision made by a majority of their colleagues do write dissenting opinions. Judges must persuade each other that their reasoning is plausible. And in celebrated cases newspapers, magazines, radio, and television provide robust forums for criticism. But at a deeper level preoccupation with this problem misses the boat. The political good that good legal reasoning serves is not the same thing as "getting the right result," either in a technical legal sense or in a social justice sense. As you know by now, there is usually no technically correct legal result, and one person's social justice is another's social folly. As intelligent critical readers of judicial opinions, we have every right to demand that the writer spell out clearly what the four elements are in the case and how his or her solution harmonizes them. We have every right to protest that when judicial writers don't do this, they fail us politically.[5] But here the work of legal reasoning ends and other criteria for evaluating results, criteria like our own political and ethical preferences, take over. We don't need to know a complete biography of an artist or composer to evaluate their paintings or symphonies. Judicial opinions stand on their own as do works of art like these.

The second practical problem is that only an infinitesimal number of people in a state or nation read appellate opinions. How can we argue that judges must build and maintain trust and impartiality by performing for an audience that is by definition very large and almost totally ignorant of the very performances we're talking about? Doesn't history show us that the actual political reaction to controversial cases depends on whose ox got gored? We have three responses to this troublesome problem. First and foremost, judges must try to persuade the parties, and particularly the losers, that the results are impartial. But these parties do come from, and share understandings of facts and values in common with, the larger and ignorant audience. In writing for "the people," judges will more likely write justly for the parties than if judges write exclusively for legal professionals in obscure legalese. Second, over time on issues that concern many, the word tends, slowly, to get out. Anthony Lewis's now-classic book, *Gideon's Trumpet*,[6] did much to explain and justify the reasoning behind extending constitutional protections to the accused. Conversely, *Roe*, the first abortion case, which was widely criticized for its unconvincing reasoning, might have forestalled so much of the subsequent litigation had it constructed a clearer and more coherent statement of what the right of privacy did and did not entail and why. And, of course, the Supreme Court's legal reasoning in *Bush v. Gore* was the stuff of television talk shows and newspaper headlines. Finally, we think preoccupation with public ignorance also misses a mark. It's a free country, and cures for the problem of ignorance may be worse than the disease. Legal reasoning is not the most important thing in politics, but it should have integrity—it should communicate constructively—in its own political sphere, just as the Federal

[5]We believe, for example, that the majority opinion in *Bush v. Gore* failed the nation (see Appendix B).
[6]Anthony Lewis, *Gideon's Trumpet* (New York: Random House, 1964).

Reserve Board, whose secretive decisions profoundly affect all our economic lives, should act with integrity.

The Value of Impartiality

What evidence might confirm that lawyers and judges actually share these values of impartiality? In a fascinating assessment of the 1992 United States Supreme Court term, Linda Greenhouse of the *New York Times* identified the unassuming Justice David Souter as the emerging leader of the coalition of justices at the center of the Court. She explained his leadership this way:

> Court observers on both ends of the political spectrum have noted that Justice Souter, much more than most judges, tends to acknowledge the weight of opposing arguments and to discuss and defend his own choices from among competing rationales.[7]

According to Greenhouse, David Souter's trustworthiness, not the political acceptability of his results, accounted for his leadership. More importantly, this is just as it should be. If legal reasoning matters politically because it convinces us that we and the judge belong to the same community, then legal reasoning should build trust in the integrity of leaders, not conviction about the correctness of the outcome.

In contrast to Justice Souter, Ronald Dworkin argues that Justice Scalia's reasoning in *Casey*, the case in which the majority reaffirmed the basic holding in *Roe*, loses our trust precisely because he fails to harmonize the four elements of legal reasoning effectively.

> Scalia, in his own partial dissent, makes even plainer his contempt for the view that the Constitution creates a system of principle. He reaches the conclusion that abortion is not a liberty protected by the Constitution, he says, "not because of anything so exalted as my views concerning the 'concept of existence, of meaning of the universe, and of the mystery of human life'" but "because of two simple facts: (1) The Constitution says absolutely nothing about it, and (2) the long-standing traditions of American society have permitted it to be legally proscribed." Scalia's flat assertion that the Constitution says nothing about abortion begs the question, of course. The Fourteenth Amendment does explicitly forbid states to abridge liberty without due process of law, and the question, in this case as in any other case involving that clause, is whether the state legislation in question does in fact do exactly that. If it does, then the Constitution does say something about it: the Constitution forbids it. The majority argues that if we accept the principles that underlie past Supreme Court decisions everyone accepts, we must also accept that forbidding abortion before viability denies liberty without due process. Scalia says nothing at all that undermines or even challenges that claim.
>
> So Scalia's entire argument depends on his assertion that since a majority of states had outlawed abortion before the Fourteenth Amendment was adopted, it would be wrong to interpret the due process clause as denying them the power to do so now. He refuses to consider whether laws outlawing abortion, no matter how popular they were or are, offend other, more general principles of liberty that are embedded in the Constitution's abstract language and in the Court's past decisions. He dis-

---

[7]"Souter: Unlikely Anchor at Court's Center," *New York Times*, 3 July 1992, pp. A1 and A12. Souter's reclusive and scholarly lifestyle has been compared to that of Benjamin Cardozo. See Richard Posner, *Cardozo: A Study in Reputation* (Chicago: University of Chicago Press, 1990). Also linking candor and trustworthiness, see Shapiro, "In Defense of Judicial Candor," 100 *Harvard Law Review* 731 (1987) and Ginsburg, "Remarks on Writing Separately," 65 *Washington Law Review* 133 (1990).

dains inquiries of that character because, he says, they involve "value judgments." Of course they do. How can any court enforce the abstract moral command of the Constitution that states may not violate fundamental liberties, without making judgments about "values"? Judges have had to make such judgments since law began.[8]

Justice Scalia's opinions, though elegant, often seem bitter and dismissive. Not only is the other side wrong, he seems to say, but its view is utter nonsense, unworthy of any consideration. Though Scalia's style amuses those who come to his opinions already in agreement with him, it is unlikely to reassure the losing party of his impartiality.

Here is a more recent example of the importance of the legal audience in judging. Justice Stephen Breyer, appointed by President Clinton to the Supreme Court in the summer of 1994, has received very positive "reviews" from both the bar and the popular press. A self-described nonideological pragmatist, Breyer believes passionately in his responsibility to communicate clearly. Not long after he first took a lower position on the federal bench, he decided never to use footnotes in his opinions. In a 1995 interview he elaborated:

> Sometimes it's awkward to use none at all, but if in fact you even use one, then you cannot make the point. And it is an important point to make if you believe, as I do, that the major function of an opinion is to explain to the audience of readers why it is that the Court has reached that decision.
>
> It's not to prove that you're right: you can't prove you're right, there is no such proof. And it's not to create an authoritative law review on the subject. Others are better doing that than I.
>
> It is to explain as clearly as possible and as simply as possible what the reasons are for reaching this decision. Others can then say those are good reasons or those are bad reasons. If you see the opinion in this way, either a point is sufficiently significant to make, in which case it should be in the text, or it is not, in which case, don't make it.[9]

Our culture reveals the same standard of integrity in many different settings beyond the law. In science, Richard Feynman has written that the ideal is

> a kind of scientific integrity, a principle of scientific thought that corresponds to a kind of utter honesty—a kind of leaning over backwards. For example, if you're doing an experiment, you should report everything that you think might make it invalid, not only what you think is right about it.[10]

We must next ask whether laypeople, those outside the legal system, also value these qualities. What evidence supports the position that trustworthiness (as opposed to, say, economic self-interest) influences political attitudes and behavior? In his book *Why People Obey the Law*, Professor Tom Tyler concludes that people obey

---

[8]Ronald Dworkin, "The Center Holds," *New York Review of Books*, August 13, 1992, pp. 29–33, 32.

[9]"In Justice Breyer's Opinion, A Footnote Has No Place," *New York Times*, 28 July 1995, p. B13. Compare this statement by legal scholar and Seventh Circuit Court of Appeals Judge Richard A. Posner, an appointee of Ronald Reagan:

> Judges have a terrible anxiety about being thought to base their opinions on guesses, on their personal views. To allay that anxiety, they rely on the apparatus of precedent and history, much of it extremely phony. I do think judges can and should get away with a lot more candor . . . [Linda Greenhouse, "In His Opinion," *New York Times Book Review*, 26 September 1999, Section 7, p. 14.]

[10]Quoted by Philip J. Hilts, "The Science Mob," *The New Republic*, May 18, 1992, p. 24 at p. 31.

the law primarily for noneconomic reasons. People do not comply because compliance costs them less. Rather, Tyler concludes they do so when they approve of the moral position the law takes and when they feel law is procedurally fair. The perception that the law is fair—and hence the willingness to comply—depends not on winning or losing, but on such moral factors as whether people trust the system to hear their arguments.[11]

Similarly, Scott Barclay concludes in *An Appealing Act: Why People Appeal in Civil Cases* that litigants decide to appeal a trial court decision not so much based on their prospect of winning in the appeal court, but rather because they felt they were treated unfairly and disrepectfully in the lower court. Even knowing they had a very small chance of having the trial court decision overturned, the appellants in Barclay's study still chose to go ahead. They thought the lower-court judges did not focus on the relevant issues and did not understand their claims, and in some cases had treated them rudely. They wanted their "day in court," a chance to tell the appellate judges how badly they had been treated in the lower court. The four losing litigants in the study who felt that the trial court was fair decided not to appeal.[12]

Applying the Theory

Let us now apply this theory of legal reasoning to some of the cases this book has applauded and some this book has criticized.

Consider first the *Prochnow* blood test case at the end of Chapter 1. We are tempted to condemn the case for flying in the face of science: The court reached a result that we all know couldn't be true. If so, we would be criticizing the case for its failure to harmonize the social background facts in the case. But the difficulties with the *Prochnow* opinion go deeper. If the opinion means to tell us that juries should be free to speculate on whether God or nature or some hidden force temporarily suspended the laws of science, the opinion should have addressed that claim head on. Such a principle would revolutionize our entire notion of how law works, for if a jury verdict based on speculations about God's will can stand, a jury can find anything it wants, and no appellate court would ever overturn a jury verdict for being inconsistent with the weight of the evidence.

We have seen another less supernatural and more plausible explanation for the *Prochnow* result. Perhaps the legislature favored fatherhood so strongly that it authorized juries to disregard science for the sake of allowing children to grow up with fathers. It might have done this in part to protect children who would otherwise be labeled illegitimate—a real disadvantage at that time. But if that was the basis on which the court acted, it should have said so, partly to give the legislature a chance to react if the court had misread the statute, and partly to explain why, if the statutory purpose was to protect children, the legislature had authorized blood tests in the first place. The majority opinion read the statute legalistically, that is, without attention to the other three elements in legal reasoning. It said the words of the statute make the tests admissible but not conclusive; therefore, the law allows juries

[11]Tom R. Tyler, *Why People Obey the Law* (New Haven: Yale University Press, 1990). In his most recent book, Tyler argues that judges and police officers can best improve compliance with the law by acting in ways that increase social trust in the legal system. See Tom R. Tyler and Yuen J. Huo, *Trust and the Rule of Law* (New Haven: Yale University Press, 2001). And see Peggy Noonan's *Present at the Creation*, which links Ronald Reagan's political success to the public's trust in him.

[12]Scott Barclay, *An Appealing Act: Why People Appeal in Civil Cases* (Evanston: Northwestern University Press, American Bar Foundation, 1999).

to disregard the tests. Instead it could have harmonized all four elements by saying, "We know all about science, and we know the blood tests in this case are incompatible. We admit that no evidence in the trial contradicted the blood tests, but we read the purpose of this law to favor paternity and we believe this value is widely shared in the community." That reasoning would give us a coherent vision of the community that we can discuss and seek to sustain or change. Instead the majority implies that we live in a confusing and unknowable world in which anything can happen, one in which we can't trust either science or God or the conventional trial court methods of fact-finding.

The legal reasoning of *Repouille v. the United States* also fails. Here a clear precedent stated law that seemed to apply directly to the case. The *Francioso* opinion said that the naturalization decision should rest on judgments about the person seeking naturalization, a generalized inquiry into the person's life and the particularities of the moral decisions the applicant has made. Yet in *Repouille* Learned Hand did quite the opposite, moving away from the facts of the applicant's life and resting his decision instead on the morality of euthanasia in the abstract. The reasoning in *Repouille* leads us to believe that law doesn't matter. It increases our mistrust.

We do not argue that *Prochnow* and *Repouille* "came out wrong." We argue that the results were not well reasoned or justified. A different opinion could have persuasively justified the result each case reached, but the opinions we read fail to do so. They are incoherent. They only confuse lawyers who must advise future clients with similar cases—confuse and thereby perhaps encourage litigation when law should instead encourage cooperation. Worse, they leave lay readers with the suspicion that those with power over them have lied to them.

You should, we hope, be able to see in each of the cases that this book has criticized one or more of the four elements that were not harmonized. The evidence introduced in trial about baseball in *Toolson* made a strong case that baseball was a business in interstate commerce that monopolized the sport. Why does the Court ignore that evidence? In *Lochner,* the bakers' hours case, the Court ignored the social background evidence that baking was unhealthy. *Repouille* ignores a legal rule created by precedent. The majority in *Fox v. Snow* ignored the ethical value of carrying out the hopes of those who write wills, and so on.

We should, of course, turn this analysis on the cases these pages have applauded. For example, *Hynes,* the diving board case, harmonizes (1) the fact in Harvey's case that the wire might have killed him had he been a swimmer lawfully using the river, and the fact that the railroad had not maintained the wires and poles; (2) the social background fact that property boundaries become increasingly hard to know and learn as life becomes more complex, urban, and interconnected; (3) a plausible reading of the thrust of the *Hoffman* and *Beck* precedents; (4) the deeply ethical value that law should promote cooperation—that the law of tort ought to encourage the railroad to prevent the dangerous wires it owns and controls from injuring others.

LEGAL REASONING AS A PUBLIC LANGUAGE

This book has emphasized the principle that law does not—and indeed cannot—provide objectively certain and correct answers to legal problems. For the same reasons, all inquiry—scientific and philosophical as well as legal—never gets to the true bottom of things. The first chapter of this book quoted a dust-jacket description of *Inventing Reality,* which said that we do not discover the physical world, we invent good ways of talking about the world. "Reality" exists in this talk that we invent.

Our political language invents our communities in much the same ways that scientific language invents physical reality and religious language invents spiritual reality. The proposition that people find reality in and through their language is hardly a unique product of postmodernism. Aristotle's *Rhetoric* and *Poetics* hint in this direction. Shaw's play *Pygmalion*—from which *My Fair Lady* became one of the most successful musicals in the history of musical theater—starts with the same premise. The works of Murray Edelman have described how language constructs political reality with special clarity.[13]

Legal reasoning is an important political language that helps invent our geographical communities. A century ago legal language, as we have seen, helped invent a community that drastically undermined the public sphere and the capacity of government to regulate the excesses of capitalism. As we step back for a final overview of legal reasoning, we shall examine how legal talk indicates both where we have been and where we may be heading.

Many books have been written about how language and narrative constructs reality, and we can only sample the phenomenon here. Much conventional research in cognitive psychology supports this perspective. It seems that all of us need to fit information into some kind of story, narrative, or drama before it makes sense to us.[14] This perspective also rests very much in the mainstream of social and political philosophy at the beginning of the twenty-first century. In fact, this view "harmonizes" a surprisingly large number of perspectives, including those in legal theory. Starting in the 1970s, critical legal scholars did much to debunk the legal profession's claim to unique insights into truth.[15]

New pragmatists, particularly Richard Rorty and Richard Bernstein, have helped fill the space created by this critical debunking. Pragmatism, as originally developed by William James and John Dewey and elaborated by Rorty and Bernstein, recognizes that for millennia people have killed each other for the sake of a doctrine or ideology that they claim to be absolutely true. In the 1990s, the horrors of "ethnic cleansing" in Bosnia, which pits Muslims and different Christian sects against one another, reminds us powerfully of the evils that pragmatic liberalism tries to overcome. The tragic deaths of the Branch Davidian cult members in Waco, Texas, in 1993 fits the same pattern. In the vein of classical liberal philosophy, pragmatism downplays the importance of ideology. It emphasizes instead that language and experience, not doctrine, should shape our beliefs and actions; and that human cooperation depends on continuously learning from experience, rather than applying abstract rules and principles dogmatically.[16] In 1985 and again in 1990, the

---

[13]See his *Constructing the Political Spectacle* (Chicago: University of Chicago Press, 1988).

[14]See, for example, Nancy Pennington and Reid Hastie, "A Cognitive Theory of Juror Decision Making: The Story Model," 13 *Cardozo Law Review* 519 (1991) and "Jurors Hear Evidence and Turn It into Stories," *New York Times*, 12 May 1992, p. B5, quoting Professor Pennington: "People don't listen to all the evidence and then weigh it at the end. They process it as they go along, composing a continuing story throughout the trial that makes sense of what they're hearing." In their research on everyday legal consciousness, Patricia Ewick and Susan S. Silbey emphasize the importance of narrative. See Ewick and Silbey, "Subversive Stories and Hegemonic Tales: Toward a Sociology of Narrative," 29 *Law and Society Review* 197–226 (1995); and *The Common Place of Law* (Chicago: University of Chicago Press, 1998).

[15]See Rogers Smith, "After Criticism: An Analysis of the Critical Legal Studies Movement," in Michael McCann and Gerald Houseman, eds., *Judging the Constitution* (Chicago: Scott Foresman, 1989), pp. 92–124.

[16]See, for example, Rorty's "Philosophy without Principles," in W. J. T. Mitchell, ed., *Against Theory* (Chicago: University of Chicago Press, 1985) and Bernstein's *Beyond Objectivism and Relativism* (Philadelphia: University of Pennsylvania Press, 1983) and *Philosophical Profiles* (Cambridgeshire: Polity Press, 1986). And see Michael Perry, *Love and Power* (New York and Oxford: Oxford University Press, 1991), especially Chapter 4.

Southern California Law Review published long symposium issues discussing many of the pragmatic elements in legal reasoning.[17] Yet these developments in contemporary legal theory may simply elaborate on the conclusion reached earlier by one of the twentieth century's most admired legal philosophers, Lon Fuller.

> If I were asked . . . to discern one central indisputable principle of what may be called substantive natural law . . . I would find it in the injunction: Open up, maintain and preserve the integrity of the channels of communication.[18]

Before examining these upcoming samples of legal language as it invents and reflects communities, we need to anticipate another potential source of confusion. This book has emphasized that even though we cannot demonstrate conclusively that certain legal answers are correct, we can distinguish between better and worse legal arguments, and we can talk about why we take the positions we do. The "harmonized" views in contemporary philosophy just summarized agree with that position, but they also make a more disturbing point. If our rhetoric defines our community, then *all* forms of legal justification are politically potent and significant. The dominant patterns of legal reasoning and rhetoric do not necessarily take us in desirable directions. Hence this final section examines the moralistic legal and political rhetoric of a prior era. It then asks you to contrast that rhetoric with a sample from our own day.

Law and Moralistic Communities: The Mann Act Revisited

Recall from the last chapter how, in 1893, Justice David Brewer defended the role of the judiciary "to restrain the greedy hand of the many from filching from the few that which they have honestly acquired" (p. 114). This is an example of moralism, a dogmatic certainty that simple rules—in this case that one should benefit from one's one work—resolve all disputes in all circumstances at all times. Moralism can be seen as the opposite of pragmatism, because it ignores the complexity of experience and rests instead on absolute rules.[19] Brewer's moralistic rhetoric captures not merely one side of a political issue; it describes a common fabric of custom and popular beliefs—one that many today would find racist, sexist, and unacceptably intolerant. This kind of legal rhetoric transcended liberal or conservative positions. Justice Harlan, dissenting from *Plessy v. Ferguson*'s separate but equal holding in 1896, spoke this way:

> The white race deems itself the dominant race in this country. And so it is, in prestige, in achievements, in education, in wealth and in power. So, I doubt not, it will continue to be for all time, if it remains true to its heritage. . . . But in view of the Constitution, . . . [t]here is no caste here. Our Constitution is color-blind, and neither knows nor tolerates classes among citizens. . . . The humblest is the peer of the most powerful.

---

[17]"Symposium on Interpretation," 58 *Southern California Law Review* (1985) and "Symposium on the Renaissance of Pragmatism in American Legal Thought," 63 *Southern California Law Review*, no. 6 (1990).

[18]*The Morality of Law* (New Haven: Yale University Press, 1964), p. 186. See also Peter Teachout's superb analysis of Fuller's jurisprudence in "The Soul of the Fugue: An Essay on Reading Fuller," 70 *Minnesota Law Review* 1073 (1986).

[19]If you are having trouble with this definition, you might consider tuning into "Ask Dr. Laura," the popular radio advice program hosted by Laura Schlessinger, who personifies moralism. When a listener struggling with a messy personal dilemma calls in, "Dr. Laura" usually responds with a simple, absolute rule that neatly resolves the situation, often in less than a minute. "Dr. Laura" can do this because the details of the listener's dilemma and the complexity of the listener's problems are irrelevant to a moralist, for whom absolute, unquestioned rules vanquish the uncertainties and ambiguities of life.

Justice Harlan reaches a "liberal" result, but starts with a moralistic certainty: that the white "race" is absolutely superior. This premise goes hand in glove with his moral reading of the equal protection clause. In other words, the language of moral absolutes that Harlan employs to support his interpretation of the Fourteenth Amendment also serves to suggest that racial differences are obvious and real.

But how do we know that moralistic rhetoric pervaded political culture generally? Because we have spent some considerable time on the Mann Act cases, we will return to the political context in which those cases arose. Prepare for a surprise or two—early Mann Act cases were headline-making national moral scandals.

The Mann Act prosecution in 1912–1914 of heavyweight boxing champion Jack Johnson, the first black champion (who had defeated "the Great White Hope" Jim Jeffries in 1910) set the tone. Johnson had paid for a girlfriend to travel from Pittsburgh to Chicago to meet him. She was white, and the appellate court implied that their racial differences converted their sexual relationship into "debauchery."

The prosecutions of Drew Caminetti and his friend, Maury Diggs—which, unlike Johnson's case, made it to the Supreme Court—were even more sensational, for both defendants were the sons of well-known Democratic politicians (Caminetti's father was U.S. Commissioner of Immigration under President Woodrow Wilson) prosecuted by a Republican U.S. attorney. Attempts were made to postpone the trial of what one Democrat called a "little fornication case from California." But Republicans forced the prosecution with rhetoric like this: "It has long been believed by the masses that there is one kind of law for the rich and the politically powerful in this country and another kind of law for the poor, the friendless, and the weak." Here are the facts.[20]

Maury Diggs and Drew Caminetti, both married men with children, publicly chased Marsha Warrington and Lola Norris, working girls with high-school degrees. The men seemed at the time to use their political connections to flaunt conventional morality.

The girls admittedly engaged in scandalous excursions with full knowledge of Diggs's and Caminetti's marital status and of the potential (and threatening) repercussions. Diggs and Caminetti enjoyed the company of the girls frequently, both publicly and privately. The couples met three or four times a week, sometimes more. They took off on numerous Saturday evening automobile rides and made stops at taverns where Diggs and Caminetti would buy drinks and bring them out to the girls. They also made trips to roadhouses, where they danced. And there was a stop in Stockton, where Maury rented a room or a cottage for just a few hours. But in her testimony, Lola said, "Nothing wrong occurred there." On their last excursion before making the trip across state lines to Reno, Marsha informed Diggs that she was pregnant with his child. But it was not until they made the trip to a bungalow in Reno that Lola had intercourse with Caminetti.

Civil suits and criminal prosecution against the four were threatened. The girls faced charges of "alienating their (the wives') husbands' affections" and being named as corespondents in divorce actions. The girls, still minors, feared the juvenile courts and "reform school." As rumors began to flare, Marsha's father went so far as to say if he ever found Diggs with his daughter he would kill them both. Ultimately, a policeman advised Diggs to leave town because their affairs had become common knowledge.

[20]This account follows that of Robert L. Anderson, *The Diggs-Caminetti Case* (Lewiston, N.Y.: E. Mellen Press, 1990).

Lola and Marsha finally agreed to leave with Diggs and Caminetti. Diggs and Caminetti both promised to divorce their wives and marry the girls. In their testimony, Lola and Marsha argued they really didn't want to go to Reno, but they had no choice given the situation.

Shortly after the trip to Reno, Diggs was brought under investigation for an incident involving a bad check. It didn't take long for the scandal involving Diggs and Lola to come under investigation as well. Shortly thereafter, charges were brought against Maury Diggs and Drew Caminetti under the Mann Act. A trial date was set for early May. The moralistic rhetoric that constituted the community at the turn of the century was about to convert a local act of adultery into a national scandal.

Commissioner Caminetti sent a recommendation from Washington that the cases be postponed for two weeks and that the trial not be set until May 19. He wanted to be present at the trial. However, during the interim between May 5 and May 19, a similar conviction was handed down for Jack Johnson. Commissioner Caminetti also requested a conference with U.S. Attorney John L. McNab.

The Republican McNab was "confident" that the cases fell under federal jurisdiction. McNab had been described as "one of the ablest lawyers and jurists in California." A local newspaper captioned McNab as: "The fighting and tireless bulldog who will prosecute Diggs and Caminetti." Nevertheless, fear had been expressed by some local citizens that Diggs and Caminetti might "escape justice." But McNab dictated the following response to the local newspaper:

> There will be no delay in the prosecution of this case. The U.S. District Attorney's office has taken charge of this prosecution and will conduct it to a finish. Those who ridicule the prosecution of these men know little or nothing of the precision and effectiveness of the Federal Court. Enough facts are already in my possession to send both of these men to the penitentiary. Under the evidence in my possession, that is where I expect to see them land.

To no one's surprise, the conference requested by Caminetti never took place, lending even more evidence to suspicions of his political motives. After the Johnson decision was handed down, yet another wire was sent to McNab, this time from Attorney General McReynolds. The Democratic attorney general requested a further delay of the Caminetti trial and asked for information regarding the case. McNab was again forced, against his recommendations, to move the trial date back to July 26th. Coincidentally, the attorney general sent yet another order to McNab. McNab was instructed to postpone the trial until autumn.

Representative Mann summed up the situation in an address to the House in late June: ". . . the present Commissioner General [Caminetti] has used both political and official influence to prevent his son from being brought to a speedy trial under the Mann Act for one of the more horrible of the offenses, the ruination of a young girl." Apparently it was an influence that an idealistic servant of justice like McNab could not stomach, and perhaps rightly so. U.S. Attorney John McNab submitted his letter of resignation shortly thereafter. He was driven from his position "for objecting to corrupt and inexcusable delay." McNab could no longer fulfill his responsibilities in the judicial "system"—a system stagnated in his view by political interference and corruption.

McNab was arguably justified in submitting his letter of resignation to both McReynolds and President Wilson. He had already informed the Department of Justice that attempts had been made to corrupt the government witnesses. Maury Diggs had made several attempts to influence the testimony of Lola and Marsha.

And the friends of the defendants publicly boasted that the wealth and political influence of Caminetti and Diggs would stay McNab's hand through influence at Washington. The friends of the defendants repeatedly stated that they could "easily fix the case" and that they had too much influence at their command to cause them to worry. McNab insisted that McReynolds had postponed the cases until autumn "with absolute indifference to the rights of this office and the honor of the Department of Justice."

McNab also sent a lengthy statement of resignation to the president reflecting his disgust with the situation in graphic detail: "In these cases two girls were taken from cultured homes, bullied and frightened, in the face of their protests, into going into a foreign state, were ruined and debauched by the defendants, who abandoned their wives and infants to commit the crime." McNab insisted Maury Diggs and Drew Caminetti were indicted for a "hideous crime, which had ruined two respectable homes and shocked the moral sense of the people of California." The district attorney reportedly said that Diggs and Caminetti had to be rushed secretly from the train and rushed into Sacramento by automobile "to avoid lynching by enraged citizens."

The scandal of the Caminetti case continued to steal the headlines, but they were no longer focused on lurid romantic interludes. Now the presidential administration and the Department of Justice were commanding the press. Political battles erupted in the House as Representative Mann launched a heated attack on the Democratic Party and President Wilson. Mann called for the removal of Commissioner Caminetti for using both political and official influence to prevent his son from being brought to a speedy trial under the Mann Act. Mann also insisted the president was interfering with upholding of the law. Mann's moral indignation contradicted his prior statement that the bill's purpose was not to interfere with the police power of the states and that it was not an attempt to regulate sexual behavior. Mann now referred to the bill in a speech to the House as "a great moral reform law." Mann also revealed in a speech: " . . . you cannot always divine motives of people. A man might be prosecuted under the law for transporting a woman, when the question of money did not enter in it at all."

You know how the *Caminetti* case came out. The majority opinion by Justice Day insisted that the words of the Mann Act plainly included the immorality involved here. In moralistic tones, Justice Day wrote that it "would shock the common understanding of what constitutes an immoral purpose" to hold that "furnishing transportation in order that a woman may be debauched, or become a mistress or a concubine" did not violate the Mann Act.[21]

Even the dissenters, who insisted that the Mann Act only applied to sexual pleasures that men purchased, wrote, "Any measure that protects the purity of women from assault or enticement to degradation finds an instant advocate in our best emotions. . . ." The dissenters suggested that the majority had failed law's internal moral test: Instead of considering and deciding "with poise of mind," the majority had yielded "to emotion. . . ."[22]

This history suggests many fascinating intersections between law and politics. Political loyalties and partisan infighting may influence the decision to prosecute. The personal values of the participants inevitably shape their perceptions of justice and fairness. The process that nominates and appoints judges and public officials generally will shift the direction the law takes, and so on. But the main political

[21]242 U.S. 470 at 486.
[22]242 U.S. 470 at 501–502.

message runs broader and deeper. Moralistic rhetoric at one time dominated American culture. Law both reflected and encouraged moralism.

How much has the United States changed since *Caminetti*? You may already be struck by the parallels between this case and the Monica Lewinsky impeachment scandal. Both cases started with a violation of sexual morality. For President Clinton it was his (alleged) vulgar propositioning of Paula Jones and White House assignations with Monica Lewinsky; for Caminetti and Diggs, it was their affair with the teenage girls. In both cases it was unclear whether the initial violation of morality was really a violation of law—many thought Jones' sexual harassment suit was legally questionable, just as others found the Mann Act prosecution of Caminetti and Diggs misguided. Both cases grew to became even larger scandals when the initial legal proceeding—Jones's suit against Clinton, Caminetti and Diggs's prosecution—was in some way interfered with by the misconduct of public officials. In Clinton's case, the interference took the form of misleading statements he gave to the court about his involvement with Lewinsky. In the *Caminetti* case, it was political influence that stalled the prosecution.

And yet there is a big difference in the outcome: in the Clinton case, moralism lost out. The president was impeached by the House, but the Senate voted not to remove him from office. The President's poll ratings rose, indicating that the great majority of Americans separated his performance in office from the misdeeds he had committed. And even those who favored impeachment declared that they were responding not to Clinton's sexual misdeeds, but to his attempt to derail the legal system through lies and the organization of a cover-up.[23] The contrast between the Caminetti and Lewinsky scandals suggest that while moralism still seems attractive to many people, it no longer dominates us. We live in a time when moralistic views compete with pragmatic judgments, and judges must take both into account. In the next section we consider the consequences of this condition for a cutting-edge legal issue, gay rights.

Law in Conditions of Diversity: Emerging Issues of Gay Rights

John Dewey pointed out many decades ago that the word *community* comes from the root word for *communication*. That root happens to be the Latin word for *common*. The preceding section suggests that at the turn of the century, people shared a common moralistic view of social arrangements, and that legal and political rhetoric inevitably (and for its time rightly) communicated that way. But law, like politics and life itself, constantly changes.

---

[23]The House Republicans who brought the impeachment charge to the Senate did, of course, employ a lot of moralistic rhetoric in their arguments for his removal. Consider this speech by Georgia Representative Bob Barr:

> What happened to these simple things that we all knew in our hearts just a few short years ago? Why do so many adults now find it so hard to call a lie a lie, when as parents, teachers, and employers, we have no such hesitancy? Why do so many now resist the search for the truth and accountability, when we do so day in and day out, in our lives at home, in business, in school, and in our religious institutions?
>
> In the short time I've served in Congress, I've learned that this place, this city, has an incredible power to complicate the simple. This staggering ability to muddle simple issues is perhaps best illustrated by the fact that much of the president's defense has hinged on defining common words in ways that shock most Americans who think they have a rather firm grasp on the meaning of words, such as "lie," "alone," "is," "perjury."

Today's political world acknowledges and accepts a diversity of interests that the world of the Mann Act did not. Diversity, you will remember, is one of the facts about the world that makes judging so difficult, because it can profoundly divide communities in ways that are hard to bridge. When judges take seriously the diversity of views on fundamental issues, they are challenged to find justifications for their decisions that appeal to the whole community, despite its divisions.

That is the challenge facing judges who are asked to resolve the many legal issues surrounding the status of gays and lesbians. A huge gulf separates Americans on these issues. Some Americans are proud of their lives as gays and lesbians, and seek full equality and integration into all aspects of social life. Others, many of them deeply religious, take a moralistic view of homosexuality. They consider homosexuality a perversion of nature and a sin, and believe that a good society should not tolerate it. [24]

That moralistic sentiment is behind the continued existence of sodomy laws, which make it a crime for gays and lesbians (and, in some states, for heterosexual couples who enjoy oral and anal sex) to engage in sexual activity, even in private. In the previous chapter, we noted that in 1986, the Supreme Court in *Bowers v. Hardwick* rejected by a 5–4 majority the argument that a Georgia antisodomy law violated the constitutional right to privacy. A concurring opinion in *Bowers* by Chief Justice Burger is filled with language about the state's interest in protecting traditional sexual morality.[25]

Bowers was the first major decision by the Supreme Court on gay and lesbian rights, and its acceptance of moralistic views on homosexuality may turn out to be an anomaly. Later decisions by state courts have struck down sodomy statutes based on state rights of privacy, including the law at issue in *Bowers*.[26] Moreover, the Supreme Court's second major gay rights decision, *Romer v. Evans* (1996), had a much different tone. *Romer* concerned a Colorado statewide initiative, "Amendment 2," that banned all state and local action aimed at protecting gays and lesbians from discrimination. The initiative was designed in part to overturn antidiscrimination ordinances enacted by the cities of Denver, Boulder, and Aspen. The Court struck down Amendment 2 as a violation of the Fourteenth Amendment Equal Protection Clause, concluding that "A State cannot so deem a class of persons a stranger to its laws."[27] Beyond the Supreme Court, federal and state courts have struggled to resolve a host of disputes involving the rights of gays and lesbians to serve in the military, to adopt children, to be treated equally on the job, and to marry.[28] Two state

---

[24]Of course most Americans belong to neither of these groups. There are plenty of heterosexuals who fully support gay rights, and there is a very large group which disapproves of homosexuality but favors social tolerance, at least in some forms. Still, in his study of middle-class public opinion, Alan Wolfe finds that the status of homosexuals is one of the most divisive and troubling issues for Americans. He concludes his analysis of public opinion regarding homosexuality on an ominous note: "Some differences cannot be talked out. This may well be one of them." Alan Wolfe, *One Nation, After All* (New York: Viking Books, 1998), 61.

[25]*Bowers v. Hardwick* 478 U.S. 186 (1986). Chief Justice Burger's concurrence rests on the argument that condemnation of sodomy "is firmly rooted in Judeo-Christian moral and ethical standards" and that to hold that the Constitution includes a right to engage in sodomy "would be to cast aside millennia of moral teaching."

[26]See for example *Powell v. Georgia*, 270 Ga. 327, 510 S.E.2d 18 (Georgia Supreme Court,1998); *Gryczan v. Montana*, 283 Mont. 433, 942 P.2d 112 (Montana Supreme Court, 1997); and *Kentucky v. Wasson*, S.W. 2d 487 (Kentucky Supreme Court, 1992).

[27]*Romer v. Evans*, 517 U.S. 620 (1996).

[28]See for example, on lesbians and gays in the military, *Thomasson v. Perry*, 80 F.3d 915 (4th Cir., en banc, 1996); and on adoption *In re Adoption of Charles B.*, 50 Ohio State 3d 88, 552 N.E.2d 884 (Ohio Supreme Court, 1990). In *Shahar v. Bowers*, 114 F.3d 1097 (11th Cir., 1997), a woman who had been hired by Georgia Attorney General Michael Bowers (the same Bowers who had defended Georgia's sodomy law in the 1986 Supreme Court case) was fired when she "married" another woman in an unofficial ceremony. The 11th Circuit Court of Appeals ruled that Bowers violated no constitutional right by firing her.

courts, in Hawaii and Vermont, ruled that laws restricting marriage to heterosexual couples violate state constitutional rights.[29] In Hawaii, voters responded by altering the state constitution to allow for this restriction, but in Vermont the legislature enacted a "civil union" law, providing same-sex couples with all the rights and privileges given to married heterosexuals.

These developments have provoked great controversy. The Hawaii decision stimulated the passage of the federal "Defense of Marriage Act," which allows states to define marriage as solely heterosexual and to refuse to recognize same-sex marriages performed in other states. As we write, the Vermont decision has created a political upheaval in a traditionally mild-mannered state. Across the nation, then, gay rights has become a major political issue.

We said in the first chapter that liberal societies often resolve deeply held differences of opinion by "agreeing to disagree." In the case of gay rights, that might work out like this: Those who disapprove of homosexuality would be free to avoid it, leaving those who approve of it—including gays and lesbians—free to associate with others who share their views. Why can't Americans agree to this simple compromise? First, the profound differences of belief about homosexuality among Americans result in widely varying perceptions of gay rights policies. Where one side sees antidiscrimination laws as merely guaranteeing that gays and lesbians have the same rights as heterosexuals, the other sees these laws as "special rights" that grant gays and lesbians special privileges—and force those who would rather not associate with homosexuals to hire and work beside them. Where one side sees gay marriage as simply extending to same-sex couples the freedoms heterosexuals enjoy, the other sees it as a subversion of a sacred institution. Diversity makes us see the world differently.

The second problem with the "live and let live" solution lies in the interconnectedness of modern life. In theory lesbians and gays could separate themselves from the homophobic and live in two different worlds. In practice, of course, they must live together, which means that the freedoms of one group almost inevitably come into conflict with the rights of the other. When such intractable conflicts develop, Americans, as Alexis de Tocqueville noted many years ago, usually turn to the courts for resolution (see page 4). That is the story of the final case we will examine, *Boy Scouts of America v. Dale.*

Scott Dale joined the Boy Scouts when he was eight, and won numerous honors and awards for his activities in the group, including the title of Eagle Scout. In 1989 Dale, then 18, was approved to become assistant scoutmaster of a troop, an adult position. Around the same time, Dale entered college at Rutgers University, where he became open about his homosexuality, joining and eventually becoming copresident of the Rutgers Gay/Lesbian Alliance. In the summer of 1990 Dale was interviewed by the New Jersey *Star Ledger* for an article about the problems facing lesbian and gay teenagers. Dale's photo appeared with the article, which identified him as copresident of the Alliance. Shortly after, Dale received a letter from the local Boy Scout Council leader revoking Dale's membership in the organization. The letter indicated that the standards of the Boy Scouts specifically excluded homosexuals from membership.

Dale eventually filed a lawsuit against the Boy Scouts of America and the local council that had expelled him. Chief among his claims was that the Boy Scouts had violated the New Jersey Public Accommodations Law, which prohibits discrimination on the basis of sexual orientation in "places of public accommodation." A New Jersey trial court threw out Dale's lawsuit, finding that the Boy Scouts was not a

---

[29]*Baher v. Lewin,* 74 Hawaii 530, 852 P.2d 44 (Hawaii Supreme Court, 1993); *Baker v. Vermont,* 98 Vt. 32, 744 A.2d 864 (Vermont Supreme Court, 2000).

place of public accommodation. Further, the court held that enforcing the accommodations law against the Boy Scouts violated the First Amendment right of freedom of association. The Boy Scouts, the court reasoned, had the right to exclude Dale if the group thought that his participation would interfere with the group's purpose of promoting morality among young people. To force the Boy Scouts to accept Dale would violate the right of group members to associate so as to express whatever message they chose to communicate about homosexuality. An appellate court reversed the trial court's decision, finding for Dale, and the New Jersey Supreme Court upheld this ruling, concluding that the Boy Scouts were covered by the accommodations law, and that applying this law to them did not violate First Amendment rights. The Boy Scouts, in turn, appealed to the U.S. Supreme Court, which in 2000 heard the case.

As you will see, the majority and dissenting opinions in *Boy Scouts v. Dale* wrestle with all four elements of legal reasoning:

- *Case facts:* To what extent does the Boy Scouts organization officially oppose homosexuality, so that requiring the group to accept openly gay members would interfere with its stated purpose? In answering this question, the two sides portray the Boy Scouts in strikingly different ways.
- *Rules of law:* Besides New Jersey's public accommodations law and the First Amendment, the opinions consider three precedents, each involving a conflict between civil rights laws and the right of private groups to exclude some people from their activities in order to express themselves as they see fit. *Roberts v. Jaycees* (1984) concerned whether the Jaycees, a business club, could be forced to admit women. The Court ruled that a Minnesota civil rights law banning discrimination on the basis of sex was constitutional as applied to the Jaycees. In *Rotary Club v. Duarte* (1987), the Court made a similar ruling admitting women to the Rotary Club, a business and service organization. Finally, in *Hurley v. Irish-American Gay, Lesbian and Bisexual Group of Boston* (1995), the Court ruled that organizers of a parade for the Irish community in Boston had a First Amendment right to exclude a gay and lesbian group, despite a Massachusetts civil rights law banning discrimination on the basis of sexual orientation.
- *Social background facts:* The opinions consider the extent to which allowing gays into the Boy Scouts would disrupt the organization's expressive goals. In doing so, the justices weigh the question of whether mandating the presence of gays and lesbians in private groups more generally might disrupt the ability of the groups to function effectively. (The justices might have looked for evidence on this point to the experiences of similar private groups that include open gays and lesbians.)
- *Shared values:* The opinions consider several shared values, but two are most prominent. First there is the value of freedom, which suggests that private groups like the Boy Scouts should have the right to choose their own members and not have their policies dictated by the government. On the other side is the value of equality, that all people should be treated with dignity and respect, which suggests that the Boy Scouts should not be allowed to discriminate against homosexuals.

As you read the majority and dissenting opinions of the Court, look for each of these elements of legal reasoning and decide how well each opinion "harmonizes" them. You should keep several levels of questions in mind:

- *The quality of judicial communication:* Does this judicial language communicate to you? That is, do you understand what each judge is saying, quite apart from whether you agree with it?
- *The political implications of judical rhetoric:* What kind of community do these justices create with their opinions? Is it a community that respects differing views on fundamental moral questions?
- *Moralism versus pragmatism:* Do the justices employ moralistic or pragmatic modes of reasoning? In other words, do they suggest that the outcome should be decided by absolute, clear rules, or does their decision focus more on the unique facts of the case?

Boy Scouts of America v. Dale
530 U.S. 640 (2000)

Justice REHNQUIST announced the judgment of the Court and delivered an opinion, in which Justice THOMAS, Justice SCALIA, Justice KENNEDY and Justice O'CONNOR joined.

. . . In *Roberts v. United States Jaycees,* we observed that "implicit in the right to engage in activities protected by the First Amendment" is "a corresponding right to associate with others in pursuit of a wide variety of political, social, economic, educational, religious, and cultural ends." This right is crucial in preventing the majority from imposing its views on groups that would rather express other, perhaps unpopular, ideas. Government actions that may unconstitutionally burden this freedom may take many forms, one of which is "intrusion into the internal structure or affairs of an association" like a "regulation that forces the group to accept members it does not desire." Forcing a group to accept certain members may impair the ability of the group to express those views, and only those views, that it intends to express. Thus "[f]reedom of association . . . plainly presupposes a freedom not to associate."

The forced inclusion of an unwanted person in a group infringes the group's freedom of expressive association if the presence of that person affects in a significant way the group's ability to advocate public or private viewpoints. But the freedom of expressive association, like many freedoms, is not absolute. We have held that the freedom could be overridden "by regulations adopted to serve compelling state interests, unrelated to the suppression of ideas, that cannot be achieved through means significantly less restrictive of associational freedoms."

To determine whether a group is protected by the First Amendment's expressive associational right, we must determine whether the group engages in "expressive association." The First Amendment's protection of expressive association is not reserved for advocacy groups. But to come within its ambit, a group must engage in some form of expression, whether it be public or private.

. . . The record reveals the following. The Boy Scouts is a private, nonprofit organization. According to its mission statement:

> It is the mission of the Boy Scouts of America to serve others by helping to instill values in young people and, in other ways, to prepare them to make ethical choices over their lifetime in achieving their full potential.

The values we strive to instill are based on those found in the Scout Oath and Law:

Scout Oath

On my honor I will do my best
To do my duty to God and my country
and to obey the Scout Law;
To help other people at all times;
To keep myself physically strong,
mentally awake, and morally straight.

Scout Law

A Scout is:

Trustworthy	Obedient
Loyal	Cheerful
Helpful	Thrifty
Friendly	Brave
Courteous	Clean
Kind	Reverent

Thus, the general mission of the Boy Scouts is clear: "[T]o instill values in young people." The Boy Scouts seeks to instill these values by having its adult leaders spend time with the youth members, instructing and engaging them in activities like camping, archery, and fishing. During the time spent with the youth members, the scoutmasters and assistant scoutmasters inculcate them with the Boy Scouts' values—both expressly and by example. It seems indisputable that an association that seeks to transmit such a system of values engages in expressive activity . . .

Given that the Boy Scouts engages in expressive activity, we must determine whether the forced inclusion of Dale as an assistant scoutmaster would significantly affect the Boy Scouts' ability to advocate public or private viewpoints. This inquiry necessarily requires us first to explore, to a limited extent, the nature of the Boy Scouts' view of homosexuality.

The values the Boy Scouts seeks to instill are "based on" those listed in the Scout Oath and Law. The Boy Scouts explains that the Scout Oath and Law provide "a positive moral code for living; they are a list of 'do's' rather than 'don'ts.'" The Boy Scouts asserts that homosexual conduct is inconsistent with the values embodied in the Scout Oath and Law, particularly with the values represented by the terms "morally straight" and "clean."

Obviously, the Scout Oath and Law do not expressly mention sexuality or sexual orientation. And the terms "morally straight" and "clean" are by no means self-defining. Different people would attribute to those terms very different meanings. For example, some people may believe that engaging in homosexual conduct is not at odds with being "morally straight" and "clean." And others may believe that engaging in homosexual conduct is contrary to being "morally straight" and "clean." The Boy Scouts says it falls within the latter category.

The New Jersey Supreme Court analyzed the Boy Scouts' beliefs and found that the "exclusion of members solely on the basis of their sexual orientation is inconsistent with Boy Scouts' commitment to a diverse and 'representative' membership . . . [and] contradicts Boy Scouts' overarching objective to reach 'all eligible youth.'" The Court concluded that the exclusion of members like Dale "appears antithetical to the organization's goals and philosophy." But our cases reject this sort of inquiry; it is not the role of the courts to reject a group's expressed values because they disagree with those values or find them internally inconsistent . . .

The Boy Scouts asserts that it "teach[es] that homosexual conduct is not morally straight," and that it does "not want to promote homosexual conduct as a legitimate form of behavior." We accept the Boy Scouts' assertion. We need not inquire further to determine the nature of the Boy Scouts' expression with respect to homosexuality . . .

We must then determine whether Dale's presence as an assistant scoutmaster would significantly burden the Boy Scouts' desire to not "promote homosexual conduct as a legitimate form of behavior." As we give deference to an association's assertions regarding the nature of its expression, we must also give deference to an association's view of what would impair its expression. That is not to say that an expressive association can erect a shield against antidiscrimination laws simply by asserting that mere acceptance of a member from a particular group would impair its message. But here Dale, by his own admission, is one of a group of gay Scouts who have "become leaders in their community and are open and honest about their sexual orientation." Dale was the copresident of a gay and lesbian organization at college and remains a gay rights activist. Dale's presence in the Boy Scouts would, at the very least, force the organization to send a message, both to the youth members and the world, that the Boy Scouts accepts homosexual conduct as a legitimate form of behavior.

Hurley is illustrative on this point. There we considered whether the application of Massachusetts' public accommodations law to require the organizers of a private St. Patrick's

Day parade to include among the marchers an Irish-American gay, lesbian, and bisexual group, GLIB, violated the parade organizers' First Amendment rights. We noted that the parade organizers did not wish to exclude the GLIB members because of their sexual orientations, but because they wanted to march behind a GLIB banner. We observed:

> [A] contingent marching behind the organization's banner would at least bear witness to the fact that some Irish are gay, lesbian, or bisexual, and the presence of the organized marchers would suggest their view that people of their sexual orientations have as much claim to unqualified social acceptance as heterosexuals. . . . The parade's organizers may not believe these facts about Irish sexuality to be so, or they may object to unqualified social acceptance of gays and lesbians or have some other reason for wishing to keep GLIB's message out of the parade. But whatever the reason, it boils down to the choice of a speaker not to propound a particular point of view, and that choice is presumed to lie beyond the government's power to control.

Here, we have found that the Boy Scouts believes that homosexual conduct is inconsistent with the values it seeks to instill in its youth members; it will not "promote homosexual conduct as a legitimate form of behavior." As the presence of GLIB in Boston's St. Patrick's Day parade would have interfered with the parade organizers' choice not to propound a particular point of view, the presence of Dale as an assistant scoutmaster would just as surely interfere with the Boy Scout's choice not to propound a point of view contrary to its beliefs.

Having determined that the Boy Scouts is an expressive association and that the forced inclusion of Dale would significantly affect its expression, we inquire whether the application of New Jersey's public accommodations law to require that the Boy Scouts accept Dale as an assistant scoutmaster runs afoul of the Scouts' freedom of expressive association. We conclude that it does . . .

We recognized in cases such as *Roberts* and *Duarte* that States have a compelling interest in eliminating discrimination against women in public accommodations. But in each of these cases we went on to conclude that the enforcement of these statutes would not materially interfere with the ideas that the organization sought to express . . .

In *Hurley,* we applied traditional First Amendment analysis to hold that the application of the Massachusetts public accommodations law to a parade violated the First Amendment rights of the parade organizers. Although we did not explicitly deem the parade in *Hurley* an expressive association, the analysis we applied there is similar to the analysis we apply here. We have already concluded that a state requirement that the Boy Scouts retain Dale as an assistant scoutmaster would significantly burden the organization's right to oppose or disfavor homosexual conduct. The state interests embodied in New Jersey's public accommodations law do not justify such a severe intrusion on the Boy Scouts' rights to freedom of expressive association. That being the case, we hold that the First Amendment prohibits the State from imposing such a requirement through the application of its public accommodations law.

Justice Stevens' dissent makes much of its observation that the public perception of homosexuality in this country has changed. Indeed, it appears that homosexuality has gained greater societal acceptance. But this is scarcely an argument for denying First Amendment protection to those who refuse to accept these views. The First Amendment protects expression, be it of the popular variety or not. And the fact that an idea may be embraced and advocated by increasing numbers of people is all the more reason to protect the First Amendment rights of those who wish to voice a different view.

Justice Stevens' extolling [in the dissenting opinion] of Justice Brandeis' comments in *New State Ice Co. v. Liebmann,* confuses two entirely different principles. In *New State Ice,* the Court struck down an Oklahoma regulation prohibiting the manufacture, sale, and distribution of ice without a license. Justice Brandeis, a champion of state experimentation in the economic realm, dissented. But Justice Brandeis was never a champion of state experimentation in the suppression of free speech. To the contrary, his First Amendment commentary provides compelling support for the Court's opinion in this case. In speaking of the Founders of this Nation, Justice Brandeis emphasized that they "believed that the freedom to think as you will and to speak as you think are means indispensable to the discovery and spread of political truth." He continued:

Believing in the power of reason as applied through public discussion, they eschewed silence coerced by law—the argument of force in its worst form. Recognizing the occasional tyrannies of governing majorities, they amended the Constitution so that free speech and assembly should be guaranteed.

We are not, as we must not be, guided by our views of whether the Boy Scouts' teachings with respect to homosexual conduct are right or wrong; public or judicial disapproval of a tenet of an organization's expression does not justify the State's effort to compel the organization to accept members where such acceptance would derogate from the organization's expressive message. "While the law is free to promote all sorts of conduct in place of harmful behavior, it is not free to interfere with speech for no better reason than promoting an approved message or discouraging a disfavored one, however enlightened either purpose may strike the government." [quoting *Hurley*]

The judgment of the New Jersey Supreme Court is reversed, and the cause remanded for further proceedings not inconsistent with this opinion.

Justice STEVENS, with whom Justice SOUTER, Justice GINSBURG and Justice BREYER join, dissenting.

New Jersey "prides itself on judging each individual by his or her merits" and on being "in the vanguard in the fight to eradicate the cancer of unlawful discrimination of all types from our society." Since 1945, it has had a law against discrimination. The law broadly protects the opportunity of all persons to obtain the advantages and privileges "of any place of public accommodation."

The New Jersey Supreme Court's construction of the statutory definition of a "place of public accommodation" has given its statute a more expansive coverage than most similar state statutes. And as amended in 1991, the law prohibits discrimination on the basis of nine different traits including an individual's "sexual orientation." The question in this case is whether that expansive construction trenches on the federal constitutional rights of the Boy Scouts of America (BSA).

Because every state law prohibiting discrimination is designed to replace prejudice with principle, Justice Brandeis' comment on the States' right to experiment with "things social" is directly applicable to this case.

> To stay experimentation in things social and economic is a grave responsibility. Denial of the right to experiment may be fraught with serious consequences to the Nation. It is one of the happy incidents of the federal system that a single courageous State may, if its citizens choose, serve as a laboratory; and try novel social and economic experiments without risk to the rest of the country. This Court has the power to prevent an experiment. We may strike down the statute which embodies it on the ground that, in our opinion, the measure is arbitrary, capricious or unreasonable. We have power to do this, because the due process clause has been held by the Court applicable to matters of substantive law as well as to matters of procedure. But in the exercise of this high power, we must be ever on our guard, lest we erect our prejudices into legal principles. If we would guide by the light of reason, we must let our minds be bold. [Citing dissenting opinion in *New State Ice Co. v. Liebmann.*]

In its "exercise of this high power" today, the Court does not accord this "courageous State" the respect that is its due. The majority holds that New Jersey's law violates BSA's right to associate and its right to free speech. But that law does not "impos[e] any serious burdens" on BSA's "collective effort on behalf of [its] shared goals," nor does it force BSA to communicate any message that it does not wish to endorse. New Jersey's law, therefore, abridges no constitutional right of the Boy Scouts . . .

In this case, Boy Scouts of America contends that it teaches the young boys who are Scouts that homosexuality is immoral. Consequently, it argues, it would violate its right to associate to force it to admit homosexuals as members, as doing so would be at odds with its own shared goals and values. This contention, quite plainly, requires us to look at what, exactly, are the values that BSA actually teaches.

BSA's mission statement reads as follows: "It is the mission of the Boy Scouts of America to serve others by helping to instill values in young people and, in other ways, to prepare them to make ethical choices over their lifetime in achieving their full potential." Its federal charter declares its purpose is "to promote, through organization, and cooperation with other agencies, the ability of boys to do things for themselves and others, to train them in scoutcraft, and to teach them patriotism, courage, self-reliance, and kindred values, using the methods which were in common use by Boy Scouts on June 15, 1916." BSA describes itself as having a "representative membership," which it defines as "boy membership [that] reflects proportionately the characteristics of the boy population of its service area." In particular, the group emphasizes that "[n]either the charter nor the bylaws of the Boy Scouts of America permits the exclusion of any boy . . . To meet these responsibilities we have made a commitment that our membership shall be representative of all the population in every community, district, and council."

To instill its shared values, BSA has adopted a "Scout Oath" and a "Scout Law" setting forth its central tenets. For example, the Scout Law requires a member to promise, among other things, that he will be "obedient." Accompanying definitions for the terms found in the Oath and Law are provided in the Boy Scout Handbook and the Scoutmaster Handbook. For instance, the Boy Scout Handbook defines "obedient" as follows:

> A Scout is OBEDIENT. A Scout follows the rules of his family, school, and troop. He obeys the laws of his community and country. If he thinks these rules and laws are unfair, he tries to have them changed in an orderly manner rather than disobey them.

To bolster its claim that its shared goals include teaching that homosexuality is wrong, BSA directs our attention to two terms appearing in the Scout Oath and Law. The first is the phrase "morally straight," which appears in the Oath ("On my honor I will do my best . . . To keep myself . . . morally straight"); the second term is the word "clean," which appears in a list of 12 characteristics together comprising the Scout Law.

The Boy Scout Handbook defines "morally straight," as such:

> To be a person of strong character, guide your life with honesty, purity, and justice. Respect and defend the rights of all people. Your relationships with others should be honest and open. Be clean in your speech and actions, and faithful in your religious beliefs. The values you follow as a Scout will help you become virtuous and self-reliant.

The Scoutmaster Handbook emphasizes these points about being "morally straight":

> In any consideration of moral fitness, a key word has to be 'courage.' A boy's courage to do what his head and his heart tell him is right. And the courage to refuse to do what his heart and his head say is wrong. Moral fitness, like emotional fitness, will clearly present opportunities for wise guidance by an alert Scoutmaster.

As for the term "clean," the Boy Scout Handbook offers the following:

> A Scout is CLEAN. A Scout keeps his body and mind fit and clean. He chooses the company of those who live by these same ideals. He helps keep his home and community clean . . .

It is plain as the light of day that neither one of these principles—"morally straight" and "clean"—says the slightest thing about homosexuality. Indeed, neither term in the Boy Scouts' Law and Oath expresses any position whatsoever on sexual matters. BSA's published guidance on that topic underscores this point. Scouts, for example, are directed to receive their sex education at home or in school, but not from the organization: "Your parents or guardian or a sex education teacher should give you the facts about sex that you must know." To be sure, Scouts are not forbidden from asking their Scoutmaster about issues of a sexual nature, but Scoutmasters are, literally, the last person Scouts are encouraged to ask: "If you have questions about growing up, about relationships, sex, or making good decisions, ask. Talk with your parents, religious leaders, teachers, or Scoutmaster." Moreover, Scoutmasters are specifically directed to steer curious adolescents to other sources of information: "If Scouts ask for information regarding . . . sexual activity, answer honestly and factually, but stay within your realm of expertise and comfort. If a Scout has serious concerns that you cannot answer, refer him to his family, religious leader, doctor, or other professional."

. . . We have recognized "a right to associate for the purpose of engaging in those activities protected by the First Amendment—speech, assembly, petition for the redress of grievances, and the exercise of religion." And we have acknowledged that "when the State interferes with individuals' selection of those with whom they wish to join in a common endeavor, freedom of association . . . may be implicated." But "[t]he right to associate for expressive purposes is not . . . absolute" [citing *Roberts*]; rather, "the nature and degree of constitutional protection afforded freedom of association may vary depending on the extent to which . . . the constitutionally protected liberty is at stake in a given case." Indeed, the right to associate does not mean "that in every setting in which individuals exercise some discrimination in choosing associates, their selective process of inclusion and exclusion is protected by the Constitution." For example, we have routinely and easily rejected assertions of this right by expressive organizations with discriminatory membership policies, such as private schools, law firms, and labor organizations. In fact, until today, we have never once found a claimed right to associate in the selection of members to prevail in the face of a State's antidiscrimination law. To the contrary, we have squarely held that a State's antidiscrimination law does not violate a group's right to associate simply because the law conflicts with that group's exclusionary membership policy.

In *Roberts v. United States Jaycees,* we addressed just such a conflict. The Jaycees was a nonprofit membership organization "'designed to inculcate in the individual membership . . . a spirit of genuine Americanism and civic interest, and . . . to provide . . . an avenue for intelligent participation by young men in the affairs of their community.'" The organization was divided into local chapters, described as "'young men's organization[s],'" in which regular membership was restricted to males between the ages of 18 and 35. But Minnesota's Human Rights Act, which applied to the Jaycees, made it unlawful to "'deny any person the full and equal enjoyment of . . . a place of public accommodation because of . . . sex.'" The Jaycees, however, claimed that applying the law to it violated its right to associate—in particular its right to maintain its selective membership policy.

We rejected that claim. Cautioning that the right to associate is not "absolute," we held that "[i]nfringements on that right may be justified by regulations adopted to serve compelling state interests, unrelated to the suppression of ideas, that cannot be achieved through means significantly less restrictive of associational freedoms." We found the State's purpose of eliminating discrimination is a compelling state interest that is unrelated to the suppression of ideas. We also held that Minnesota's law is the least restrictive means of achieving that interest. The Jaycees had "failed to demonstrate that the Act imposes any serious burdens on the male members' freedom of expressive association." Though the Jaycees had "taken public positions on a number of diverse issues, [and] . . . regularly engage in a variety of . . . activities worthy of constitutional protection under the First Amendment," there was "no basis in the record for concluding that admission of women as full voting members will impede the organization's ability to engage in these protected activities or to disseminate its preferred views." "The Act," we held, "requires no change in the Jaycees' creed of promoting the interest of young men, and it imposes no restrictions on the organization's ability to exclude individuals with ideologies or philosophies different from those of its existing members."

The evidence before this Court makes it exceptionally clear that BSA has, at most, simply adopted an exclusionary membership policy and has no shared goal of disapproving of homosexuality. BSA's mission statement and federal charter say nothing on the matter; its official membership policy is silent; its Scout Oath and Law—and accompanying definitions—are devoid of any view on the topic; its guidance for Scouts and Scoutmasters on sexuality declare that such matters are "not construed to be Scouting's proper area," but are the province of a Scout's parents and pastor; and BSA's posture respecting religion tolerates a wide variety of views on the issue of homosexuality. Moreover, there is simply no evidence that BSA otherwise teaches anything in this area, or that it instructs Scouts on matters involving homosexuality in ways not conveyed in the Boy Scout or Scoutmaster Handbooks. In short, Boy Scouts of America is simply silent on homosexuality. There is no shared goal or collective effort to foster a belief about homosexuality at all—let alone one that is significantly burdened by admitting homosexuals . . .

Equally important is BSA's failure to adopt any clear position on homosexuality. BSA's temporary, though ultimately abandoned, view that homosexuality is incompatible with being "morally straight" and "clean" is a far cry from the clear, unequivocal statement necessary to prevail on its claim. Despite the solitary sentences in the 1991 and 1992 policies, the group continued to disclaim any single religious or moral position as a general matter and actively eschewed teaching any lesson on sexuality. It also continued to define "morally straight" and "clean" in the Boy Scout and Scoutmaster Handbooks without any reference to homosexuality. As noted earlier, nothing in our cases suggests that a group can prevail on a right to expressive association if it, effectively, speaks out of both sides of its mouth. A State's antidiscrimination law does not impose a "serious burden" or a "substantial restraint" upon the group's "shared goals" if the group itself is unable to identify its own stance with any clarity.

The majority's argument relies exclusively on *Hurley v. Irish-American Gay, Lesbian and Bisexual Group of Boston.* In that case, petitioners John Hurley and the South Boston Allied War Veterans Council ran a privately operated St. Patrick's Day parade. Respondent, an organization known as "GLIB," represented a contingent of gays, lesbians, and bisexuals who sought to march in the petitioners' parade "as a way to express pride in their Irish heritage as openly gay, lesbian, and bisexual individuals." When the parade organizers refused GLIB's admission, GLIB brought suit under Massachusetts' antidiscrimination law. That statute, like New Jersey's law, prohibited discrimination on account of sexual orientation in any place of public accommodation, which the state courts interpreted to include the parade. Petitioners argued that forcing them to include GLIB in their parade would violate their free speech rights.

We agreed. We first pointed out that the St. Patrick's Day parade—like most every parade—is an inherently expressive undertaking. Next, we reaffirmed that the government may not compel anyone to proclaim a belief with which he or she disagrees. We then found that GLIB's marching in the parade would be an expressive act suggesting the view "that people of their sexual orientations have as much claim to unqualified social acceptance as heterosexuals." Finally, we held that GLIB's participation in the parade "would likely be perceived" as the parade organizers' own speech—or at least as a view which they approved—because of a parade organizer's customary control over who marches in the parade. Though *Hurley* has a superficial similarity to the present case, a close inspection reveals a wide gulf between that case and the one before us today.

First, it was critical to our analysis that GLIB was actually conveying a message by participating in the parade—otherwise, the parade organizers could hardly claim that they were being forced to include any unwanted message at all. Our conclusion that GLIB was conveying a message was inextricably tied to the fact that GLIB wanted to march in a parade, as well as the manner in which it intended to march. We noted the "inherent expressiveness of marching [in a parade] to make a point," and in particular that GLIB was formed for the purpose of making a particular point about gay pride. More specifically, GLIB "distributed a fact sheet describing the members' intentions" and, in a previous parade, had "marched behind a shamrock-strewn banner with the simple inscription 'Irish American Gay, Lesbian and Bisexual Group of Boston.' [A] contingent marching behind the organization's banner," we said, would clearly convey a message . . .

Second, we found it relevant that GLIB's message "would likely be perceived" as the parade organizers' own speech. That was so because "[p]arades and demonstrations . . . are not understood to be so neutrally presented or selectively viewed" as, say, a broadcast by a cable operator, who is usually considered to be "merely 'a conduit' for the speech" produced by others. Rather, parade organizers are usually understood to make the "customary determination about a unit admitted to the parade."

Dale's inclusion in the Boy Scouts is nothing like the case in *Hurley*. His participation sends no cognizable message to the Scouts or to the world. Unlike GLIB, Dale did not carry a banner or a sign; he did not distribute any fact sheet; and he expressed no intent to send any message. If there is any kind of message being sent, then, it is by the mere act of joining the Boy Scouts. Such an act does not constitute an instance of symbolic speech under the First Amendment . . .

Unfavorable opinions about homosexuals "have ancient roots." Like equally atavistic opinions about certain racial groups, those roots have been nourished by sectarian doctrine. Over the years, however, interaction with real people, rather than mere adherence to traditional ways of thinking about members of unfamiliar classes, have modified those opinions. A few examples: The American Psychiatric Association's and the American Psychological Association's removal of "homosexuality" from their lists of mental disorders; a move toward greater understanding within some religious communities; Justice Blackmun's classic opinion in *Bowers;* Georgia's invalidation of the statute upheld in *Bowers;* and New Jersey's enactment of the provision at issue in this case . . .

That such prejudices are still prevalent and that they have caused serious and tangible harm to countless members of the class New Jersey seeks to protect are established matters of fact that neither the Boy Scouts nor the Court disputes. That harm can only be aggravated by the creation of a constitutional shield for a policy that is itself the product of a habitual way of thinking about strangers. As Justice Brandeis so wisely advised, "we must be ever on our guard, lest we erect our prejudices into legal principles."

If we would guide by the light of reason, we must let our minds be bold. I respectfully dissent.

CONCLUSION

This book began by reprinting a telling confession by Judge (and later Justice) Benjamin Cardozo, one of this country's most progressive legal thinkers. Cardozo had looked for certainty in the law. When he found that his search was futile, he became depressed until he discovered that at its highest levels legal reasoning doesn't discover something, it creates it. By now we trust you understand this truth: judicial opinions create things. They create more than winners and losers in particular cases. The judicial opinion creates an image of an ethical political life.

In this book we have taken the position that legal reasoning, done well, necessarily creates an ethical world we cannot out of hand reject. In *Boy Scouts v. Dale* both sides attempt to do this. The majority opinion acknowledges the growing sense that gays and lesbians are entitled to equal treatment in society, but nevertheless concludes that in a good society, groups must be allowed to express themselves as they wish, even by excluding some community members from their ranks. The minority respects the importance of group autonomy, but argues that the Boy Scouts have failed to prove that including gays would significantly impair the group's mission. A good society, the minority opinion says, is inclusive and pluralistic, and sometimes a courageous government must step in on behalf of the excluded. Each opinion creates a vision of a good community that many Americans would accept. The judges could not, of course, have done this by merely citing the words of the First Amendment, or of the New Jersey Accommodations Law, or of the precedents. They had to make those words meaningful by drawing them together with facts about the world and values that we share.

You may find one opinion persuasive, the other completely obtuse. Or you may find yourself torn between them, unable to decide. You may even find both unconvincing. Legal reasoning is, as we have argued, political, and people with different political beliefs will necessarily judge the persuasiveness of opinions differently. We urge you to discuss this case with your classmates, paying particular attention to points that seemed unconvincing or weakly argued. As we argued in the first chapter, if you look closely, you will find in every opinion gaps in logic, distortions, and oversimplifications.

That reflects a basic disjunction between the way the world works and what we seek in legal opinions. In the world there are no right answers to legal questions. The world is filled with disputed facts, ambiguous words and old precedents that must be applied to new circumstances. Moreover, the world is tragic because it often pulls us in two inconsistent but equally good directions at once—toward on the one hand recognizing the freedom of the Boy Scouts to act as they wish, but on the other toward the right of gays and lesbians to be treated with dignity and respect. We know this about the world, yet we require judges to smooth out the edges, to make the world somehow fit. The job of judges, we have said, is to make the uncertain *seem* certain.

But a judge's ruling doesn't end the matter. Lon Fuller (page 139) wrote that the morality of law lies in keeping the lines of communication open. Practically speaking, of course, judges render judgments. They are in business to settle disputes, and settling disputes shuts the lines of communication as far as they are concerned. Parties can, however, appeal, and even truly final Supreme Court opinions in specific cases do not end the chance for further political and legal conversations.[30] Americans are engaging in a continuing conversation about gay rights, and courts—in controversies over the rights of lesbians and gays to marry, to adopt, to serve in the military, and to be treated equally in the workplace—have become a major part of the dialogue. We believe that good legal reasoning provokes constructive conversations and spirited debates, and that conversations and debates beat shooting at each other to settle differences.

Illustrative Case

Professor Sanford Levinson of the University of Texas School of Law has presented his students with the following problem at the beginning of their study of constitutional law. It is the concluding piece in the long symposium on interpretation cited in this chapter.[31] We urge you to use Levinson's "adulterer's hypothetical" to further explore the many facets of legal reasoning that we've discussed in this book. How would you answer the questions he poses?

In 1970 a number of concerned citizens, worried about what they regarded as the corruption of American life, met to consider what could be done. During the course of the discussion, one of the speakers electrified the audience with the following comments:

The cure for our ills is a return to old-time religion, and the best single guide remains the Ten Commandments. Whenever I am perplexed as to what I ought to do, I turn to the Commandments for the answer, and I am never disappointed. Sometimes I don't immediately like what I discover, but then I think more about the problem and realize

---

[30]In the wake of *Dale*, both private and public groups are deciding whether to drop their support of the Boy Scouts because of the organization's anti-gay stance. Kate Zernike, "Scouts' Successful Ban on Gays Is Followed by Loss in Support," *New York Times*, 29 August 2000, p. A1; "L.A. Cuts Ties to Boy Scouts, Charging Bias," *Washington Post*, 28 November 2000, p. A19.

[31]On Interpretation: The Adultery Clause of the Ten Commandments," 58 *Southern California Law Review* 719 (1985).

how limited my perspective is compared to that of the framer of those great words. Indeed, all that is necessary is for everyone to obey the Ten Commandments, and our problems will all be solved.*

Within several hours the following plan was devised: As part of the effort to encourage a return to the "old-time religion" of the Ten Commandments, a number of young people would be asked to take an oath on their eighteenth birthday to "obey, protect, support, and defend the Ten Commandments" in all of their actions. If the person complied with the oath for seventeen years, he or she would receive an award of $10,000 on his or her thirty-fifth birthday.

The Foundation for the Ten Commandments was funded by the members of the 1970 convention, plus the proceeds of a national campaign for contributions. The speaker quoted above contributed $20 million, and an additional $30 million was collected—$15 million from the convention and $15 million from the national campaign. The interest generated by the $50 million is approximately $6 million per year. Each year since 1970, 500 persons have taken the oath. *You* are appointed sole trustee of the Foundation, and your most important duty is to determine whether the oath-takers have complied with their vows and are thus entitled to the $10,000.

It is now 1987, and the first set of claimants comes before you:

(1) Claimant *A* is a married male. Although freely admitting that he has had sexual intercourse with a number of women other than his wife during their marriage, he brings to your attention the fact that "adultery," at the time of Biblical Israel, referred only to the voluntary intercourse of a married woman with a man other than her husband. He specifically notes the following passage from the article *Adultery*, I JEWISH ENCYCLOPEDIA 314:

> The extramarital intercourse of a married man is not *per se* a crime in biblical or later Jewish law. This distinction stems from the economic aspect of Israelite marriage: The wife as the husband's possession . . . , and adultery constituted a violation of the husband's exclusive right to her; the wife, as the husband's possession, had no such right to him.

A has taken great care to make sure that all his sexual partners were unmarried, and thus he claims to have been faithful to the original understanding of the Ten Commandments. However we might define "adultery" today, he argues, is irrelevant. His oath was to comply with the Ten Commandments; he claims to have done so. (It is stipulated that *A*, like all the other claimants, has complied with all the other commandments; the only question involves compliance with the commandment against adultery.)

Upon further questioning, you discover that no line-by-line explication of the Ten Commandments was proffered in 1970 at the time that *A* took the oath. But, says *A*, whenever a question arose in his mind as to what the Ten Commandments required of him, he made conscientious attempts to research the particular issue. He initially shared your (presumed) surprise at the results of his research, but further study indicated that all authorities agreed with the scholars who wrote the *Jewish Encyclopedia* regarding the original understanding of the Commandment.

(2) Claimant *B* is *A*'s wife, who admits that she has had extramarital relationships with other men. She notes, though, that these affairs were entered into with the consent of her husband. In response to the fact that she undoubtedly violated the ancient understanding of "adultery," she states that that understanding is fatally outdated:

---

*Cf. Statement of President Ronald Reagan, Press Conference, February 21, 1985, reprinted in the *New York Times*, February 22, 1985, § 1, at 10, col. 3: "I've found that the Bible contains an answer to just about everything and every problem that confronts us, and I wonder sometimes why we won't recognize that one Book could solve a lot of problems for us." [note in original]

(a) It is unfair to distinguish between the sexual rights of males and females. That the Israelites were outrageously sexist is no warrant for your maintaining the discrimination.

(b) Moreover, the reason for the differentiation, as already noted, was the perception of the wife as property. That notion is a repugnant one that has been properly repudiated by all rational thinkers, including all major branches of the Judeo-Christian religious tradition historically linked to the Ten Commandments.

(c) She further argues that, insofar as the modern prohibition of adultery is defensible, it rests on the ideal of discouraging deceit and the betrayal of promises of sexual fidelity. But these admittedly negative factors are not present in her case because she had scrupulously informed her husband and received his consent, as required by their marriage contract outlining the terms of their "open marriage."

(It turns out, incidentally, that *A* had failed to inform his wife of at least one of his sexual encounters. Though he freely admits that this constitutes a breach of the contract he had made with *B*, he nevertheless returns to his basic argument about original understanding, which makes consent irrelevant.)

(3) *C*, a male (is this relevant?), is the participant in a bigamous marriage. *C* has had no sexual encounters beyond his two wives. (He also points out that bigamy was clearly tolerated in both pre- and post-Sinai Israel and indeed was accepted within the Yemenite community of Jews well into the twentieth century. It is also accepted in a variety of world cultures.)

(4) *D*, a practicing Christian, admits that he has often lusted after women other than his wife. (Indeed, he confesses as well that it was only after much contemplation that he decided not to sexually consummate a relationship with a co-worker whom he thinks he "may love" and with whom he has held hands.) You are familiar with Christ's words, *Matthew* 5:28: "Whosoever looketh on a woman to lust after, he hath committed adultery with her already in his heart." (Would it matter to you if *D* were the wife, who had lusted after other men?)

(5) Finally, claimant *E* has never even lusted after another woman since his marriage on the same day he took his oath. He does admit, however, to occasional lustful fantasies about his wife, *G*, a Catholic, and is shocked when informed of Pope John Paul II's statement that "adultery in your heart is committed not only when you look with concupiscence at a woman who is not your wife, but also if you look in the same manner at your wife." The Pope's rationale apparently is that all lust, even that directed toward a spouse, dehumanizes and reduces the other person "to an erotic object."

Which, if any, of the claimants should get the $10,000? (Remember, *all* can receive the money if you determine that they have fulfilled their oaths.) What is your duty as Trustee in determining your answer to this question?

Introduction to Legal Procedure and Terminology

H ere is a relatively short but complete judicial opinion. This "case of the stolen airplane" made a brief appearance in Chapter 1 and plays a more important analytical role in Chapter 4. At the end of the case, this appendix introduces you to most of the more common terms of judicial organization and procedure, using the case to illustrate each term as it arises.

THE CASE

McBoyle v. United States
Supreme Court of the United States
283 U.S. 25 (1931)

Mr. Justice HOLMES delivered the opinion of the Court.

The petitioner was convicted of transporting from Ottawa, Illinois, to Guymon, Oklahoma, an airplane that he knew to have been stolen, and was sentenced to serve three years' imprisonment and to pay a fine of $2,000. The judgment was affirmed by the Circuit Court of Appeals for the Tenth Circuit. 43 F.(2d) 273. A writ of *certiorari* was granted by this Court on the question whether the National Motor Vehicle Theft Act applies to aircraft. Act of October 29, 1919, c. 89, 41 Stat. 324, U.S. Code, title 18, § 408. That Act provides: "Sec. 2. That when used in this Act: (a) The term 'motor vehicle' shall include an automobile, automobile truck, automobile wagon, motor cycle, or any other self-propelled vehicle not designed for running on rails. . . . Sec. 3. That whoever shall transport or cause to be transported in interstate or foreign commerce a motor vehicle, knowing the same to have been stolen, shall be punished by a fine of not more than $5,000, or by imprisonment of not more than five years, or both."

Section 2 defines the motor vehicles of which the transportation in interstate commerce is punished in Section 3. The question is the meaning of the word "vehicle" in the phrase "any other self-propelled vehicle not designed for running on rails." No doubt etymologically it is possible to use the word to signify a conveyance working on land, water, or air, and sometimes legislation extends the use in that direction, e.g., land and air, water being separately provided for, in the Tariff Act, September 21, 1922, c. 356, § 401 (b), 42 Stat. 858, 948. But in everyday speech "vehicle" calls up the picture of a thing moving on land. Thus in Rev. St. § 4, intended, the Government suggests, rather to enlarge than to restrict the definition, vehicle includes every contrivance capable of being used "as a means of transportation on land." And this is repeated, expressly excluding aircraft, in the Tariff Act, June 17, 1930, c. 497, § 401 (b), 46 Stat. 590, 708. So here, the phrase under discussion calls up the popular picture. For after including automobile truck, automobile wagon, and motor cycle, the words "any other self-propelled vehicle not designed for running on rails" still indicate that a vehicle in the popular sense, that is a vehicle running on land, is the theme. It is a vehicle that runs, not something, not commonly called a vehicle, that flies. Airplanes were well known in 1919 when this statute was passed, but it is admitted that they were not mentioned in the reports or in the debates in Congress. It is impossible to read words that so carefully enumerate the different forms of motor vehicles and have no reference of any kind to aircraft, as including airplanes under a term that usage more and more precisely confines to a different class. The counsel for the petitioner have shown that the phraseology of the statute as to motor vehicles follows that of earlier statutes of Connecticut, Delaware, Ohio, Michigan, and Missouri, not to mention the late Regulations of Traffic for the District of Columbia, title 6, c. 9, § 242, none of which can be supposed to leave the earth.

Although it is not likely that a criminal will carefully consider the text of the law before he murders or steals, it is reasonable that a fair warning should be given to the world in language that the common world will understand, of what the law intends to do if a certain line is passed. To make the warning fair, so far as possible the line should be clear. When a rule of conduct is laid down in words that evoke in the common mind only the picture of vehicles moving on land, the statute should not be extended to aircraft simply because it may seem to us that a similar policy applies, or upon the speculation that if the legislature had thought of it, very likely broader words would have been used. *United States v. Bhagat Singh Thind*, 261 U.S. 204, 209, 43 S.Ct. 338.

Judgment reversed.

LEGAL TERMS

When a person feels disappointed by the result a court reaches in a lawsuit in which he or she is a **party,** he or she may (unless the highest court has already heard their case) **appeal** to a higher court. In an appeal the **appellant** (the party taking the appeal up) argues that the lower-court judge interpreted and applied the law of the case erroneously. Appeals do not reopen the facts of the case or consider new testimony or evidence. Appeals are limited to questions about whether the lower court reasoned well about the legal issues in the case. In *McBoyle,* the appellant (Mr. McBoyle) argued successfully that the lower courts wrongly interpreted the National Motor Vehicle Theft Act to include airplanes. Thus in this case the **appellee,** the U.S. government, lost in the "court of last resort."

In this and all cases, the initial **plaintiff** (in this case the United States) must prove it has a **cause of action.** That is, the plaintiff must find some official legal text somewhere that says that what the initial **defendant** (McBoyle) did was wrong. A cause of action clearly exists in this case, since McBoyle obviously helped transport something stolen. But not all harms are legal causes of action. If, for example, a professor wears an offensively ugly necktie to class and a student sues him for the pain he suffers at having to stare at rank ugliness for 50 minutes, the student will lose because no legal text makes such an offense **actionable.** Note, however, that the student can sue the professor. The interesting question in the legal system is never "Can I sue?" (The answer is always *yes.* All it takes to sue is to fill out the appropriate forms and pay the appropriate fees at a courthouse.) The question is whether the court will have some reason to throw the suit out without hearing its merits. If an official legal text made recovery actionable for the tort of having to look at ugly neckties, then the plaintiff might recover money **damages** from the professor or might win a court **injunction** in which a court would order him never to wear such a tie again.[1]

A cause of action existed in *McBoyle* because the plaintiff, in this case the United States government, could claim that the defendant, Mr. McBoyle, violated a legal rule enacted by Congress: the National Motor Vehicle Theft Act. No statutes, common-law cases, or bureaucratic regulations protect against the hurt we call embarrassment, so

[1]For a thorough (and dramatic) description of the details of litigation at the trial level, see Jonathan Harr, *A Civil Action* (New York: Random House, 1995).

embarrassment does not constitute a legal cause of action. There are, however, common-law rules of negligence. If a professor wears a combination of pants, jacket, and necktie that causes a student to have a severe seizure, and if that student then explains to the professor the problem and asks him not to wear that combination again, and if the professor then forgets and causes a second seizure requiring medical attention, the rules of negligence would give the student a cause of action.

The legal system normally classifies legal actions as either **civil** or **criminal.** As long as we don't think about it too much, we think we know the difference: In a criminal case like McBoyle's a governmental official—a **prosecutor**—has the responsibility for filing complaints for violations of laws that authorize the judge to impose a punishment—usually fine, imprisonment, or both—on behalf of the polity. *McBoyle* is a criminal case, prosecuted by a U.S. attorney working for the U.S. Department of Justice, because the National Motor Vehicle Theft Act prescribes a punishment for those convicted under it.

In a civil case, on the other hand, the plaintiff seeks a judicial decision that will satisfy him personally. Civil remedies usually consist of a court award of money damages to compensate for harm already done or of a court order commanding the defendant to stop doing (or threatening to do) something injurious.

In practice these distinctions between civil and criminal actions tend to break down. Units of government, acting as civil plaintiffs, may file lawsuits to enforce policies that benefit the entire country. The United States government does so when it files civil antitrust actions. A private citizen may file and win a civil rights complaint in which the judge imposes "punitive damages" on defendants. Then damages awarded can far exceed the harm the plaintiff actually experienced.

Occasionally in public debate there is talk about "decriminalizing" some form of behavior. To decriminalize something does not automatically legalize it. In 1996 there was considerable discussion about decriminalizing physician-assisted suicide. To do so would prevent prosecutors from seeking criminal convictions of physicians who assist others who are terminally ill to take their own lives. However, civil remedies might remain in place, so that surviving family members might still bring successful civil lawsuits against doctors for the tort of wrongful death, particularly in the event that the deceased may not have made a fully knowing and voluntary decision to end his or her life. When a legal issue is civil rather than criminal, the rules of evidence change significantly. For example, in the civil trial brought against O. J. Simpson for wrongful death by the heirs of Ron Goldman and Nicole Brown, Mr. Simpson could not refuse to testify. Double jeopardy protections apply only to defendants in criminal cases, and Simpson no longer faced criminal prosecution for these deaths.

The kind of rule on which a lawsuit is based very much shapes the **evidence** that the parties introduce in trial. We can, for example, imagine that when the owner of the airplane McBoyle transported got it back, he found that it needed $1,000 of repairs. The owner of the plane might file a civil suit against McBoyle seeking to recover damages from McBoyle to pay for the repairs plus the damage the owner suffered by not having use of his vehicle. At this imaginary trial, McBoyle's lawyers might try to introduce evidence that the airplane needed the repairs before McBoyle transported it. In the actual criminal case, however, the facts at issue and the evidence presented are completely different. The evidentiary questions at this trial might wrestle with whether McBoyle knew the plane was stolen. In the actual criminal trial, McBoyle denied any involvement, but the trial court found that he had hired a Mr. Lacey to steal the airplane directly from the manufacturer and fly it to Oklahoma. The jury found that McBoyle paid Lacey over $300 to do so. See *McBoyle v. United States*, 43 F. (2d) 273 (1930).

The four elements of legal reasoning introduced in Chapter 1 include two kinds of facts about which lawyers and judges may reason. One set of facts we may call the facts of the dispute at issue between the parties. These are events and observations that the people in the lawsuit must either prove or disprove through their evidence to prevail at trial. Thus the United States government had to prove that McBoyle knew the plane he transported was indeed stolen. These facts are settled one way or the other by the **trier of fact:** a jury or a judge sitting without a jury. (Jury trials are longer and more costly than "bench trials." The large majority of lawsuits filed are in fact settled by negotiation without any trial, and most trial court proceedings take place without juries.)

A second kind of fact, which we have labeled "social background facts," also influences legal reasoning. In *McBoyle*, the court, including the trial judge, must interpret the word *vehicle* in this statute so as to decide whether it covers airplanes. Social background facts help decide that question: How common were airplanes when Congress passed the statute in 1919? Did congressional debates discuss and reject the idea of including the word *airplanes* in the statute? What social problem prompted busy Congress members to pass the National Motor Vehicle Theft Act? Every state had laws prohibiting theft. Why, historically, was a national law about stealing and transporting motor vehicles necessary in 1919?

Notice that, unlike the facts at issue between the parties, these social background issues have no direct connection with the parties at all. They do not have to be proved at trial. Sometimes lawyers at trial will address them, but just as often these factual issues will arise only on appeal, where the lawyers will argue them orally or in their written briefs. Furthermore, judges are free to research such issues on their own or through their clerks with no help from the parties before them, and base their legal conclusions on them. Often the social background facts appear only implicitly in the opinion. They are the judge's hunches about the way the world works that we can only infer from what the judge does say. Every appellate opinion reviewed in these pages rests on such explicit or implicit hunch assertions.

In addition to the requirement of a cause of action, litigants must meet a number of other procedural requirements before courts will decide their case "on the merits." For our purposes we may divide these procedures into requirements for **jurisdiction** and **justiciability.**

"Jurisdiction" prescribes the legal authority of a court to decide the case at all. More specifically, a court must have (a) **jurisdiction over the subject matter** and (b) **jurisdiction over the person** before it can decide. Neither of these requirements is terribly mysterious. Subject matter jurisdiction refers to the fact that all courts are set up by statutes that authorize the court to decide some kinds of legal issues but not others. A local "traffic court" has jurisdiction to hear only a small subset of cases: criminal traffic violations. State probate courts hear issues about the wills and estates of the deceased. The federal court system has a variety of specialized courts, such as the United States Customs Court and the United States Court of International Trade. In both federal and state judicial systems, some courts have statutory authority to hear a broad scope of cases. These are called courts of "general jurisdiction." The U.S. District Court and (in most states) state "superior courts" serve as the trial courts in which most serious lawsuits begin. The U.S. District Court for the Western District of Oklahoma is such a court, and it therefore had subject matter jurisdiction to try the criminal case against McBoyle.

Jurisdiction over the person refers to the fact that agents of a court must catch the defendant and serve him with the papers notifying him that a suit has been filed against him before the court can enter a judgment against him. The agents who "serve process" on defendants—sheriffs in the states and U.S. marshalls in the federal system—have authority to find people and serve notice on them only within the geographic territory the court governs. A sheriff working for a Superior Court in Georgia cannot serve someone who lives in Alabama unless the sheriff can catch the person (or attach land of his) in Georgia. This jurisdiction over the person is sometimes called **territorial jurisdiction.**[2]

McBoyle's case raises an interesting problem of jurisdiction over the person. Federal law requires that defendants be tried in the district where the crime was committed. McBoyle claimed that because he never flew the airplane, or left Illinois for that matter, he could not have committed a crime in the Western District of Oklahoma, Mr. Lacey's destination. The U.S. Court of Appeals for the Tenth Circuit rejected that argument, saying that the crime ran with the airplane, and that the crime was committed in Oklahoma, even if McBoyle wasn't in Oklahoma at the time. See 43 F. (2d) 273 at 275 (1930).

Most courts in the United States possess authority to decide what the U.S. Constitution (in Article III) calls "cases" and "controversies." Over the years this phrase has become synonymous with a genuinely adversarial contest in which plaintiff and defendant desire truly different outcomes. Judges cannot initiate lawsuits. They respond to the initiatives taken by the litigants.

Rules of **justiciability** ensure that judges decide true adversary contests. These rules serve three functions: (a) To avoid wasting judicial time and resources on minor matters; (b) to improve the quality of information that reaches them by hearing different points of view; (c) to justify refusing to decide politically delicate cases that might damage the courts' political popularity.

Thus courts generally refuse to hear **moot** cases, cases in which the harm the plaintiff tried to prevent never happened or, for whatever reasons, cannot happen in the future. Plaintiffs must have **standing,** which means that the plaintiff must be among those directly injured (or directly threatened) by the defendant's actions. To illustrate, in 1996 federal courts held that the city seal of Edmond, Oklahoma, violated the Constitution because it contained a Christian cross. The plaintiffs in that case, Unitarian and Jewish residents of Edmond, argued successfully that their very membership in a community with a religious symbol directly injured them enough to have standing to sue. **Exhaustion** requires that plaintiffs exploit their primary opportunities for settling a case, especially through bureaucratic channels, before going to court, and **ripeness** requires that the defendant actually threaten what the plaintiff fears. Thus, partly to avoid getting itself in hot political water, the U.S. Supreme Court at first refused to consider the constitutionality of Connecticut's laws against distribution and use of birth control devices. It insisted that Connecticut wasn't bothering to enforce these laws and that therefore the case wasn't ripe. No justiciability problems arose in *McBoyle.*

McBoyle's case reached the U.S. Supreme Court in this fashion: The trial court found McBoyle guilty. (In criminal cases the trial court expresses its **disposition** in terms of guilt and innocence. Civil dispositions find defendant "liable" or "not liable.") McBoyle appealed, and the Court of Appeals, ruling on both the jurisdictional claim and the statutory interpretation claim, **affirmed** (upheld) the trial court's decisions on these two matters of law. McBoyle appealed again, and the U.S. Supreme Court **reversed.**

---

[2]Courts are just beginning to wrestle with the problems of jurisdiction presented by legal conflicts that arise in cyberspace. See "Trying to Resolve Jurisdictional Rules on the Internet" *New York Times,* 14 April 1997, p. B1.

Bush v. Gore

*Although we may never know with complete certainty the identity of the
winner of this year's Presidential election, the identity of the loser is perfectly
clear. It is the Nation's confidence in the judge as an impartial guardian of
the rule of law.*

—JUSTICE JOHN PAUL STEVENS, dissenting in *Bush v. Gore*

INTRODUCTION

O n December 12, 2000, the United States Supreme Court called an end to a
manual recounting of ballots cast in the November 7 presidential election in the
state of Florida. The Supreme Court announced its decision at a time when
Democrat Vice President Al Gore trailed Republican Governor George Bush in
Florida by a mere 154 votes (out of about 6 million cast). The Court, by a 5–4 vote,
reversed a 4–3 Florida Supreme Court decision calling for a completion of the
count. The Florida Supreme Court had interpreted Florida's election statutes as requiring a hand recount of "undercounted" ballots, i.e., those votes that a variety of
voting machine technologies in Florida initially read as indicating no vote for any
presidential candidate. Since Florida's electoral votes tipped the balance of electoral votes, and hence the presidency, to Bush, the U.S. Supreme Court's decision
effectively ended Al Gore's chance to win the presidency.

The legal drama that culminated in *Bush v. Gore*, 121 S.Ct. 525, dominated
front-page headlines for weeks. For the first time in U.S. history, federal courts directly intervened in a presidential election and may have determined its outcome.
The dramatic events of the 2000 presidential election prove the fundamental contention of this book: Legal reasoning matters. After the U.S. Supreme Court made its
ruling, journalists, legal scholars, and everyday people analyzed the Court's reasoning. Among those sympathetic to Gore, few were persuaded that the Court had acted
impartially; even some conservative commentators voiced their doubts. Some legal
scholars concluded that the reputation of the Court as an impartial tribunal had
been deeply scarred. (See, for example, the statement of Professor Pierce, quoted in
Chapter 1 on page 2.)

We do not argue in this appendix that either the U.S. Supreme Court or the
Florida Supreme Court reached the "right" legal answer in this history-making case.
The questions we pose at the end of this appendix, however, reveal our conclusion
about the adequacy of the legal reasoning used to justify these decisions: While the
Florida Supreme Court's opinions pass our test of impartial legal reasoning, the U.S.
Supreme Court's majority opinion falls woefully short. Justice Stevens, in dissent,
thought that the majority had dealt a serious blow to "the Nation's confidence in the
judge as impartial guardian of the rule of law."

This appendix allows you to formulate your own conclusion about this momentous decision by using the principles of legal reasoning you have learned in this book. In reading through the various opinions, you should consider whether they harmonize the case facts, social background facts, rules of law, and widespread social values presented by this case. Then you can decide for yourself whether the Florida and U.S. Supreme Courts served effectively as impartial umpires. Space doesn't permit us to include every fascinating facet of this controversy, but this appendix covers the critical materials as accurately as possible. For a complete review of this historic legal and political drama, you can find all the major court decisions as well as the supporting briefs and oral argument transcripts through a variety of Web sources. For U.S. Supreme Court materials, start with www.findlaw.com. Thus to read the briefs in this case, you would go to http://supreme.lp.findlaw.com/supreme_court/briefs/index.html. To hear the oral arguments try www.Oyez.nwu.edu. For Florida materials, go to http://guide.lp.findlaw.com/11stategov/fl/courts.html. Try also www.flcourts.org/sct/clerk/briefs/2000.

The legal controversy began with the "protest" of the election by Vice President Gore. Both the Florida and U.S. Supreme Courts issued opinions regarding conflicts and ambiguities in Florida law about the time allowed to "protest" an election prior to the time the secretary of state "certifies" the election result. After the "protest" phase, Florida law then specifies procedures for "contesting" the validity of the certified election. The U.S. Supreme Court's decision on December 12 ended this "contest" phase, and the contest for the presidency.

THE PROTEST PHASE

On Wednesday, November 8, 2000, the Division of Elections of the State of Florida reported that, in balloting on the previous day for President of the United States, Republican candidate George Bush had received 2,909,135 votes and Democratic candidate Al Gore had received 2,907,351 votes. Florida by law organizes and supervises elections through its counties and their "county canvassing boards." The head of the county canvassing board is an official elected every four years, except in Miami-Dade, where he is appointed. A county court judge and the head of the county commission make up the rest of the canvassing board.

Under Florida law, when the margin of victory is under .5 percent (and in this case the margin was less than .03 percent), each county canvassing board automatically recounts its ballots by machine. This automatic machine recount reduced Governor Bush's lead slightly. In addition to the machine recount, under Florida statute 102.166, each canvassing board may, if petitioned within 72 hours of the official announcement of vote totals, order a hand recount of a sample of ballots in the county. If this sample recount shows a change in vote totals such that a manual recount of the entire county could affect the outcome of the election, then Florida law says the board, in the absence of technical failures in the machines themselves, "shall . . . manually recount all ballots" in the county.

Because Florida, like most states, gives its counties primary responsibility for conducting elections, different counties in Florida use different technologies for casting and counting votes. Miami-Dade and Palm Beach, urban counties with large populations of low-income and minority populations, had chosen not to spend limited revenues to update their voting technologies. Unlike more affluent counties that used more reliable and more expensive optical scanning devices, these counties used a system in which voters punched holes in cards through a template. In theory the cardboard rectangle, called a "chad," should fall away from the card when the voter punches the ballot for her candidate. The machine then "reads" the presence of a hole in the card to indicate the intended vote. But due to the nature of the technology and the age of the machines, some chads do not fall away when punched. If they are still attached to the card, the machine reading the card may suck the chad back into place and record no vote. Only a ballot-by-ballot physical inspection by a human can tell if a voter tried but unintentionally failed to punch out the chad by his or her candidate's name.

Democratic Party officials in four counties—Broward, Miami-Dade, Palm Beach, and Volusia—requested that the sample hand recounts be done. Miami-Dade ultimately refused to complete and report its manual recount. The other three counties eventually completed their recounts, which reduced the Bush margin to a few hundred votes.

Here the Florida courts faced their first legal reasoning challenge. Florida statute 102.111, enacted in 1951, states that "If the County returns are not received by the Department of State by 5:00 p.m. of the seventh day following an election, all missing counties shall be ignored and the results shown by the returns shall be certified." But in 1989, the Florida legislature added statute 102.112, which says that returns not filed by the 5 p.m. deadline "may be ignored." This law also specified that canvassing board members "shall" be fined $200 per day for every day the returns are late, to be payable only out of their personal funds.

On Tuesday, November 21, the Florida Supreme Court, in *Palm Beach Canvassing Board v. Harris,* 772 So. 2d 1220 (Fla. 2000), resolved the conflict. It reasoned that no county could plausibly recount all ballots by hand in the time between the end of the 72-hour period (which starts not on election day but on the day the county canvassing board announces its official vote totals) and the seventh day after the election, the day for statewide certification. (Approximately 1.5 million ballots were cast in Miami-Dade and Palm Beach counties alone.) In light of the more recent use of the phrase "may be ignored," the court by a 7–0 vote ordered the Secretary of State, Katherine Harris, to accept recounted ballots submitted for certification until 5:00 p.m. on Sunday, November 26:

> Twenty-five years ago, this court commented that the will of the people, not a hyper-technical reliance upon statutory provisions, should be our guiding principle in election cases. . . .
>
> The right to vote is the right to participate; it is also the right to speak, but more importantly, the right to be heard. . . .
>
> In light of this [statutory] ambiguity, the court must resort to traditional rules of statutory construction. . . .
>
> First, it is well settled that where two statutory provisions are in conflict, the specific statute controls the general statute. In the present case . . . Section 102.111 in title and text addresses the general makeup and duties of the Elections Canvassing Commission. . . . Section 102.112, on the other hand, directly addresses in its title and text both the "deadline" for submitting returns and the "penalties" for submitting returns after a certain date. . . .
>
> Second, it is also well settled that when two statutes are in conflict, the more recently enacted statute controls the older statute. . . .
>
> Third, a statutory provision will not be construed in such a way that it renders meaningless or absurd any other statutory provision. [Here the court points out that the provisions in 102.112 for fining board members for filing late returns would be meaningless if the late returns could never count, since in this event board members would file no returns at all and pay no fine.]

Fourth, related statutory provisions must be read as a cohesive whole. [Here the court points out that a full manual recount could not be completed between the end of the period allowed to file a protest and the 5:00 p.m. deadline seven days after the election.]

Courts must not lose sight of the fundamental purpose of election laws: The laws are intended to facilitate and safeguard the right of each voter to express his or her will in the context of our representative democracy. . . .

The Court also pointed out that under Florida 101.5614, the official vote totals are not the same as the certified totals because the official vote totals by law must include "write-in, absentee and manually counted results."

The court gave the county canvassing boards until 5 p.m. November 26th to complete their recounts. Miami-Dade County concluded that it could not meet this deadline, and declined to complete a manual recount. Palm Beach County held a recount, but missed the deadline by 90 minutes. The "official" certification by Secretary of State Harris concluded that Bush won Florida's electoral votes with a margin of 537 votes over Gore, but on this date many thousands of challenged votes had still not been recounted, far more votes than the margin of difference between the two candidates. The struggle for the presidency thus entered a second phase, the "contest" phase, leading to the decision in *Bush v. Gore* excerpted below.

On the road to *Bush v. Gore*, however, the U.S. Supreme Court reviewed the 7–0 Florida decision that gave the counties extra time to conduct recounts during the "protest" phase. In *Bush v. Palm Beach County Canvassing Board,* 121 S.Ct. 471 (2000), the Supreme Court on December 4 vacated the Florida order and sent it back for reconsideration to the Florida Supreme Court. In vacating the state court's ruling, the U.S. Supreme Court raised questions about whether the Florida court's order had violated Article II of the U.S. Constitution, which holds:

Each state shall appoint, in such manner as the legislature thereof may direct, a number of electors, equal to the whole number of senators and representatives to which the state may be entitled in Congress. . . .

This provision, the U.S. Supreme Court said, leaves it entirely to the state legislature to decide how electors should be selected. The Court noted that the Florida opinion had included some references to the Florida Constitution's guarantees of popular election. These references, the Court concluded, could indicate a violation of Article II because they suggested that the Florida court had relied on the state constitution rather than the statutes created by the legislature in reaching a decision about Gore's protest. Under Article II, the U.S. Supreme Court ruled, delegate selection was left to the legislature, and nothing in the state constitution could be used to alter what the legislature had commanded.

The U.S. Supreme Court also raised questions about the meaning of U.S. Code Title 3, Section 5:

If any State shall have provided, by laws enacted prior to the day fixed for the appointment of the electors, for its final determination of any controversy or contest concerning the appointment of all or any of the electors of such State, by judicial or other methods or procedures, and such determination shall have been made at least six days before the time fixed for the meeting of the electors, such determination made pursuant to such law so existing on said day, and made at least six days prior to said time of meeting of the electors, shall be conclusive, and shall govern in the counting of the electoral votes as provided in the Constitution, and as hereinafter regulated, so far as the ascertainment of the electors appointed by such State is concerned.

This provision means that Congress, in counting the electoral votes for president when it meets the following January, must accept a state's selection of electors that was made "by judicial or other methods or procedures," "provided by laws enacted prior to," election day. The U.S. Supreme Court raised concerns about whether the Florida Supreme Court had in fact changed the law governing selection of delegates, thus putting the state outside of the boundaries of this statute.

Gore lawyers argued that since all Florida statutes interpreted by the Florida Supreme Court were made by the legislature prior to election day, and since Florida Statute 102.168(1) assigns to Florida courts the power to resolve disputes about presidential elections, the Florida Supreme Court seemed to be acting fully within the "manner" that the legislature directed for choosing electors under Article II. To allay doubts about the fairness of the proposed manual recounts, Gore forces pointed out that Florida's 102.166(7) itself calls for bipartisanship in the recount, with members of each party being present to observe and protest readings of am-biguous ballots that might go aginst its candidate. 102.166(7) also contained this important provision:

> . . . If a counting team is unable to determine a voter's intent in casting a ballot, the ballot shall be presented to the county canvassing board for it to determine the voter's intent.

As Gore attorneys noted, to conclude that the Florida Supreme Court's decision in *Palm Beach Canvassing Board v. Harris* violated 3 U.S.C. 5, one must accept two very questionable propositions. First, the Florida Supreme Court would have to have made "new law" after the election. By resetting the certification date to November 26, attorneys for Bush argued that the Florida court had done just that. But clearly the Florida court was caught in a Catch-22. To rule that the state must stick to the November 14 certification date, the court would equally have revised state law by nullifying the statutory provisions for a hand recount and making the language about accepting late returns and fining officials for filing late returns meaningless. The court chose instead to harmonize each of these provisions so as to make the statutory scheme "to determine the voter's intent" coherent. As we have seen, appellate judges in common-law systems commonly "change the law" when they decide any case. To say that the Florida court violated 3 U.S.C. 5 because it exercised its standard judi-cial power of statutory interpretation, granted to it specifically by the Florida legisla-ture, would fly in the face of the American common-law legal tradition.

Second, one would have to read 3 U.S.C. 5 as *ordering* the states to choose elec-tors by a single system prior to the national election day. But such a reading would violate the very Article II of the Constitution we have just reviewed! Also, the his-tory of Section 5 provides no evidence for such a statutory purpose. Congress passed Section 5, the "Electoral Count Act" on February 3, 1887, in order to prevent a re-play of the historic Hayes-Tilden fight of 1876. In that battle Congress was forced to decide which of competing slates of electoral votes (some from Florida!) would count in presidential elections. Title 3 U.S.C. 5 created a default (or "safe harbor") rule in such controversies which provided that as long as the state followed proper proce-dures in selecting delegates, Congress would recognize them. Title 3 U.S.C. 5 can thus be read as a statutory promise from Congress not to accept any group of electors other than those chosen by the state's ordinary election machinery. Also, 3 U.S.C. Section 15 provides elaborate procedures for how Congress should resolve a dispute over whether a slate of electors has met the requirements of Section 5. This provi-sion would make no sense if Section 5 already settled the matter, or empowered the federal courts to step in to do so.

THE CONTEST PHASE

Florida statutes provide that losing candidates may contest an election *after* it is certified. Hence in the final frenzy of litigation, the issue of resetting the certification date, the main point of contention in the protest phase, faded into the legal background.

The primary rule of law applicable to the "contest" phase of this litigation is section 102.168 of the Florida election code. Its relevant parts read:

> (1) [T]he certification of election or nomination of any person to office, or of the result on any question submitted by referendum, may be contested in the circuit court by any unsuccessful candidate for such office or nomination thereto or by any elector qualified to vote in the election related to such candidacy, or by any taxpayer, respectively. . . .
>
> (3) The complaint shall set forth the grounds on which the contestant intends to establish his or her right to such office or set aside the result of the election on a submitted referendum. The grounds for contesting an election under this section are:
>
> (a) Misconduct, fraud, or corruption on the part of any election official or any member of the canvassing board sufficient to change or place in doubt the result of the election.
>
> (b) Ineligibility of the successful candidate for the nomination or office in dispute.
>
> (c) Receipt of a number of illegal votes or rejection of a number of legal votes sufficient to change or place in doubt the result of the election.
>
> (d) Proof that any elector, election official, or canvassing board member was given or offered a bribe or reward in money, property, or any other thing of value for the purpose of procuring the successful candidate's nomination or election or determining the result on any question submitted by referendum.
>
> (e) Any other cause or allegation which, if sustained, would show that a person other than the successful candidate was the person duly nominated or elected to the office in question or that the outcome of the election on a question submitted by referendum was contrary to the result declared by the canvassing board or election board. . . .
>
> (8) The circuit judge to whom the contest is presented may fashion such orders as he or she deems necessary to ensure that each allegation in the complaint is investigated, examined, or checked, to prevent or correct any alleged wrong, and to provide any relief appropriate under such circumstances.

The Gore campaign filed a lawsuit under 102.168 claiming primarily that Florida Secretary of State Harris (herself a co-chair of the Bush campaign in Florida) had illegally refused to count a number of legal votes "sufficient to change or place in doubt the result of the election." In the case of Miami-Dade, approximately 9,000 votes had never been manually recounted at all, even though recounts in other counties had showed significant vote changes due to the failure of the machines to dislodge chads properly. Also, Gore attorneys argued that the certification, though properly completed on November 26, excluded manually recounted votes that unambiguously revealed the intent of the voter as required by 102.166. Attorneys for Gore reinforced their argument by citing a prominent Florida precedent, *Beckstrom v. Volusia County Canvassing Board* 707 So. 2d 720 (Fla. 1998), which ordered the manual recount of over 8,000 absentee ballots in a contest phase. No fraud or corruption was alleged in that case, but election officials had refused to count ballots that unambiguously indicated the voters' candidate preference because voters had used the wrong kind of marker (in many cases a pen rather than a no. 2 pencil) to mark their ballots.

In the expedited trial before Leon County Judge Sanders Sauls, Gore attorneys introduced into evidence the "undercounted" ballots—those on which the voting machines had not counted a presidential vote—from Miami-Dade. Without inspecting them, Judge Sauls ruled against Gore on the ground that Gore had not shown a "reasonable probability that the results of the election would have been changed."

Alleging, among other things, that Judge Sauls had obviously failed to investigate, examine, or check the allegation that the recount of the 9,000 votes might "place in doubt the result of the election" (102.168 (3c), above), Gore filed an expedited appeal to the Florida Supreme Court. The Bush team responded that Judge Sauls's decision was (like the trial court's decision in the *Prochnow* case in Chapter 1) a matter of fact for the trial court and so not reversible on appeal. Bush lawyers also argued for the first time that a hand recount based on varying standards, in which some counties would accept ballots that others rejected, violated the due process and equal protection clauses of the Fourteenth Amendment of the U.S. Constitution. Such a count would be unfair because it would treat voters unequally, depending on where they happened to live, the Bush campaign argued.

The Bush team further claimed that since Gore was contesting the election of presidential electors for the entire state of Florida, not just Miami-Dade, the contest statute required a uniform recounting of all votes in Florida. And this argument in turn opened up another avenue of attack. Time was running out. Congress had set December 18 as the date for the electors to meet and cast their ballots for president. III U.S.C. 5 guarantees the "safe harbor" protection of a state's electoral slate only if controversies about it are resolved "at least six days before the date specified for meeting of the electors," i.e., December 12. Judge Sauls issued his ruling on December 4. The Florida Supreme Court scheduled oral argument in Gore's appeal from Sauls's ruling for December 7. If it ruled that a manual recount of all challenged ballots had to be completed by December 12, and according to uniform standards, would there be enough time left to finish the job?

On December 8, the Florida Supreme Court ruled, 4–3, that the count of the "undervote" should resume. Gore had asked for recounts in heavily Democratic counties, which were likely to produce more votes for him than for his opponent. Perhaps for this reason, the majority ordered a statewide recount of all "undervotes."

Here is the majority opinion. We omit without notation footnotes and most source law citations. We indicate all omissions of substantive text with ellipses. We urge all readers to read the unedited opinions at the Web sources noted earlier.

Albert Gore, Jr., and Joseph I. Lieberman, Appellants,
v. Katherine Harris, as Secretary, etc., et al., Appellees
Supreme Court of Florida
772 So.2d 1243
Per Curiam

I. Background

The appellants' election contest is based on five instances where the official results certified involved either the rejection of a number of legal votes or the receipt of a number of illegal votes. These five instances, as summarized by the appellants' brief, are as follows:

(1) The rejection of 215 net votes for Gore identified in a manual count by the Palm Beach Canvassing Board as reflecting the clear intent of the voters [but submitted after Secretary of State Harris's deadline on November 26];

(2) The rejection of 168 net votes for Gore, identified in the partial recount by the Miami-Dade County Canvassing Board [the partial result of the Miami-Dade recount before the county suspended its recount altogether];

(3) The receipt and certification after Thanksgiving of the election night returns from Nassau County, instead of the statutorily mandated machine recount tabulation, in violation of section 102.14, Florida Statutes, resulting in an additional 51 net votes for Bush;

(4) The rejection of an additional 3,300 votes in Palm Beach County, most of which Democrat observers identified as votes for Gore but which were not included in the Canvassing Board's certified results; and

(5) The refusal to review approximately 9,000 Miami-Dade ballots, which the counting machine registered as non-votes and which have never been manually reviewed.

For the reasons stated in this opinion, we find that the trial court erred as a matter of law in not including (1) the 215 net votes for Gore identified by the Palm Beach County Canvassing Board and (2) in not including the 168 net votes for Gore identified in a partial recount by the Miami-Dade County Canvassing Board. However, we find no error in the trial court's findings, which are mixed questions of law and fact, concerning (3) the Nassau County Canvassing Board and the (4) additional 3,300 votes in Palm Beach County that the Canvassing Board did not find to be legal votes. Lastly, we find the trial court erred as a matter of law in (5) refusing to examine the approximately 9,000 additional Miami-Dade ballots placed in evidence, which have never been examined manually.

II. Applicable Law

Article II, section I, clause 2 of the United States Constitution, grants the authority to select presidential electors "in such Manner as the Legislature thereof may direct." The Legislature of this State has placed the decision for election of President of the United States, as well as every other elected office, in the citizens of this State through a statutory scheme. These statutes established by the Legislature govern our decision today. We consider these statutes cognizant of the federal grant of authority derived from the United States Constitution and derived from III U.S.C. 5 (1994) entitled "Determination of controversy as to appointment of electors." . . .

This case today is controlled by the language set forth by the Legislature in section 102.168, Florida Statutes (2000). Indeed, an important part of the statutory election scheme is the State's provision for a contest process, section 102.168, which laws were enacted by the Legislature prior to the 2000 election. . . .

Although courts are, and should be, reluctant to interject themselves in essentially political controversies, the Legislature has directed in section 102.168 that an election contest shall be resolved in a judicial forum. This Court has recognized that the purpose of the election contest statute is "to afford a simple and speedy means of contesting election to stated offices." *Farmer v. Carson*, 148 So. 557, 559 (Fla. 1933).

In carefully construing the contest statute, no single statutory provision will be construed in such a way as to render meaningless or absurd any other statutory provision. In interpreting the various statutory components of the State's election process, then, a common-sense approach is required, so that the purpose of the statute is to give effect to the legislative directions ensuring that the right to vote will not be frustrated. . . .

Although the right to contest an election is created by statute, it has been a long-standing right since 1845 when the first election contest statute was enacted. As well-established in this State by our contest statute, "the right to a correct count of the ballots in an election is a substantial right which it is the privilege of every candidate for office to insist on, in every case where there has been a failure to make a proper count, call, tally, or return of the votes as required by law, and this fact has been duly established as the basis for granting such relief."

The Staff Analysis of the 1999 legislative amendment expressly endorses this important principle. Similarly, the Florida House of Representatives Committee on Election Reform 1997 Interim Project on Election Contests and Recounts expressly declared:

Recounts are an integral part of the election process. For one's vote, when cast, to be translated into a true message, that vote must be accurately counted, and if necessary, recounted. The moment an individual's vote becomes subject to error in the vote tabulation process, the easier it is for that vote to be diluted.

Furthermore, with voting statistics tracing a decline in voter turnout and an increase in public skepticism, every effort should be made to ensure the integrity of the electoral process.

Integrity is particularly crucial at the tabulation stage because many elections occur in extremely competitive jurisdictions, where very close election results are always possible. In addition, voters and the media expect rapid and accurate tabulation of election returns, regardless of whether the election is close or one sided. Nonetheless, when large numbers of votes are to be counted, it can be expected that some error will occur in tabulation or in canvassing.

It is with the recognition of these legislative realities and abiding principles that we address whether the trial court made errors of law in rendering its decision.

III. Order on Review

Vice President Gore claims that the trial court erred in the following three ways: (1) The trial court held that an election contest proceeding was essentially an appellate proceeding where the County Canvassing Board's decision must be reviewed with an "abuse of discretion," rather than "de novo," standard of review; (2) The court held that in a contest proceeding in a statewide election a court must review all the ballots cast throughout the state, not just the contested ballots; (3) The court failed to apply the legal standard for relief expressly set forth in section 102.168(3)(c).

A. The Trial Court's Standard of Review

[In this section of the opinion the court explains why the trial court judge, Sanders Sauls, should not have limited his review to an "abuse of discretion standard."]

B. Must All the Ballots Be Counted Statewide?

Appellees contend that even if a count of the undervotes in Miami-Dade were appropriate, section 102.168, Florida Statutes (2000), requires a count of all votes in Miami-Dade County and the entire state as opposed to a selected number of votes challenged. However, the plain language of section 102.168 refutes Appellees' argument.

Section 102.168(2) sets forth the procedures that must be followed in a contest proceeding, providing that the contestant file a complaint in the circuit court within ten days after certification of the election returns or five days after certification following a protest pursuant to section 102.166(1), whichever occurs later. Section 102.168(3) outlines the grounds for contesting an election, and includes: "Receipt of a number of illegal votes or rejection of a number of legal votes sufficient to change or place in doubt the result of the election." Finally, section 102.168(8) authorizes the circuit court judge to "fashion such orders as he . . . deems necessary to ensure that each allegation in the complaint is investigated, examined, or checked, to prevent or correct any alleged wrong, and to provide any relief appropriate under the circumstances."

As explained above, section 102.168(3)(c) explicitly contemplates contests based upon a "rejection of a number of legal votes sufficient to change the outcome of an election." Logic dictates that to bring a challenge based upon the rejection of a specific number of legal votes under section 102.168(3)(c), the contestant must establish the "number of legal votes" which the county canvassing board failed to count. This number, therefore, under the plain language of the statute, is limited to the votes identified and challenged under section 102.168(3)(c), rather than the entire county. Moreover, counting uncontested votes in a contest would be irrelevant to a determination of whether certain uncounted votes constitute legal votes that have been rejected. On the other hand, a consideration of "legal votes" contained in the category of "undervotes" identified statewide may be properly considered as evidence in the contest proceedings and, more importantly, in fashioning any relief.

We do agree, however, that it is absolutely essential in this proceeding and to any final decision, that a manual recount be conducted for all legal votes in this State, not only in

Miami-Dade County, but in all Florida counties where there was an undervote, and, hence a concern that not every citizen's vote was counted. This election should be determined by a careful examination of the votes of Florida's citizens and not by strategies extraneous to the voting process. This essential principle, that the outcome of elections be determined by the will of the voters, forms the foundation of the election code enacted by the Florida Legislature and has been consistently applied by this Court in resolving elections disputes.

We are dealing with the essence of the structure of our democratic society; with the inter-relationship, within that framework, between the United States Constitution and the statutory scheme established pursuant to that authority by the Florida Legislature. Pursuant to the authority extended by the United States Constitution, in section 103.011, Florida Statutes (2000), the Legislature has expressly vested in the citizens of the State of Florida the right to select the electors for President and Vice President of the United States:

> Electors of President and Vice President, known as presidential electors, shall be elected on the first Tuesday after the first Monday in November of each year the number of which is a multiple of 4. Votes cast for the actual candidates for President and Vice President shall be counted as votes cast for the presidential electors supporting such candidates. The Department of State shall certify as elected the presidential electors of the candidates for President and Vice President who receive the highest number of votes.

In so doing, the Legislature has placed the election of presidential electors squarely in the hands of Florida's voters under the general election laws of Florida. Hence, the Legislature has expressly recognized the will of the people of Florida as the guiding principle for the selection of all elected officials in the State of Florida, whether they be county commissioners or presidential electors.

When an election contest is filed under section 102.168, Florida Statutes (2000), the contest statute charges trial courts to:

> fashion such orders as he or she deems necessary to ensure that each allegation in the complaint is investigated, examined, or checked, to prevent or correct any alleged wrong, and to provide any relief appropriate under such circumstances.

Through this statute, the Legislature has granted trial courts broad authority to resolve election disputes and fashion appropriate relief. In turn, this Court, consistent with legislative policy, has pointed to the "will of the voters" as the primary guiding principle to be utilized by trial courts in resolving election contests:

> The real parties in interest here, not in the legal sense but in realistic terms, are the voters. They are possessed of the ultimate interest and it is they whom we must give primary consideration. The contestants have direct interests certainly, but the office they seek is one of high public service and of utmost importance to the people, thus subordinating their interests to that of the people. Ours is a government of, by and for the people. Our federal and state constitutions guarantee the right of the people to take an active part in the process of that government, which for most of our citizens means participation via the election process. The right to vote is the right to participate; it is also the right to speak, but more importantly the right to be heard. [*Boardman v. Esteva*, 323 So. 2d 259, 263 (Fla. 1975).]

For example, the Legislature has mandated that no vote shall be ignored "if there is a clear indication of the intent of the voter" on the ballot, unless it is "impossible to determine the elector's choice. . . ." 101.5614(5)-(6) Fla. Stat. (2000). Section 102.166(7), Florida Statutes (2000), also provides that the focus of any manual examination of a ballot shall be to determine the voter's intent. The clear message from this legislative policy is that every citizen's vote be counted whenever possible, whether in an election for a local commissioner or an election for President of the United States. . . .

The demonstrated problem of not counting legal votes inures to any county utilizing a counting system which results in undervotes and "no registered vote" ballots. In a countywide election, one would not simply examine such categories of ballots from a single precinct to insure the reliability and integrity of the countywide vote. Similarly, in this statewide election, review should not be limited to less than all counties whose tabulation has resulted in such categories of ballots. Relief would not be "appropriate under [the] circumstances" if it failed to address the "otherwise valid exercise of the right of a citizen to vote" of all those citizens of this State who, being similarly situated, have had their legal votes rejected. This is particularly important in a Presidential election, which implicates both State and uniquely important national interests. The contestant here satisfied the threshold requirement by demonstrating that, upon consideration of the thousands of undervote or "no registered vote" ballots presented, the number of legal votes therein were sufficient to at least place in doubt the result of the election. However, a final decision as to the result of the statewide election should only be determined upon consideration of the legal votes contained within the undervote or "no registered vote" ballots of all Florida counties, as well as the legal votes already tabulated.

C. The Plaintiffs Burden of Proof

[Here the court shows that the trial court, in concluding that Gore had failed to show a "reasonable probability" that the election would have come out differently, was relying on precedents created prior to the addition in 1999 of the statutory phrase "or place in doubt" the result of the election.]

Legal Votes[1]

Having first identified the proper standard of review, we turn now to the allegations of the complaint filed in this election contest. To test the sufficiency of those allegations and the proof, it is essential to understand what, under Florida law, may constitute a "legal vote," and what constitutes rejection of such vote.

Section 101.5614(5), Florida Statutes (2000), provides that "no vote shall be declared invalid or void if there is a clear indication of the intent of the voter as determined by the canvassing board." Section 101.5614(6) provides, conversely, that any vote in which the board cannot discern the intent of the voter must be discarded. Lastly, section 102.166(7)(b) provides that, "if a counting team is unable to determine a voter's intent in casting a ballot, the ballot shall be presented to the county canvassing board for it to determine the voter's intent." This legislative emphasis on discerning the voter's intent is mirrored in the case law of this State, and in that of other states.

This Court has repeatedly held, in accordance with the statutory law of this State, that so long as the voter's intent may be discerned from the ballot, the vote constitutes a "legal vote" that should be counted. See . . . also *State ex rel. Peacock v. Latham*, 125 Fla. 6 (1936) (holding that the election contest statute "affords an efficient available remedy and legal procedure by which the circuit court can investigate and determine, not only the legality of the votes cast, but can correct any inaccuracies in the count of the ballots by having them brought into the court and examining the contents of the ballot boxes if properly preserved"). As the State has moved toward electronic voting, nothing in this evolution has diminished the long-standing case law and statutory law that the intent of the voter is of paramount concern and should always be given effect if the intent can be determined. . . .

Here, then, it is apparent that there have been sufficient allegations made which, if analyzed pursuant to the proper standard, compel the conclusion that legal votes sufficient to place in doubt the election results have been rejected in this case.

---

[1]Here, perhaps due to the press of time, the original published opinion appears to shift to a different scheme for outlining its headnotes.

This Case

. . . [W]e again note the focus of the trial court's inquiry in an election contest authorized by the Legislature pursuant to the express statutory provisions of section 102.168 is not by appellate review to determine whether the Board properly or improperly failed to complete the manual recount. Rather, as expressly set out in section 102.168, the court's responsibility is to determine whether "legal votes" were rejected sufficient to change or place in doubt the results of the election. Without ever examining or investigating the ballots that the machine failed to register as a vote, the trial court in this case concluded that there was no probability of a different result. First, as we stated the trial court erred as a matter of law in utilizing the wrong standard. Second, and more importantly, by failing to examine the specifically identified group of uncounted ballots that is claimed to contain the rejected legal votes, the trial court has refused to address the issue presented. Appellants have also been denied the very evidence that they have relied on to establish their ultimate entitlement to relief. The trial court has presented the plaintiffs with the ultimate Catch-22, acceptance of the only evidence that will resolve the issue but a refusal to examine such evidence. We also note that whether or not the Board could have completed the manual recount by November 26, 2000, or whether the Board should have fulfilled its responsibility and completed the full manual recount it commenced, the fact remains that the manual recount was not completed through no fault of the Appellant. . . .

Conclusion

Through no fault of appellants, a lawfully commenced manual recount in Dade County was never completed and recounts that were completed were not counted. Without examining or investigating the ballots that were not counted by the machines, the trial court concluded there was no reasonable probability of a different result. However, the proper standard required by section 102.168 was whether the results of the election were placed in doubt. On this record there can be no question that there are legal votes within the 9,000 uncounted votes sufficient to place the results of this election in doubt. We know this not only by evidence of statistical analysis but also by the actual experience of recounts conducted. The votes for each candidate that have been counted are separated by no more than approximately 500 votes and may be separated by as little as approximately 100 votes. Thousands of uncounted votes could obviously make a difference.

Although in all elections the Legislature and the courts have recognized that the voter's intent is paramount, in close elections the necessity for counting all legal votes becomes critical. However, the need for accuracy must be weighed against the need for finality. The need for prompt resolution and finality is especially critical in presidential elections where there is an outside deadline established by federal law. Notwithstanding, consistent with the legislative mandate and our precedent, although the time constraints are limited, we must do everything required by law to ensure that legal votes that have not been counted are included in the final election results. As recognized by the Florida House of Representatives Committee on Election Reform 1997 Interim Project on Election Contests and Recounts:

> All election contests and recounts can be traced to either an actual failure in the election system or a perception that the system has failed. Public confidence in the election process is essential to our democracy. If the voter cannot be assured of an accurate vote count, or an election unspoiled by fraud, they will not have faith in other parts of the political process. Nonetheless, it is inevitable that legitimate doubts of the validity and accuracy of election outcomes will arise. It is crucial, therefore, to have clearly defined legal mechanisms for contesting or recounting election results.

Only by examining the contested ballots, which are evidence in the election contest, can a meaningful and final determination in this election contest be made. As stated above, one of the provisions of the contest statute, section 102.168(8), provides that the circuit court judge may "fashion such orders as he . . . deems necessary to ensure that each allegation in the complaint is investigated, examined or checked, to prevent any alleged wrong, and to provide any relief appropriate under such circumstances. . . .

Accordingly, for the reasons stated in this opinion, we reverse the final judgment of the trial court dated December 4, 2000, and remand this cause for the circuit court to immediately tabulate by hand the approximate 9,000 Miami-Dade ballots, which the counting machine registered as non-votes, but which have never been manually reviewed, and for other relief that may thereafter appear appropriate. The circuit court is directed to enter such orders as are necessary to add any legal votes to the total statewide certifications and to enter any orders necessary to ensure the inclusion of the additional legal votes for Gore in Palm Beach County and the 168 additional legal votes from Miami-Dade County.

Because time is of the essence, the circuit court shall commence the tabulation of the Miami-Dade ballots immediately. The circuit court is authorized, in accordance with the provisions of section 102.168(8), to be assisted by the Leon County Supervisor of Elections or its sworn designees. Moreover, since time is also of the essence in any statewide relief that the circuit court must consider, any further statewide relief should also be ordered forthwith and simultaneously with the manual tabulation of the Miami-Dade undervotes.

In tabulating the ballots and in making a determination of what is a "legal" vote, the standard to be employed is that established by the Legislature in our Election Code which is that the vote shall be counted as a "legal" vote if there is "clear indication of the intent of the voter." Section 101.5614(5), Florida Statutes (2000).

It is so ordered.

ANSTEAD, PARIENTE, LEWIS, and QUINCE, JJ., concur.

WELLS, CJ., dissents with an opinion [omitted].

HARDING, J., dissents with an opinion, in which SHAW, J., concurs [omitted].

We, the authors, do not of course claim that the four-judge majority in *Gore v. Harris* "got the right answer." (Justices Harding and Shaw in their dissent indicate another coherent solution that would produce a victory for Bush: Gore's initial challenge of the vote in the four counties was illegal because he had won the vote in those counties and was obligated from the beginning to contest the vote statewide.) But we do not hesitate to say that the Florida Supreme Court majority created a well-reasoned and trustworthy opinion. That is, it harmonized clear statutory language with its own state case law, the admitted factual difficulties about counting votes done with punch-card technology, and the widespread democratic values that the candidate with the most votes should win and that all votes should count.

The effect of the 4–3 decision was to reduce Bush's vote lead to 154. Immediately upon receiving the order to supervise the statewide recount of the undervote, Florida circuit judge Terry Lewis of Leon County organized election officials and judges from around the state to begin the final recount of approximately 140,000 ballots. From all reports, the initial recount, begun the morning of December 9, ran smoothly. Judge Lewis and media sources began to predict that the count could finish by late on December 10.

But in the mid-afternoon of December 9, in a 5–4 decision, the United States Supreme Court granted the Bush campaign's request for an injunction to halt the recounts. The Court granted certiorari and scheduled oral arguments in *Bush v. Gore* for Mon. Dec. 11. This was, of course, just one day before the safe-harbor provision of 3 U.S.C. 5 would take effect.

In a concurring opinion explaining the order to suspend the recount, Justice Scalia wrote that "the issuance of the stay suggests that a majority of the Court, while not deciding the issues presented, believe that the petitioner has a substantial probability of success." Bush would suffer an "irreparable harm" if the stay was not issued, Scalia said, because "the counting of votes that are of questionable legality [threatens] irreparable harm to petitioner, and to the country, by casting a cloud upon what he claims to be the legitimacy of his election. Count first, and rule upon legality afterwards, is not a recipe for producing election results that have the public acceptance democratic stability requires."

The four dissenters—Stevens, Souter, Ginsburg, and Breyer—responded that "there is a danger that a stay may cause irreparable harm to the respondents—and, more importantly, the public at large—because of the risk that the entry of the stay would be tantamount to a decision on the merits in favor of the applicants . . . Preventing the recount from being completed will inevitably cast a cloud on the legitimacy of the election." In other words, the dissenters insisted that Bush's interest in not having his presidency embarrassed by the possibility that he did not actually win it was less than Gore's interest in having legal votes counted under Florida law.

George W. Bush, et al., Petitioners v. Albert Gore, Jr., et al.
Supreme Court of the United States
121 S.Ct. 525
Per Curiam

. . . The petition presents the following questions: whether the Florida Supreme Court established new standards for resolving Presidential election contests, thereby violating Art. II, §1, cl. 2, of the United States Constitution and failing to comply with 3 U. S. C. §5, and whether the use of standardless manual recounts violates the Equal Protection and Due Process Clauses. With respect to the equal protection question, we find a violation of the Equal Protection Clause . . .

The individual citizen has no federal constitutional right to vote for electors for the President of the United States unless and until the state legislature chooses a statewide election as the means to implement its power to appoint members of the Electoral College. U. S. Const., Art. II, §1. This is the source for the statement in *McPherson v. Blacker*, 146 U. S. 1, 35 (1892), that the State legislature's power to select the manner for appointing electors is plenary; it may, if it so chooses, select the electors itself, which indeed was the manner used by State legislatures in several States for many years after the Framing of our Constitution. Id., at 28–33. History has now favored the voter, and in each of the several States the citizens themselves vote for Presidential electors. When the state legislature vests the right to vote for President in its people, the right to vote as the legislature has prescribed is fundamental; and one source of its fundamental nature lies in the equal weight accorded to each vote and the equal dignity owed to each voter. The State, of course, after granting the franchise in the special context of Article II, can take back the power to appoint electors. ("[T]here is no doubt of the right of the legislature to resume the power at any time, for it can neither be taken away nor abdicated.")

The right to vote is protected in more than the initial allocation of the franchise. Equal protection applies as well to the manner of its exercise. Having once granted the right to vote on equal terms, the State may not, by later arbitrary and disparate treatment, value one person's vote over that of another. See, e.g., *Harper v. Virginia Bd. of Elections*, 383 U. S. 663, 665 (1966) ("[O]nce the franchise is granted to the electorate, lines may not be drawn which are inconsistent with the Equal Protection Clause of the Fourteenth Amendment"). It must be remembered that "the right of suffrage can be denied by a debasement or dilution of the weight of a citizen's vote just as effectively as by wholly prohibiting the free exercise of the franchise." *Reynolds v. Sims*, 377 U. S. 533, 555 (1964).

There is no difference between the two sides of the present controversy on these basic propositions. Respondents say that the very purpose of vindicating the right to vote justifies the recount procedures now at issue. The question before us, however, is whether the recount procedures the Florida Supreme Court has adopted are consistent with its obligation to avoid arbitrary and disparate treatment of the members of its electorate. Much of the controversy seems to revolve around ballot cards designed to be perforated by a stylus but which, either through error or deliberate omission, have not been perforated with sufficient precision for a machine to count them. In some cases a piece of the card—a chad—is hanging, say by two corners. In other cases there is no separation at all, just an indentation.

The Florida Supreme Court has ordered that the intent of the voter be discerned from such ballots. For purposes of resolving the equal protection challenge, it is not necessary to decide whether the Florida Supreme Court had the authority under the legislative scheme for resolving election disputes to define what a legal vote is and to mandate a manual recount implementing that definition. The recount mechanisms implemented in response to the decisions of the Florida Supreme Court do not satisfy the minimum requirement for non-arbitrary treatment of voters necessary to secure the fundamental right. Florida's basic command for the count of legally cast votes is to consider the "intent of the voter." *Gore v. Harris*, _____ So. 2d, at _____ (slip op., at 39). This is unobjectionable as an abstract proposition and a starting principle. The problem inheres in the absence of specific standards to ensure its equal application. The formulation of uniform rules to determine intent based on these recurring circumstances is practicable and, we conclude, necessary.

The law does not refrain from searching for the intent of the actor in a multitude of circumstances; and in some cases the general command to ascertain intent is not susceptible to much further refinement. In this instance, however, the question is not whether to believe a witness but how to interpret the marks or holes or scratches on an inanimate object, a piece of cardboard or paper which, it is said, might not have registered as a vote during the machine count. The factfinder confronts a thing, not a person. The search for intent can be confined by specific rules designed to ensure uniform treatment.

The want of those rules here has led to unequal evaluation of ballots in various respects. See *Gore v. Harris*, _____ So. 2d, at _____ (slip op., at 51) (Wells, J., dissenting) ("Should a county canvassing board count or not count a 'dimpled chad' where the voter is able to successfully dislodge the chad in every other contest on that ballot? Here, the county canvassing boards disagree."). As seems to have been acknowledged at oral argument, the standards for accepting or rejecting contested ballots might vary not only from county to county but indeed within a single county from one recount team to another.

The record provides some examples. A monitor in Miami-Dade County testified at trial that he observed that three members of the county canvassing board applied different standards in defining a legal vote. And testimony at trial also revealed that at least one county changed its evaluative standards during the counting process. Palm Beach County, for example, began the process with a 1990 guideline which precluded counting completely attached chads, switched to a rule that considered a vote to be legal if any light could be seen through a chad, changed back to the 1990 rule, and then abandoned any pretense of a per se rule, only to have a court order that the county consider dimpled chads legal. This is not a process with sufficient guarantees of equal treatment.

The State Supreme Court ratified this uneven treatment. It mandated that the recount totals from two counties, Miami-Dade and Palm Beach, be included in the certified total. The court also appeared to hold sub silentio that the recount totals from Broward County, which were not completed until after the original November 14 certification by the Secretary of State, were to be considered part of the new certified vote totals even though the county certification was not contested by Vice President Gore. Yet each of the counties used varying standards to determine what was a legal vote. Broward County used a more forgiving standard than Palm Beach County, and uncovered almost three times as many new votes, a result markedly disproportionate to the difference in population between the counties.

In addition, the recounts in these three counties were not limited to so-called undervotes but extended to all of the ballots. The distinction has real consequences. A manual recount of all ballots identifies not only those ballots which show no vote but also those which contain more than one, the so-called overvotes. Neither category will be counted by the machine. This is not a trivial concern. At oral argument, respondents estimated there are as many as 110,000 overvotes statewide. As a result, the citizen whose ballot was not read by a machine because he failed to vote for a candidate in a way readable by a machine may still have his vote counted in a manual recount; on the other hand, the citizen who marks two candidates in a way discernable by the machine will not have the same opportunity to have his vote count, even if a manual examination of the ballot would reveal the requisite indicia of intent. Furthermore, the citizen who marks two candidates, only one of which is discernable by the machine, will have his vote counted even though it should have been read as an invalid ballot. The State Supreme Court's inclusion of vote counts based on these variant standards exemplifies concerns with the remedial processes that were under way.

That brings the analysis to yet a further equal protection problem. The votes certified by the court included a partial total from one county, Miami-Dade. The Florida Supreme Court's decision thus gives no assurance that the recounts included in a final certification must be complete. Indeed, it is respondent's submission that it would be consistent with the rules of the recount procedures to include whatever partial counts are done by the time of final certification, and we interpret the Florida Supreme Court's decision to permit this. This accommodation no doubt results from the truncated contest period established by the Florida Supreme Court in *Bush I*, at respondents' own urging. The press of time does not diminish the constitutional concern. A desire for speed is not a general excuse for ignoring equal protection guarantees.

In addition to these difficulties the actual process by which the votes were to be counted under the Florida Supreme Court's decision raises further concerns. That order did not specify who would recount the ballots. The county canvassing boards were forced to pull together ad hoc teams comprised of judges from various Circuits who had no previous training in handling and interpreting ballots. Furthermore, while others were permitted to observe, they were prohibited from objecting during the recount. The recount process, in its features here described, is inconsistent with the minimum procedures necessary to protect the fundamental right of each voter in the special instance of a statewide recount under the authority of a single state judicial officer. Our consideration is limited to the present circumstances, for the problem of equal protection in election processes generally presents many complexities.

The question before the Court is not whether local entities, in the exercise of their expertise, may develop different systems for implementing elections. Instead, we are presented with a situation where a state court with the power to assure uniformity has ordered a statewide recount with minimal procedural safeguards. When a court orders a statewide remedy, there must be at least some assurance that the rudimentary requirements of equal treatment and fundamental fairness are satisfied.

Given the Court's assessment that the recount process underway was probably being conducted in an unconstitutional manner, the Court stayed the order directing the recount so it could hear this case and render an expedited decision. The contest provision, as it was mandated by the State Supreme Court, is not well calculated to sustain the confidence that all citizens must have in the outcome of elections. The State has not shown that its procedures include the necessary safeguards. The problem, for instance, of the estimated 110,000 overvotes has not been addressed, although Chief Justice Wells called attention to the concern in his dissenting opinion.

Upon due consideration of the difficulties identified to this point, it is obvious that the recount cannot be conducted in compliance with the requirements of equal protection and due process without substantial additional work. It would require not only the adoption (after opportunity for argument) of adequate statewide standards for determining what is a legal vote, and practicable procedures to implement them, but also orderly judicial review of any disputed matters that might arise. In addition, the Secretary of State has advised that the recount of only a portion of the ballots requires that the vote tabulation equipment be used to screen out undervotes, a function for which the machines were not designed. If a recount of overvotes were also required, perhaps even a second screening would be necessary. Use of the equipment for this purpose, and any new software developed for it, would have to be evaluated for accuracy by the Secretary of State, as required by Fla. Stat. §101.015 (2000).

The Supreme Court of Florida has said that the legislature intended the State's electors to "participat[e] fully in the federal electoral process," as provided in 3 U. S. C. §5. That statute, in turn, requires that any controversy or contest that is designed to lead to a conclusive selection of electors be completed by December 12. That date is upon us, and there is no recount procedure in place under the State Supreme Court's order that comports with minimal constitutional standards. Because it is evident that any recount seeking to meet the December 12 date will be unconstitutional for the reasons we have discussed, we reverse the judgment of the Supreme Court of Florida ordering a recount to proceed.

. . . Because the Florida Supreme Court has said that the Florida Legislature intended to obtain the safe-harbor benefits of 3 U. S. C. §5, JUSTICE BREYER's proposed remedy—remanding to the Florida Supreme Court for its ordering of a constitutionally proper contest until December 18—contemplates action in violation of the Florida election code, and hence could not be part of an "appropriate" order authorized by Fla. Stat. §102.168(8) (2000).

None are more conscious of the vital limits on judicial authority than are the members of this Court, and none stand more in admiration of the Constitution's design to leave the selection of the President to the people, through their legislatures, and to the political sphere. When contending parties invoke the process of the courts, however, it becomes our unsought responsibility to resolve the federal and constitutional issues the judicial system has been forced to confront.

The judgment of the Supreme Court of Florida is reversed, and the case is remanded for further proceedings not inconsistent with this opinion. Pursuant to this Court's Rule 45.2, the Clerk is directed to issue the mandate in this case forthwith.

It is so ordered.

Chief Justice REHNQUIST, with whom Justice SCALIA and Justice THOMAS join, concurring [omitted].

Justice STEVENS, with whom Justice GINSBURG and Justice BREYER join, dissenting.

The Constitution assigns to the States the primary responsibility for determining the manner of selecting the Presidential electors. See Art. II, §1, cl. 2. When questions arise about the meaning of state laws, including election laws, it is our settled practice to accept the opinions of the highest courts of the States as providing the final answers. On rare occasions, however, either federal statutes or the Federal Constitution may require federal judicial intervention in state elections. This is not such an occasion.

The federal questions that ultimately emerged in this case are not substantial. Article II provides that "[e]ach State shall appoint, in such Manner as the Legislature thereof may direct, a Number of Electors." It does not create state legislatures out of whole cloth, but rather takes them as they come—as creatures born of, and constrained by, their state constitutions. Lest there be any doubt, we stated over 100 years ago in *McPherson v. Blacker*, 146 U. S. 1, 25 (1892), that "[w]hat is forbidden or required to be done by a State" in the Article II context "is forbidden or required of the legislative power under state constitutions as they exist." In the same vein, we also observed that "[t]he [State's] legislative power is the supreme authority except as limited by the constitution of the State." The legislative power in Florida is subject to judicial review pursuant to Article V of the Florida Constitution, and nothing in Article II of the Federal Constitution frees the state legislature from the constraints in the state constitution that created it. Moreover, the Florida Legislature's own decision to employ a unitary code for all elections indicates that it intended the Florida Supreme Court to play the same role in Presidential elections that it has historically played in resolving electoral disputes. The Florida Supreme Court's exercise of appellate jurisdiction therefore was wholly consistent with, and indeed contemplated by, the grant of authority in Article II.

It hardly needs stating that Congress, pursuant to 3 U. S. C. §5, did not impose any affirmative duties upon the States that their governmental branches could "violate." Rather, §5 provides a safe harbor for States to select electors in contested elections "by judicial or other methods" established by laws prior to the election day. Section 5, like Article II, assumes the involvement of the state judiciary in interpreting state election laws and resolving election disputes under those laws. Neither §5 nor Article II grants federal judges any special authority to substitute their views for those of the state judiciary on matters of state law.

Nor are petitioners correct in asserting that the failure of the Florida Supreme Court to specify in detail the precise manner in which the "intent of the voter," Fla. Stat. §101.5614(5) (Supp. 2001), is to be determined rises to the level of a constitutional violation. We found such a violation when individual votes within the same State were weighted unequally, see, e.g., *Reynolds v. Sims,* 377 U. S. 533, 568 (1964), but we have never before called into question the substantive standard by which a State determines that a vote has been legally cast. And there is no reason to think that the guidance provided to the factfinders, specifically the various canvassing boards, by the "intent of the voter" standard is any less sufficient—or will lead to results any less uniform—than, for example, the "beyond a reasonable doubt" standard employed every day by ordinary citizens in courtrooms across this country.

Admittedly, the use of differing substandards for determining voter intent in different counties employing similar voting systems may raise serious concerns. Those concerns are alleviated—if not eliminated—by the fact that a single impartial magistrate will ultimately adjudicate all objections arising from the recount process. Of course, as a general matter, "[t]he interpretation of constitutional principles must not be too literal. We must remember that the machinery of government would not work if it were not allowed a little play in its joints." *Bain Peanut Co. of Tex. v. Pinson,* 282 U. S. 499, 501 (1931) (Holmes, J.). If it were otherwise, Florida's decision to leave to each county the determination of what balloting system to employ—despite enormous differences in accuracy—might run afoul of equal protection. So, too, might the similar decisions of the vast majority of state legislatures to delegate to local authorities certain decisions with respect to voting systems and ballot design.

Even assuming that aspects of the remedial scheme might ultimately be found to violate the Equal Protection Clause, I could not subscribe to the majority's disposition of the case. As the majority explicitly holds, once a state legislature determines to select electors through a popular vote, the right to have one's vote counted is of constitutional stature. As the majority further acknowledges, Florida law holds that all ballots that reveal the intent of the voter constitute valid votes. Recognizing these principles, the majority nonetheless orders the termination of the contest proceeding before all such votes have been tabulated. Under their own reasoning, the appropriate course of action would be to remand to allow more specific procedures for implementing the legislature's uniform general standard to be established.

In the interest of finality, however, the majority effectively orders the disenfranchisement of an unknown number of voters whose ballots reveal their intent—and are therefore legal votes under state law—but were for some reason rejected by ballot-counting machines. It does so on the basis of the deadlines set forth in Title 3 of the United States Code. But, as I have already noted, those provisions merely provide rules of decision for Congress to follow when selecting among conflicting slates of electors. They do not prohibit a State from counting what the majority concedes to be legal votes until a bona fide winner is determined. Indeed, in 1960, Hawaii appointed two slates of electors and Congress chose to count the one appointed on January 4, 1961, well after the Title 3 deadlines. Thus, nothing prevents the majority, even if it properly found an equal protection violation, from ordering relief appropriate to remedy that violation without depriving Florida voters of their right to have their votes counted. As the majority notes, "[a] desire for speed is not a general excuse for ignoring equal protection guarantees."

Finally, neither in this case, nor in its earlier opinion in *Palm Beach County Canvassing Bd. v. Harris,* did the Florida Supreme Court make any substantive change in Florida electoral law. Its decisions were rooted in long-established precedent and were consistent with the relevant statutory provisions, taken as a whole. It did what courts do—it decided the case before it in light of the legislature's intent to leave no legally cast vote uncounted. In so doing, it relied on the sufficiency of the general "intent of the voter" standard articulated by the state legislature, coupled with a procedure for ultimate review by an impartial judge, to resolve the concern about disparate evaluations of contested ballots. If we assume—as I do—that the members of that court and the judges who would have carried out its mandate are impartial, its decision does not even raise a colorable federal question.

What must underlie petitioners' entire federal assault on the Florida election procedures is an unstated lack of confidence in the impartiality and capacity of the state judges who would make the critical decisions if the vote count were to proceed. Otherwise, their position is wholly without merit. The endorsement of that position by the majority of this Court can only lend credence to the most cynical appraisal of the work of judges throughout the land. It is confidence in the men and women who administer the judicial system that is the true backbone of the rule of law. Time will one day heal the wound to that confidence that will be inflicted by today's decision. One thing, however, is certain. Although we may never know with complete certainty the identity of the winner of this year's Presidential election, the identity of the loser is perfectly clear. It is the Nation's confidence in the judge as an impartial guardian of the rule of law.

I respectfully dissent.

[Additional dissenting opinions by Justices Souter, Ginsburg, and Breyer omitted.]

QUESTIONS

We began this appendix with Justice Stevens's conclusion. We believe this book has given you the materials you need to decide whether you agree with him, and why. We conclude by asking some questions about each of the four elements of legal reasoning that we trust will shape your answers.

The Law in the Case

Chapter 5 has already introduced you to the equal protection clause, so you already know that, since Bush did not claim that Florida was injuring the right to vote of a "suspect class" like racial minorities, the test is one of minimum rationality. (Indeed, the equal protection clause voting cases cited by the five in the majority, for example, *Harper v. Virginia Board of Elections,* support judicial intervention precisely because certain classes of voters were systematically excluded from full political participation. *Harper* specifically struck down a poll tax that was deemed disproportionately to discourage racial minorities from voting.) So what is it about Florida's system that makes it fail the minimum rationality test? What is irrational about decentralizing the organization and management of elections? Most states do it this way because decentralization maximizes hands-on local political participation and prevents an all-controlling central state authority from easily corrupting the outcome. Is this goal totally irrational? Is it rational, in the name of uniform counting, *not* to count some votes altogether, particularly when the votes that *were* counted were not counted by a uniform counting system to begin with? Doesn't the majority's reasoning implicitly invalidate every election in the entire country? If equal protection law does not apply here, does not every other principle of federal law relevant to this case, especially Article II of the Constitution and the long-standing principle of federalism that state courts have final authority to say what their state laws mean, suggest that the U.S. Supreme Court should not even hear such a case?

The Facts in the Case

What evidence did the U.S. Supreme Court have before it that the statewide count could not be completed before the December 12th date? Was it not the Supreme Court's own staying of the recount that made it impossible after its December 12 decision? And why should this fact matter? Since Congress's "safe harbor" law cannot, according to Article II, tell Florida what to do, couldn't the recount continue at least until the meeting of Florida's electors on the 18th? Further, what factual evidence before the Supreme Court told it that the recount would not be uniform? How could it tell this before the recount was finished? Members of both parties observed the inspection of every chad and every ballot. When they disagreed, a single judge would determine whether the ballot unambiguously indicated a vote for one and only one candidate.

Social Background Facts

Consider the *Welosky* case from Chapter 4. Recall there that the Massachusetts court merely invented a fictional "intent of the legislature" and ignored issues of statutory purpose altogether. What evidence on the record of *Bush v. Gore* did the majority have before it to show that the legislature of Florida intended to take advantage of the December 12 deadline? Nothing in federal law compels it to do so. Do the statute books of Florida express such an intention? Remember that the statutes governing contests and protests were written for all Florida elections, not simply presidential elections. How likely is it that Florida legislators, in writing these statutes, had any intention at all about what to do in the unlikely event that a deadlocked and contested presidential election hinged on the selection of Florida electors? Florida's Republican-dominated legislature threatened in late November to appoint Bush electors if Gore had won the recount, but can legislative posturing create law? Even if it could, did not the U.S. Supreme Court itself say that only laws in place at the time of the election on November 7 could govern? Chief Justice Rehnquist in his concurring opinion joined by Justices Scalia and Thomas wrote, "Surely when the Florida Legislature empowered the courts of the state to grant 'appropriate' relief, it must have meant relief that would have become final by the cut-off date of 3 U.S.C., Section 5." What background facts in Florida's legislative history support this claim? Not one word in Florida's election statutes even hints at an adoption of the December 12 deadline. Does not the Florida Supreme Court describe a convincing purpose behind the election statutes as they are written?

Widely Held Social Values

In a democracy, what values should trump the value of determining as best as possible which of two candidates got more votes? Perhaps more important, what values justify federal judges, appointed for life, setting aside a state's resolution of a conflict over an election, given that Article II of the Constitution explicitly empowers the states—not the federal government—to choose presidential electors? The Supreme Court, a court that in recent years has worked to shift political responsibility to the states in many cases, did not have to hear *Bush v. Gore*. It heard the case under its certiorari procedures, which are completely discretionary for the Court. How convincing, therefore, is the following conclusion of the "per curiam" opinion? What democratic values justify this statement?

> None are more conscious of the vital limits on judicial authority than are the members of this court, and none stand more in admiration of the Constitution's design to leave the selection of the president to the people, through their legislatures and the political sphere. When contending parties invoke the process of the courts, however, it becomes our unsought responsibility to resolve the federal and constitutional issues the judicial system has been forced to confront.

Can you reconcile the political values this statement takes for granted with the political values so thoughtfully embodied in the *Carolene* footnote 4, discussed in Chapter 5 (p. 115)?[2]

CONCLUSION: WHY LEGAL REASONING MATTERS

Why should we, apart from our own political preferences, care about good legal reasoning? Why bother to say, as *The Economist* (December 16, 2000, p. 30) wrote of *Bush v. Gore*, "The justices' decision could have been worse. But not much."? We suggested in this book's opening section that by the time you finished it, you would see that *Reason in Law* "is at its deepest level a book about political morality" (p. 3). We hope you see that point now. We should care that our judges reason impartially and with integrity because the rule of law is not possible unless judges do so. It is nothing short of hypocritical to mouth "rule of law" talk for public consumption while ignoring the very principle in practice.

But the morality of law goes much further than a rejection of hypocrisy. The morality of law itself rests on the hard-won lesson of history that political life becomes a "war of all against all," and "nasty, brutish, and short," when people in communities no longer share common institutions that they trust. The presence of an active, independent, and impartial judiciary distinguishes peaceful countries—like the United States, Canada, Great Britain, and contemporary Germany—from murderous and strife-ridden countries like Nazi Germany and Milosovic's Yugoslavia. Other dynamics distinguish these countries as well, but an independent judiciary is as important as any of them.

In endorsing the morality of internally coherent legal reasoning, we are not being "moralistic." Reason in law does not and should not endorse any one political ideology or religious morality. The popular analogy of a game may help here. We rarely think that one team or another should win because it is "right." We don't say that it is "fairer" for the Yankees to win over the Mets, or "right" that the U.S. Women's Soccer team beat China for the World Cup in 1999 (one of the most thrilling sports events of its entire decade). Rather, we value the game itself. We know that good play beats bloody warfare, hands down. And we know that good games happen only when we, as players and as spectators, trust that the umpires and referees do not care who wins but simply try to make the best calls they can with the material they've got. Should we not expect the same of our courts, and particularly of the highest court in the land?

[2]Books devoted exclusively to the 2000 election controversy include E. J. Dionne and William Kristol, *Bush v. Gore: The Court Cases and the Commentary* (Washington, D.C.: The Brookings Institute, 2001); *36 Days: The Complete Chronicle of the 2000 Presidential Election Crisis* (New York: The New York Times, 2001); *Deadlock: The Inside Story of America's Closest Election* (Washington, D.C.: The Washington Post, 2001); Howard Gillman, *The Votes That Counted: How the Court Decided the 2000 Presidential Election* (Chicago: University of Chicago Press, forthcoming); Richard A. Posner, "Florida 2000: A Legal and Statistical Analysis of the Election Deadlock and the Ensuing Litigation," 2000 *Supreme Court Review* 1 (2001).

Credits

Index

Index of Cases

Boldface page numbers indicate pages on which a significant excerpt from an opinion in the case begins. All other page numbers denote in-text case references. This index excludes cases of minor significance—cases, for example, cited only within other quoted cases and secondary citations, particularly in footnotes.